COMMERCIAL REAL ESTATE INVESTING

COMMERCIAL REAL ESTATE INVESTING

12 EASY STEPS TO GETTING STARTED

JACK CUMMINGS

WILEY

John Wiley & Sons, Inc.

Published by John Wiley & Sons, Inc., Hoboken, New Jersey.
Published simultaneously in Canada.

For general information on our other products and services please contact our Customer Care Department within the U.S. at (800) 762-2974, outside the United States at (317) 572-3993 or fax (317) 572-4002.

Wiley also publishes its books in a variety of electronic formats. Some content that appears in print may not be available in electronic books. For more information about Wiley products, visit our web site at www.Wiley.com.

Library of Congress Cataloging-in-Publication Data:
Cummings, Jack, 1940-
    Commercial real estate investing : 12 easy steps to getting started / Jack Cummings.
        p. cm.
    Includes index.
    ISBN 0-471-64714-4 (pbk.)
        1. Commercial real estate.   2. Real estate investment.   3. Commercial real estate—United
    States.   4. Real estate investment—United States.   I. Title.
HD1393.55.C86 2004
332.63'24—dc22

                                                                    2004042221

Printed in the United States of America.

10   9   8   7   6   5   4   3   2   1

CONTENTS

CONTENTS

Contents

CONTENTS

Contents

FOREWORD

As a multi-decade friend of Jack Cummings and perhaps one of the few around who has a copy of every one of his books (all speed-read, by the way) in his personal library, I feel uniquely qualified to write the following, not only about Jack, but about *Commercial Real Estate Investing* as well.

If you have followed the extraordinary and unique investing, writing, teaching, lecturing, Renaissance-man–like career of Jack's over the last 40-plus years, you already know what you are about to learn and experience in this latest of his books. Jack is a man who lives Life (notice that capital L!) to the fullest and is able to share everything that his sponge-like mind absorbs and his keen eyes see. All you will read about and all that has been recounted on these pages has actually been lived by the author. He has done it all, seen it all, profited from it all (as you can and will when you put these lessons to work for yourself), and made all of the mistakes that this book will teach you how to avoid.

When I first read the manuscript, I realized there is much more to this book than simply commercial real estate investing. Sure, all the techniques, the how-to-get-started ins and outs, the pitfalls, the step-by-step lessons, the terminology, and so on, are here. But, *but*, and an even bigger BUT, everything contained in these pages can be applied to how to invest in *anything*.

In Chapter 1 you'll learn how to find your own "comfort zone" and how to set realistic goals. Chapter 2 talks about other people's money and the dynamics of any investment. You can apply the "Rule of Small" and the factors of motivation to buy or sell, illustrated in Chapter 3, to virtually any investment you are looking at. And the most useful thing you'll get out of Chapter 4 is the "Key Factors to Becoming an Expert in Your Own Backyard."

No investor into any investment vehicle should take one step forward without understanding the sections in Chapter 5 about what you must know and the "Easy Steps to Ascertain Data and What to Look For." Jack also urges you to do your due diligence and points out at least eight things you can do when you find problems."

By now you must see that this book not only walks you through all the steps necessary to become a successful commercial real estate investor, but actually sets down in an easy-to-follow format the answer to that question all investors ask themselves (usually after the investment has been made and little can be done to fix it): "Now, why didn't I think of that." Jack thought about it, experienced it, profited from it, and is now showing you how to do the same thing.

I could comment on the techniques outlined and taught in the remaining chapters, but I think that you not only get the idea but now have the incentive to apply every page and every technique to your entire investment experience, in your financial life and personal life as well. Why not do what I've done with every book I've reviewed on the air over the last 5,000-plus broadcast/interviews. Speed-read it first and then snail-read all of those sections Jack has outlined that apply to you. If you're a first-time investor in anything, I would suggest that you start with that snail read. Ultimately, I snail-read everything that will serve to expand my knowledge of what I'm investing in and eventually produce greater profits for me. This book does every bit of that, and I am thrilled, honored, flattered, and glad to have been invited to comment on it by my good friend Jack Cummings. I'm still learning from him, and so can you!

Bill Bresnan

Broadcaster, author, lecturer, educator

Life is full of mysteries that, when uncovered, turn out to be neither sinister nor complex. Generally they fall into the "Now, why didn't I think of that" category, once their truth has been discovered they often become commonplace, taken for granted. The Wright brothers uncovered some such mysteries, as did Leonardo da Vinci and countless other philosophers, scientists, and average people who simply figured things out by themselves. In this book, Jack Cummings uncovers the mystery of commercial real estate and reveals that successful investing in this sometimes-intimidating category of real estate is as simple as following 12 easy steps.

Why This Book?

This book is the first of its kind. Until now no author has had the experience in commercial real estate to share with you the insider secrets that will allow you to make the big money jump from casual real estate investing to fortune-building properties.

Why Jack Cummings?

Jack Cummings is a household name in many real estate circles. He is an internationally recognized author and lecturer in real estate investing. He is a hands-on broker and investor who keeps his investment expertise current. Jack Cummings is also the most published contemporary author on the subject of real estate investing. His many books have become investment bibles for countless real estate investors around the world. His hands-on techniques and easy style of writing will take any wannabe investor into the world of successful investments.

Yet Jack Cummings is far more than an author on the subject of real estate. He is an example to follow. He made his first real estate investment over 40 years ago, and since then has bought and sold millions of dollars of real estate around the world, just for his own account. As a broker and investment consultant, his dollar volume of real estate transactions exceeds $700 million and is growing. Client transactions for the 12 months ending October 2003 exceeded $42 million.

Commercial Real Estate Investing is a composite of Jack's 40 years of experience, written in such a way that any reader can take Jack's hand and be led through the book toward a successful future investing in commercial real estate. As Cummings puts it, "Investing in income-producing properties is the easiest possible way to build your fortune and insure a life of financial independence." He continues, "Where else can you buy something and invest only a fraction of its value, get income for years from that property, and profit handsomely, even if you sell it at half of what you paid for it?" Does that sound like one of those mysteries that need to be uncovered? Well, Jack does that in his first chapter.

This book is many things to many people. It is easy and fun to read. It is sharp and to the point in such a way that examples and lessons are easily retained by the reader. The goals of each chapter are clear and the steps to take are laid out in simple and clear language for the reader to embrace. This book is filled with "Now, why didn't I think of that" ideas, techniques, and strategies. It is packed with Cummings' own real-life investing experience, offering many examples of success and failure to learn from. This book uncovers the real insider mysteries of how to be successful in real estate investing.

What this book is not: This book is not heavy theory with what-if examples that are unrealistic and difficult to follow. There are no complex mathematical and analytical processes such as are found in many real estate books today. That kind of investing often loses more great deals for the investor than it produces. Besides, as Cummings puts it, "The key to success in any kind of real estate is to know your local market, and to build your own comfort zone." This simple factor will be your springboard to success in commercial real estate.

Commercial Real Estate Investing is written for all would-be real estate investors. This book is Cummings' best choice for the first-time investor who needs to get out of the rental rut or is tired of dealing with get-rich-quick schemes that sound good but don't work. This book is designed for whatever level of real estate expertise the reader may have, and is neither condescending nor complicated. It is a building block of tried-and-true steps designed to let any investor succeed in commercial real estate at his or her own pace.

CHAPTER 1

How to Get Started Investing in Commercial Real Estate

Every author has a goal for the book he/she is writing. I suppose it is logical to assume that the goal for many writers is to become financially independent by virtue of the books they author. That is a worthy goal, provided that the author has first grasped the concept that, to achieve your worthy goals, you must help others attain their worthy goals. By *worthy* I mean a goal that is realistic to your abilities, is task oriented, is measurable, has a timetable attached to it, and has worth other than simply a dollar amount. A writer following this scenario would then be required to provide the reader with all the elements essential to attain the principal task of his book.

In my case, the mandate is to give my reader the tools and the road map for success in investing in commercial real estate. To rephrase a rather old saying, "Only if your better mousetrap works will they beat a path to your door."

This section of the book gives you a heads-up on what to expect in the chapters to follow and how to make the most of them. Each chapter begins with a description of its principal goals. To help you stay on track, each chapter also lists key words and concepts, which are then discussed in some detail. While these elements pertain mainly to the goals of the chapter, they also introduce insider secrets and other concepts and techniques that will be important tools as you begin to implement the interim steps which will lead you to success later on. These key words and concepts are introduced in an order that will enhance your understanding of later elements in the book. The following paragraph begins with the format that each succeeding chapter will follow:

The goal of this chapter is:

How to Get Started in Commercial Real Estate

Key Words and Concepts to Build Your Insider Knowledge

Commercial Real Estate Defined
Investment vs Use
Comfort Zone
Setting Realistic Goals

Commercial Real Estate Defined

For the purpose of this book, commercial real estate is considered to be any real estate that has the ability to produce outside revenue or income for you as an investor in that property. This can include a vacant lot or tract of land on which you intend to construct a building to rent out, or land that can itself be leased to a user and thereby produce income. A duplex or apartment building in which you live while you rent out the other units is considered a commercial property. A single family home where you live is not, at that moment, a commercial property. If you later make changes to the property such that you can generate income, whether or not you still live there, then the property becomes a form of commercial property.

Investment versus Use

It is essential to distinguish between the two elements of investment and use. Let's start with an investment property. When you find a property you wish to *invest* in, it is a property that you anticipate will return a profit to you at a future date. A property you intend to *use* may end up being a good investment, but your original goal is not to profit directly from the real estate but, rather, to profit from your personal use of it. You might need an office to house your business, so you buy one to use. Or you may need a home and, rather than rent, you buy one to use. The concept of use is important, because it includes other factors that make a property valuable for more reasons than just profit from income or a future sale.

This book delves deeply into the different reasons people buy real estate. To set the stage, consider that a person buys a home or apartment near a great school or work or medical care for reasons oriented to those services, and not solely for future profit. Grasp the idea that use may be the ultimate deciding factor in the purchase of a property, and that it may even be the sole reason for its value to a specific user. Keep in mind right from the start, not all properties can be used for every possible use. By the time you have completed this book you will understand that the key insider secret to investing in commercial real estate is *use* and in the long run *use* governs profit.

Comfort Zone

I use the term *comfort zone* to refer to the investment area that you establish. It will begin as a small part of your neighborhood or other area of town, perhaps where you work. Your long-range goal is to become an expert in everything that goes on, from a real estate and value point of view, within that comfort zone. You will slowly expand the zone until it contains more of the kind of properties which you might eventually want to own. Your task is to become comfortable in every way with the kind of real estate you are going to buy. For example, if you want to own small apartment buildings, you will define the area of town where you will become knowledgeable of what is going on in the apartment rental business in that area as well as in adjoining areas that may also affect your area. (I will give you details on what you will need to do in Chapter 4).

Setting Realistic Goals

I have already mentioned the importance of goals. To reinforce the earlier statement: A worthy goal is one that is realistic to your abilities, is task oriented, is measurable, has a timetable attached to it, and has merit or worth other than simply the dollar sign at its end. It is easy to say, "My goal is to have ten million dollars" and truly want that to happen. But that kind of goal generally brings you only disappointment. The missing ingredients are those other elements.

- *Goals should be realistic to your abilities.* First of all, what are your abilities? By this I don't mean the list of things you are capable of doing right now. You need to include those talents that you can unleash or expand. A class in general contracting or in decorating might be a good start, if that is something you have a good feel for. "Realistic to your abilities" would not mean becoming an airline pilot, for example, unless you have the time to learn how to fly, get the needed experience to be hired by an airline, and enjoy flying in the first place.

- *The goal must be task oriented.* This means you have to do something to make the goal come about. Sitting on your duff waiting for the lotto number you picked to come up is not exactly a task-oriented event. "I will become an expert in my comfort zone" is a good goal only if you then go out and do what is necessary to become that expert. Good news on that front: I can show you exactly what you will need to do, and the rest will be up to you. Becoming an expert in your comfort zone is exactly what one of your primary goals will be. You might as well write that one down right now. Everything this book points to is how to obtain that status, then how to use the status and your newfound knowledge to reach your financial targets.

- *The goal must be measurable.* The goal to be rich is one you will likely never reach, because most rich people I know are driven by the dollar sign and never feel they are rich enough. So, by *measurable*, I'm not talking about the concept of being rich, but an obtainable amount of money. To do this, first think of the end result—say, to become financially independent. As you move toward that long-range goal, check on your progress from time to time. How far along are you in reaching that point? A good measuring point might be to set, as the goal you first target, the amount of money you are currently earning from your present job. Write down your present wages and then aim to obtain that amount over and above what you earn from your current job from your real estate investments.

- *The goal must have a timetable tied to it.* If you have carefully followed the idea of a realistic goal, then you should have some idea of how long it might take to get there. If you set a deadline of two years to own your own home, and a year goes by and you have not even been out looking for homes or haven't even picked a neighborhood you would like to live in, I'd say you need to reevaluate your timetable. It might be that you underestimated the steps you need to accomplish before you know enough to achieve the goal. It's okay to change your goal once you have set it up, timetable and all, but don't wait two years to do that. And when you do make a change, be sure you understand the reason for making it.

- *The goal must have merit or worth beyond a dollar amount.* Ask this question of yourself: "Why do I want to own several small apartment buildings?" The right answer is not "to become a millionaire." The answer should fit into a longer-range plan. A longer-range plan is, in essence, a goal on a bigger scale. All goals should be structured so that short-range goals are designed to be steps up the ladder. As you achieve them, you are moving in the direction of the longer-range goal.

Far too many people set long-range goals but then fail to grasp that while their goal—for instance, to move to Paris—might be okay, there is something missing. For example, how do you get to the point that you will be able to support yourself (and family) once you got there? Or, perhaps, what do you do to obtain sufficient funds to be so financially independent that you will be able to retire? Each element that leads you toward your long-range goal is in itself nothing more than an achieved segment on a road map to your desired destination.

Whether real estate is to be a part of the destination or only a step that takes you there, this book will allow you to develop a plan that will help you achieve your goal. Once you are on your way and begin to move up the ladder of attainment of goals, you can keep raising your sights. Start with the smallest elements possible until you discover that all the goals you set, you attain. How about this as your next goal: "I will read this book within the next 20 days." Then go on to, "I will start to follow the steps to develop a comfort zone and become a real estate insider."

The next chapter of this book will begin your formation—or reformation, as the case may be—into a highly effective and successful real estate investor.

How to Get the Most out of This Book

You will get the maximum benefit from this book if you begin to implement the steps as you read about them. The majority of the tasks you will be asked to do are designed to turn you into a real estate insider. As you begin to learn the real insider secrets from the book, and build your real estate vocabulary of words and concepts, you will also see how easy it is to rub elbows with other real estate insiders. If there is any doubt as to who they are, don't worry. I not only tell you how to find them, but I give you tips on how to get the most out of your new sphere of friends and future business associates.

By the time you have completed the first eight chapters, you will be ready to start some of the major steps necessary to make your entry into the circle of real estate insiders. This is when you will start attending city commission meetings and planning and zoning board meetings. Wait until you are finished with Chapter 8 before going to those meetings. You will appreciate them far more than you might now, and until you are ready, the people you will meet are not yet ready for you.

By reading each chapter in order, the material will flow better, and you will have time to use the information in your everyday activities. Even a drive to work can be a step in the right direction at learning how to become a real estate expert in your comfort zone. How? Learn to observe what is going on. Change routes from time to time so as to know what is happening on the back streets and not just along the thriftiest route between your residence and place of work. Look for signs of change. Are there new buildings in the works, or old ones being torn down? All of this activity will give you insight into what makes for potential profit and what almost guarantees a loss. Learn to be curious, and learn whom you need to contact to satisfy that curiosity.

Each chapter builds your knowledge with terms and concepts, and offers examples, tips, techniques, and steps to maximize your desired goals. No single chapter is so long that it can't be read in one sitting. But don't worry if you cannot get through it all at once. This book is designed for your success, whoever you are.

CHAPTER 2

Why Commercial Real Estate Is a Dynamic Investment

The goals of this chapter are:

To Introduce You to the World of Commercial Real Estate

To Illustrate the Ease in Building Financial Independence with Commercial Real Estate

All real estate that is not solely used as your personal residence can become commercial in nature. If it produces rental income or is a part of your business, then it is commercial real estate.

The steps outlined in this book are directed toward commercial real estate, and all the examples provided are of a commercial nature. Nonetheless, the essence of becoming a true real estate insider is much the same no matter what kind of real estate you choose as your investment. The fact that few books are written about commercial real estate does not mean that this category of real estate is more complicated, difficult, or impossible for a first-timer to excel in. Commercial real estate is a more direct and faster way to build your fortune.

Key Words and Concepts to Build Your Insider Knowledge
Invested Amount = Cash + Debt + Time
Other People's Money
Leveraged Cash Flow
Equity Buildup
Appreciation You Can Accelerate
Management Postures 1, 2, 3 and 4
Supply & Demand

Invested Amount = Cash + Debt + Time

The real cost of every real estate investment can be broken down to this simple equation. The amount of your investment is ultimately the total of the cash you invest, the debt you take on, and the value of the time you spend. Each of these elements has its importance, and the degree of importance differs relative to each investor's circumstance. If you have a lot of free cash, then the debt and time you spend may be reduced. It can go the other way too: If you are short of cash and have to max out your mortgage and other debt potentials, then you might have to spend a lot more time to turn the investment into a real winner. Nowhere in this equation should you consider that the invested amount is the same as what you paid for the property, without including your time as a part of that overall value. It is okay for you to discount the value of your time to a certain degree, as being your own boss has its own real value. But do put a value to your time.

Other People's Money

Other people's money is a factor available to the real estate investor that simply is not a realistic option to an investor in any other commodity. Sure, you can buy stocks on a margin account, or commodities like pork bellies and gold at a fraction of what they sell for, but those items won't give you rental income. And if your margin is called and you don't have cash or credit to meet the shortage, then you can get wiped out overnight.

Real estate is where it is at, and other people's money (or just OPM for short) is the name of that game. OPM comes in many forms. It is the money you borrow from the local savings and loan association when you buy your home, or the loan you get from FHA on a four-unit apartment building, or the loan from an insurance company for a shopping center you want to build. It can come from many other sources, including a second mortgage from the seller, or your brother-in-law, or a guy you know who hangs around your local pub. It is all money that either you have to pay back or get when you give up a piece of the action. In the case of using OPM to buy your home, it is money that you owe for which you make payments every month. Those payments come out of your pocket and, while it is better than paying rent, it is still a reduction from the amount of money you have in your pocket.

When you use OPM in investing in commercial real estate, you are able to double-dip at the OPM wells. This means simply that you dip into the lender's well, and then you dip into your tenant's well when you pay back the lender. Many examples used in this book demonstrate how important OPM is in all kinds of real estate investing. Your maximum benefit from using this book will come through your ability to become as comfortable as you can with as many OPM techniques as possible. My book *Investing in Real Estate With Other People's Money* (McGraw Hill, 2004) is a recommended addition to your investment reference library.

Leveraged Cash Flow

A lever is used to pry up something. In commercial real estate investing, you use OPM as a lever to increase the yield (rate of return) on your investments. You obtain leveraged cash flow when you obtain OPM at a lower cost than the return you are getting from your investments. For example, if you are able to invest $100,000 in an apartment building that gives you a cash flow (money left at the end of the year) of $15,000 a year, after all operational expenses (excluding possible income taxes), you have just received 15 percent on the invested $100,000. However, if you invest only $20,000 in cash and borrow $80,000 of OPM at an annual cost of $7,000, and all other expenses remain the same, then you end up with $8,000 clear. As your cash investment is only $20,000 and the cash in your pocket is $8,000, that is a 40 percent return. The increase from 15 percent to 40 percent is the *leverage* you have obtained.

Expenses to own and operate real estate vary depending on the type of property, the level of maintenance and upgrades you give to that property, and the cost of real estate tax and insurance. Other minor expenses include management and other professional fees. The greatest variables from place to place will be real estate tax, insurance, and utilities. If you can handle the management part yourself, and an occasional weekend with a paint brush to handle the maintenance and upgrade part, it will mean more cash in your pocket. Take a look at these numbers:

Purchase price of the property	$100,000	
Other people's money (mortgage)	80,000	
Cash you invest	20,000	
Annual cash flow in this example	15,000	(Prior to Mortgage Payment)
Debt service	7,000	(Your Mortgage Payment)
Cash flow (in your pocket)	$8,000	
Return on your cash invested	40 percent	

Note: Your annual income is still $15,000. Deducting the $7,000 you pay for the $80,000 loan leaves you with $8,000, which is 40 percent of the $20,000 you invested. The key is getting OPM at a lower cost than your return.

On the other hand, if the cost of the $80,000 was $14,000, you would be left with only $1,000 at the end of the year ($15,000–$14,000 = $1,000), and that is only a 5 percent return on your invested $20,000. You have not leveraged your return at all. Is this all bad? That depends. If the only way you could buy this property was to finance the $80,000 at that higher cost, and you ended up with an apartment building in which you could improve the rental income to your favor, then you might be able to build the income to $20,000 or more and still come out like a bandit. Besides, as you will discover before finishing this chapter, even if you eventually sold the apartment building for less than $100,000 you might still profit very nicely indeed.

Equity Buildup

As you pay off a mortgage or any other debt, you may be increasing your equity. I say "may be" because if you are letting the property go into disrepair at the same time, it may drop in value faster than you are paying off the debt. But, with prudent investing, you should be able to increase rents and have the benefit of appreciation, as well as pay off a mortgage. Even if the property value does not go up one cent, by the time you pay off that $80,000 debt on the apartment house, you have an equity buildup of $80,000. Remember, you invested only $20,000 and double-dipped by having tenants pay off the $80,000 for you.

Appreciation You Can Accelerate

Appreciation refers to the increase in the value of a property over a period of time. The reasons that property values go up are the principal subject of Chapter 3, so I won't spend much time on them at this juncture. The key element here is the fact that there are things you can do to increase the amount of appreciation over a set period of time.

Consider two identical apartment buildings across the street from each other. Even though these two buildings are in the same immediate area, they might be in different cities. Boundary lines between cities and even counties generally run down the center of a street. The very fact that one property is in a different city than the other can greatly affect it's value. Why? Zoning, setbacks, and other local building rules may differ. The flexibility of ultimate use may also vary. For example, one building may sit on a lot that is zoned to allow professional offices, whereas the other, directly across the street, can only be used for residential apartments. This fact alone may have a profound effect 10 years from now when professional offices are better suited for the street, which by then has become a major traffic artery in town and too noisy for high-priced apartment rentals. The savvy investor would have checked these factors out prior to buying and, by recognizing the future advantage of a broader-use zoning, would have made the moves to quickly take advantage of a higher economic return from professional offices if the trend goes that way.

One of the best ways to accelerate the appreciation is to let nature do it for you. Well-landscaped commercial properties can take on a mature value that the barren parking lot of a similar property never achieves. But remember, landscaping is something that most communities are very particular about, so do not jump in and plant trees that may not be approved by the city. Sit down with the appropriate person in the city and get a list of what is allowed, and what they think would be the best plant for the intended area. Keep in mind that some plants tend to drop nasty things on cars parked under them, or millions of leaves each fall, and hard round things, like coconuts, that can damage property as well as people.

One of the most prudent ways to accelerate appreciation is through the right kind of management for the specific property.

Management Postures 1, 2, 3, and 4

Each owner has the choice to do one of the following forms of management. Let's call them management postures 1, 2, 3, and 4. I refer to these management postures periodically throughout this book, so you may want to mark this page for easy reference.

Management posture 1:   Do nothing to maintain the property.

Management posture 2:   Do very little to maintain the property unless it is actually broken.

Management posture 3:   Maintain the property in its original condition.

Management posture 4:   Maintain the property in a constant upgrade mode.

It should be obvious that if the property has the potential for a long economic life, management posture (MP) 4 is the least expensive in the long run because the value of the property goes up faster than with MP 1, 2, or 3. There is no single reason for this, but one important lesson to learn is that investors who constantly strive to upgrade their properties are able to increase rent and, in the long run, reduce the percentage of gross income that is spent on maintenance.

How so? Assume your property grosses $100,000 in rents, and after all expenses and debt service you have a cash flow of $15,000. Assume also that all other expenses remain the same, except you increase your maintenance by $2,000. If you spent 6 percent of your gross rents on maintenance last year, or $6,000, and you increase that sum to $8,000, and the improved condition of the property allows you to bring in a new gross rent of $105,000, your cash flow has jumped up to $18,000 for the year. That $2,000 added cost brought you in an additional $3,000 in revenue. But more important, if an investor wanted 10 percent return on his or her investment, it increased the value of the property by $30,000.

Last year's gross rent	$100,000
Less all expenses and debt payments	85,000
Cash flow in your pocket	$ 15,000

Next year's gross rent	$105,000
Less all expenses	87,000
New cash flow	$ 18,000
Added value	$ 30,000

This occurs because an additional price of $30,000 will be justified because of the added $3,000 of cash flow.

Chapter 3 introduces the Rule of Small, which should open your eyes to how important your management posture is to your overall value.

Supply and Demand

The interplay between supply and demand is an economic function that has to do with the level of demand for something and the amount of that "something" that is available. The only open cold drink stand on a busy street in downtown Phoenix in July will make more money than the cold drink stand in Buffalo, New York, in January. By the way, a solitary cold drink stand in the middle of the desert is only valuable if there are people who want (and can afford) cold drinks. When you apply this to real estate, you find that you don't have to start out today with what will be in greater demand five years from now—all you have to do is end up with it.

For example, assume the current trend in an area is the development of new luxury rental apartment buildings. It would be safe to assume that this is because there is a demand for that product now. So you look around the same area and find apartment buildings that are not quite up to the same quality level as the new apartments. This would mean lower cost to buy, and less rent to collect. However, if you buy apartment buildings that are less than luxury rentals now and augment a plan to upgrade the units over a period of about five years, your buildings will continue to stay rented because there will always be tenants who cannot afford the higher-priced luxury apartments.

As you implement the management plan (MP 4) to bring your apartments up to a status much higher than you began with, you continually accelerate the appreciation of your property. Five years later your apartments are at the level the luxury rentals started at, and you are easily able to rent your apartments at a small discount over the now five-year-old luxury apartments.

The Seven Dynamics of Commercial Real Estate

There are seven factors that apply to commercial real estate to a much greater degree than to single family real estate. Let's look at each of these incentives in detail.

1. Ability to produce income
2. High yield through double-dipping
3. Job security
4. Tax shelter
5. Easy-to-Create New Value
6. Inflation Fighter
7. Sell for Less than You Paid and Still Make a Huge Profit

Ability to Produce Income

Commercial real estate will generally produce a higher rental return than single family homes can produce. This statement takes into consideration the fact that if you have one single family home and it is vacant, you have, for that period of time at least, a 100 percent vacancy factor to consider. Single family homes may require a higher mainte-nance cost than other properties and, in general, the single family home as a rental property does not appreciate as rapidly because of overall wear and tear. A portfolio of 100 single family homes spread all over town would be far more of a management headache than a single complex of 200 rental apartments. The synergy of income potential goes up as you reduce the cost to keep the facility in operation. Remember that fact when you consider single family homes over multifamily housing or other kinds of commercial real estate.

High Yield through Double-Dipping

I have already touched on the double-dipping effect of getting your OPM for the purchase from one well and the payments to meet your debt obligation from another well. This factor alone can create a great win-win situation. Let's say you have $50,000 to invest, and you find a $500,000 commercial building containing seven shops that are all rented. You have negotiated the deal to the point where you are able to obtain financing in the total amount of $450,000. To show you how easy that might be, consider a first mortgage in the amount of $400,000 from a local savings and loan association, and the seller holding the remaining $50,000 which is secured by your mother's oceanfront condo (naturally you get her approval first!). Assume that you use all but $5,000 a year of the income to pay off the debt and are able to do that in 12 years. What do you have?

If you elected to use MP 4, it is likely that in those 12 years the property has increased in value to over $1,000,000. Your equity buildup has been 100 percent, so there is no debt on the property at all. You have received a 10 percent return on your investment for each year of your ownership, which would be a total of $60,000. What if you could only sell the property for $400,000 ($100,000 less than you paid for it)? Well, you would put that $400,000 in your pocket. Not such a bad situation, is it.

Price	$500,000	
Mortgage	450,000	
Cash invested	$ 50,000	Price less mortgage (OPM)

Cash Flow	$ 5,000	per year, which is a 10 percent yield
Cash in your pocket	$ 60,000	over 12 years
Mortgage in 12 years	0	
Blowout sale	$400,000	$100,000 less than your original purchase price
Profit	$350,000	plus you also get back your original $50,000 invested

Job Security

Many people find that real estate can provide them with the most important benefit of all: job security. Many family businesses are tied to real estate—farms, roadside fruit stands, landscaping nurseries, restaurants, motels and hotels, and so on. Often it is the food business that first attracts foreigners who come to the United States with little more than the knowledge of how to cook their own ethnic dishes.

Hunger is a great motivator, and how many such restaurants have you entered where most of the staff are members of the same family? Many more than you might realize. I know of families who have worked their way up the financial ladder of success, building grand fortunes in the motel and hotel business, starting with a small facility and ending up with oceanfront flagship hotels worth millions of dollars. One of the factors that all of these people ultimately learn is that owning their place of business is the best way to go. It is in these family-run businesses that all the value-producing aspects of real estate can come together. Any business that adopts as its mission statement that it will succeed only by delivering to its customers the best service possible (food, hotel rooms, plants, or whatever) ensures that its own goals will be achieved. As the owners build a business that has value, they also cause the real estate in which it is situated to have increases in value.

Tax Shelter

A tax shelter is another form of OPM. This occurs because the Internal Revenue Service (IRS) allows investors to deduct operational expenses, which are real dollars spent, from the gross income collected to arrive at the taxable income. The IRS also allows the owner to deduct a "paper-entry" amount from the gross revenue for depreciation of the value of the property. You can depreciate 100 percent of an improvement, except for the actual land value, and any salvage value that can be calculated. The amount deducted from the gross revenue that falls into this paper-entry category of deduction (depreciation and, in the case of groves and mines, depletion) is like borrowing OPM from the government. As this deduction is a paper-entry only, it reflects a decrease in the book value of your property and not an actual cash payout. But best of all, it is taken directly from the bottom line at the end of the year.

This means that if you have $20,000 cash left over after all real expenses (operational expenses for the property, including interest on the mortgage), and then can take another paper-entry deduction of $5,000, then you pay tax on $15,000 of income but actually have $20,000. If you do that over 10 years you have put a total of $50,000 in your pocket that you did not pay tax on. The tax bite might have been a total of $10,000 or more, but you don't ever have to pay that to Uncle Sam (or the IRS) unless you sell the property and have a profit above your new tax basis.

Without Depreciation

Rents you collect after paying operational expenses	$20,000	(cash in your pocket)
Tax you might have had to pay on the $20,000	4,000	(at 20 percent rate)
Cash left over as spendable cash	$16,000	

With Depreciation

Rents you collect after paying operational expenses	$20,000	
Depreciation allowed by the IRS	5,000	
The amount you report as earnings to the IRS	$15,000	
The amount you actually got	$20,000	
Tax you pay (assume minimum of 15 percent)	1,750	(paid on the lower $15,000)
Spendable cash	$18,250	
Additional money in your pocket over 10 years	$22,500	

The tax basis of any improved property is the book value of the property which you have created by lowering the original purchase value by the amount of depreciation taken on its improvements while you owned the property. Tax shelter is less of an issue today because the tax rates have come down over past years and the amount of depreciation taken must be spread out over a longer period of time. However, it is a factor to keep in mind when every penny might count.

Easy-to-Create New Value

There are many ways to create nearly instant value at a very low cost when it comes to real estate. I have purchased buildings that simply needed to be cleaned up to double my investment. One such example was an office condo where my present office is located. The space I purchased had been trashed by the previous owners when they moved out to larger offices downtown. It was twice the area I needed, but I had done my research on the building and the site (due diligence—discussed in Chapter 5) and discovered that I could actually split the office into two separate condo units. With a local carpenter/painter doing the work, we installed a new entrance into the main hallway for half of the suite of offices. I then put both units on the market.

My decision was to sell one side of the office (whichever side first sold) and keep the remaining one. For one side, I was able to get a price that was equal to what I had paid for the total area, plus enough to cover almost all of the cleaning, painting, and carpentry needed to turn it into two offices.

Another building I purchased was a very old, wooden, single family home in the downtown part of Fort Lauderdale. It had not been painted, inside or out, for 20 years or longer and was a shambles. It was located on a busy business street and had been occupied by a frame shop for the previous 10 years. Many of the rooms were filled with leftover frame stock and simply needed to be emptied, cleaned up, and painted. I offered a local summer camp all the old frame stock if they came and got it (they used it in their summer arts and craft department of the camp). I hired day labor to scrub the place down with TSP (trisodium phosphate is one of the best cleaning compounds you will ever buy, and is found in any hardware store or paint shop) and then pressure-clean the results. A painter arrived a few days later and, using a pressure spray machine, gave the inside and out several new coats of white paint. The building sold a week later at a nice profit of twice the price I paid.

Landscaping is another great way to create both instant and long-improving value. Many older properties suffer from deteriorating landscaping around them or are overgrown with plants. Each situation presents different challenges, but the end result can be an instant improvement with the longer-term growth of a beautiful yard at a relatively low cost. If you are looking for a longer period of growth (say you are going to use the building for five years yourself) then spend less money by purchasing the kinds and sizes of plants that will reach their greater value in five years. This book gives many such examples of instant or near-instant creation of value.

Inflation Fighter

All my friends have heard this story. In 1963 my bride and I moved from Spain to Fort Lauderdale. I had completed my graduate studies in Europe, was out of the Air Force, and was returning to reality in the United States. We borrowed $1,000 from my parents and used it as a down payment on a vacant lot, on which we proceeded to build a four-unit apartment building. I was able to obtain 100 percent financing from a local savings and loan, and slowly paid off what I owed the lot owner. We moved into the single two-bedroom apartment in the building and rented out the three one-bedroom units. Three years later we moved out into a new home we had built, but kept the apartment building.

Today, as was the case in 1967, the rent from one of those apartments pays the electric bill of our current home, plus the real estate tax on the apartment building. Mind you, the rents in 1963 were $87 per month on an annual rental. Today they are in the $700 range. Over the years the taxes on the apartment building also continued to rise, as did the electric bill of our different (and continually larger) homes. But for me, those increases in the cost of living remain equal to the rent of one apartment unit in that original building.

Commercial property is a great inflation fighter because the owner is able to dip, and double-dip, into the OPM wells. If you can lock up a large percentage of the original cost of the property in the form of a mortgage or other debt used to purchase the property, at an interest rate that will still allow you to have a positive cash flow (some money left over at the end of the year), then all the inflation in the world will only benefit you. This is what makes real estate such a sweet form of investing.

Sell for Less than You Paid and Still Make a Big Profit

One of the sweetest aspects of real estate is that through the combination of OPM and a sound investment strategy, you have a built-in safety net. This safety net is so good that even if you make a pretty bad mistake, you can come out smelling like a rose.

Here is another example of this magic:

Say you buy a small strip store for a total price of $600,000. You invest a total of $100,000 in up-front value (cash and/or exchange of services or property), and the balance of $500,000 is made up of total debt (first mortgage from a bank and some seller-held financing). The terms are set so that you pocket only $7,000 each year after all expenses (which include your accountant and lawyer), but you are also able to pay off the total debt over a 15 years so that at the end of that time you own the property free and clear of debt.

Let's look at two situations. In the first scenario, you made a great investment, and over the years you raise rents to the extent that your total cash earnings for the 15 years is $220,000. This translates to an average cash flow of $14,666.67 per year—a comfortable 14.67 percent annual return on your investment. After a 15-year holding period, the property should have appreciated to at least $1,000,000 in value and is all yours, free and clear. Your cash income for the 16th year should be over $120,000 because you no longer have any debt to pay.

Now let the safety net come into play. Your investment starts out okay, but after the third year your income stays at a lower level. You end up, after 15 years, having earned a cash flow of only $125,000 for the entire time. So you decide to sell, and the best offer you can get is $500,000 after selling costs—less than you paid for the property. But wait—you only invested $100,000, and you did earn interest on that at double or more what you could get in the bank. On top of that, you had some tax shelter along the way and are still able to walk away from the closing office with a check for $500,000. That is still a profit of $400,000 over what you started with. Only in real estate can this happen.

A Recap of This Example

Original price of the property	$600,000
Cash invested	100,000
Mortgage (OPM)	500,000

Total cash in your pocket over 15 years	$125,000	
Ultimate sales price	$500,000	
Your profit	$400,000	plus your $100,000 investment back

How *Not* to Be Intimidated by Commercial Real Estate

I frequently give courses at the Fort Lauderdale Board of Realtors on the subject of "Successful Commercial Real Estate Brokerage." There is generally a good turnout of salesmen and saleswomen who come to learn how they can escape the housing market and get into the part of brokerage where the real money is to be found. They leave the program with a new respect for what they thought they needed to escape from, because they recognize that the same fundamentals that work for successful home brokers will also work for real estate firms that specialize in selling large commercial or investment properties.

However, there is one major element that they must overcome. They need to stop being intimidated by the aspect of commercial real estate. Over the years I have discovered that this fear or intimidation extends well beyond the salesmen and saleswomen who deal with this kind of property—it also affects the investors who might otherwise seek to buy and invest in commercial properties. I believe this happens because people think that commercial or investment properties require a level of investment savvy or financial education that is greater than they possess or are capable of obtaining. I can assure you that I know many people who have made a great success out of owning strip stores, shopping plazas, office buildings, rental apartments, and other kinds of commercial properties, but who have never graduated from college. Many have worked hard to attain their success, even those who have come to the United States unable to speak English with just a few dollars in their pockets. Why were they not intimidated? My guess is simply because they didn't know they were supposed to be intimidated.

Even so, the aura of complication still hovers and is just one of the many myths that exist about real estate. Once you face them and discover that even many of the real insiders don't know the truth about them, you will be able to face them down and no longer be intimidated about any aspect of the real estate investment arena.

The Four Real Estate Myths That Need to Be Unveiled

Commercial Real Estate Is Complicated

The proponents of this myth will fill their arguments with statements such as "Commercial real estate is filled with heavy and complex math, international finance, reams of forms and applications and reports to be filed, mystifying tax complications, and legal ramifications that can send you to jail if you screw up." Now, as with all myths, it takes some truth to keep the myth alive. There is some math involved, only you don't have to do it. The same is true with forms and taxes and all that. That is what accountants and lawyers are for. They are cheap if you start with them and only expensive if you try to do it yourself and need them to bail you out of a jam. The fact is that the benefits of getting into multitenant investment property far outweigh the complications that you will be able to farm out to hired help. The investor who is trying to make his investment capital work for him by keeping the books, collecting the rents, inspecting the property, and doing the year-end tax reporting is doing more than he should be doing. So don't get caught in that trap.

By the time you are halfway into this book, you will understand that knowing what is going on in the marketplace is 90 percent of the effort. Arriving at this level of knowledge is simple, easy, and fun, and does take some time. This is the time that you will devote to making contacts that will work for you year after year and cost you nothing more than the time it took to meet them and to cultivate them as your friends and business associates. It is also the time you will spend getting to know what creates value within your comfort zone, and how you can take advantage of the obvious signals that have been sitting right on the next-door neighbor's fence all the time, only you didn't recognize them.

The other 10 percent of the ingredients needed to fill out the formula for success are elements that you will absorb all by yourself as you work your way up the ladder of becoming a true real estate insider. It is to meet these ends that this book is dedicated. As you may suspect, 90 percent of the book is designed to hold your hand and lead you through the initial 90 percent of your effort. Not once will you be asked to take an SAT test, or attend graduate school, or apply to law school. No one will ask to see your diploma.

This book and the lessons it provides will get you started on the right path and propel you as far as your own motivation and ability will carry you. You will be asked to do everything you can to expand your sphere of reference (the people around you and your knowledge of what is going on in your own growing backyard). Is this book the last book you will ever read on the subject? I truly hope not. Not only do I continue to write more books on the subject, but I also am an avid reader of many aspects of this exciting field. I know the necessity to maintain a current posture in the marketplace, and that requires me (and you too) to become a student of real estate for as long as I hope to be successful in it. Become a sponge and absorb all you can about the subject. But never be intimidated again—never.

Real Estate Is Management Intensive

Remember management postures 1, 2, 3, and 4? They are the foundations to all the real estate management you need to begin with. You will add finesse to each of them as you go along. You will discover that MP 4 is not always the best approach to real estate management. Sure, MP 4 is ideal for property you plan to keep for a while, and property that is not already near its economic obsolescence. There are times when you simply want to keep the property producing income, at its highest level, for a short period of time. This means you do not want to plow more capital into a property that is going to be torn down in a few years. In such cases, MP 2 or MP 3 might be all that is needed. You will also discover that the Rule of Small works with almost every aspect of real estate and especially applies to the management side of things. The Rule of Small, which governs the financial mastery of real estate where small moves give big end results, is discussed in detail in Chapter 3.

The most important aspect of real estate management is to deal with it quickly and decisively without big moves. Tenant complaints should be addressed and not ignored, problem tenants removed if possible, and rents kept at or below the market rate of similar properties. If the property is in a constant upgrade program (MP 4), then stay at or above market rates.

The Three Most Important Words Are "Location, Location, Location"

I love to discuss this subject because virtually everyone I come across has it all wrong. The idea of "location, location, location" as the three most important words was coined by an unknown person, or surely by someone too embarrassed to admit to having coined that phrase. I can only suspect that the point this person was trying to make was that where a property is located is the most important aspect of that property. Now, there is a smidgin of truth in this statement. Location does have both merit and value. But as you will shortly understand, it is not the location that makes the property most valuable.

Let's begin by looking at two corners of a very busy intersection in a prosperous city in the United States. Each corner is exactly the same size, and each street that makes up this intersection is equally important, with the same amount of traffic at all times of the day. All four corners of the intersection have the same advantage as to location, with only very small differences. These differences would apply to the direction of the heaviest traffic at certain times of the day, as at most intersections traffic flow tends to shift to a certain degree; bright sun reflections in morning or afternoon drivers' eyes; and existing buildings that adjoin the corner can influence where a person decides to turn in. But let's ignore those minor elements, as the question at hand is the location only.

These four corners have essentially the same value. But are there other factors we should be looking at? Is location alone enough of a criterion to establish value? No. The most important aspect of any property is the allowed use. This aspect comes in several packages. First, what is the use the buyer intends for that property? This is important because if you are an investor looking to make a great investment, and you believe you have found a great location in town and can buy the remaining corner at half the price that the other three have sold for, that should be all you need to know. Right?

Wrong. As an investor, you may not have a clue what the future use of this property will be. Will it be a fast food facility, a bank, a parking lot, or what? So the word *use* must be viewed as referring to the possible uses that the local zoning and other restrictions will allow. In essence, what will they let you put there? If you are the actual user looking for a place to put one of your existing businesses—say a tire store, or a muffler shop, or a full service restaurant with lounge—your first choice may be to find a good location, but you need a location that allows the use that you need. The best location in the world, if it does not allow a muffler shop, will have no value to Midas Muffler stores, or any other muffler shop for that matter.

Use, then, is a critical element that needs to be understood. Use is controlled by a number of factors, some governmental in nature, such as zoning ordinances, controls dealing with fire issues, and regulations about hazardous substances (relating to such things as gas storage, paint booths, and chemical sales). Deed restrictions imposed by past owners or developers can also restrict use, as can setbacks from other similar uses or prohibitions on activities within so many feet of their front door. Use is the key to the value of any location.

The subject of use and all the elements that control it is discussed in the balance of this book. It will be very important for you to recognize these elements because they are often hidden, and only the real insider is able to sort them out.

Real Estate Is a Universal Commodity, and All Universal Commodities Are Complicated

I am sure that this is a statement invented by a stock broker. Real estate is found everywhere, to be sure, but if you think that you can invest in Fort Lauderdale by being the expert in real estate in San Francisco, then you are headed for a disappointment. Trends do follow certain similarities, but they can occur for different reasons and last for different periods of time. What is going on in Fort Lauderdale may not be the same thing that is happening only 25 miles away in Miami. Local trends are really *local*. Certain neighborhoods suddenly become hot and start to go through a phase of rebuilding. If you get in early enough, that might be the only ticket you need to your fortune. If a local growth phase is nearing an end (because there is no more viable property to buy on which to rebuild), then you need to look at nearby or adjoining neighborhoods that will take off due to the supply-and-demand effect of the market.

Real estate is so local, in fact, that many people who have had good success investing in their neighborhood have run into difficulty because they believed they could relate that success to anywhere they went. They go on a vacation and fall into what I call the "greener grass syndrome." You know about the green grass on the other side of the fence, don't you? Well, this happens to real estate investors too. What suddenly looks like greener grass than they have at home seems to be a bargain because it is one-third or less the price of a similar piece of grass at home. Uh oh, not so! It might turn out that there are too many restrictions, only one-fourth the traffic, building and zoning won't allow more than two floors of building, and on and on.

Rely on your comfort zone (which is discussed in great detail in Chapter 4). The idea is to build your comfort zone in your own backyard first. Expand it and then, if you are so inclined, begin another comfort zone in another neighborhood where, at first at least, the grass looks pretty green.

CHAPTER 3

What Makes Real Est
Value Go Up or Down

The goals of this chapter are:

To Demonstrate the Key Factors that Cause Real Estate Values to Go Up or Down

To Learn How to Take Advantage of These Factors and Avoid Their Downside Consequences

---

The factors that affect the value of real estate are generally obvious once they are at work, causing real estate to rise or fall in value. It's important to understand exactly what those factors are and how they can cause the value to move either up or down. The key to success in real estate is to use this knowledge in determining when and what to buy, and how to maximize your profit on a sale. Interestingly, the same factor can cause one property to go up in value while causing another similar property in the same town to go down in value, even if it is just across the street.

Ironically, most of the factors do not just suddenly appear. They are elements that have been in place for years, such as local zoning or building codes. Those and other factors may not be noticed or their real impact not unleashed until the owner of a property attempts to take advantage of what he previously thought was the property's real value.

By understanding the six factors covered in this chapter, you will learn to recognize how to take advantage of a situation when it arises, as well as how and when to avoid potential problems that could diminish the value of a property you are about to purchase.

Key Words and Concepts to Build Your Insider Knowledge

Community Planning
Departments of Transportation
Fire and Health Codes
Lack of Concurrency
Land Use Changes
Condemnation and Eminent Domain Proceedings
Building Moratoriums
Economic Obsolescence
The Rule of Small

Community Planning

Nearly every community in the United States, Canada, and most of Europe has some form of community planning. Within cities this may come in the form of a planning and zoning department that deals with matters such as "How is this city to be developed?" The county is further controlled by broader mandates from the state, which requires that each county adhere to standards of building and development to fit the scheme of things that the state legislature has decided. Naturally, there is also a higher order of things, and the federal government gets its fingers into the pie through its federal matching funds that local communities vie for—funds for road development, bridges, tollways, airports, schools, and countless other federal projects.

Each of these elements of community planning will impose something that may affect the value of your property so that you win or lose value because of it. Because this chapter and others in this book show different ways these factors can affect the value of your property or investments, it is important that you get a good grasp on everything presented here.

The whole concept of community planning is in constant flux—nothing remains fixed. One planning team may be prodevelopment and encourage construction and new urban development, while two elections away a new city council votes to change all zoning laws to effectively stop development in its tracts. Both situations can occur for good reasons, or at least good intentions, but they can have disastrous effects on your property's value, and your rights as a property owner.

Departments of Transportation

Each level of community planning may have a Department of Transportation. This is a powerful factor in controlling development, because development doesn't flourish unless there is good traffic flow in the community. So what goes on in your city will be greatly affected by the planning that is going on in all the different departments of transportation, as well as other departments in city, county, and state planning bureaus. The good news is that, of all the departments in local, state, and federal governments, transportation is the one that can sow your fortunes right under your nose. Once you understand how transportation planning functions, you will be able to avoid most of its potential bite and reap most of its benefits. Why? How?

First of all, understand that decisions and plans of departments of transportation are slow to evolve. Their future plans take years to draft, and years longer to implement. New roads and bridges, and revamping, expanding, and even resurfacing old roads are very expensive undertakings, and when something is expensive it takes a lot of yesses along the way to get final approval. Public hearings are generally required, and the public that shows up not to complain but to observe is the public that will ultimately benefit the most.

World history demonstrates how this works. When one tribe left a foot path marked in the sand, other surrounding tribes began to use it, and it became a traffic way. Soon someone built a trading post at the juncture of two such paths. The Romans were successful because they were great road builders. They knew and understood the value of their avenues of transportation and what it would do to a community if their road went through it instead of through another town 50 miles away. The Romans took advantage of this knowledge and were able to rule vast parts of the world by virtue of the commerce they would bring to an area and the tax they would collect on it. Today, the simple announcement of a new turnpike entrance/exit in an otherwise remote area of the county will bring nearly instant value to the property located at that entrance/exit—or it might bring a sudden devaluation of what was once a high-priced, exclusive residential subdivision.

Keep in mind that transportation is not just about cars; it includes pedestrians, trains, planes, and ships. All of these people- and goods-moving elements of your community are strongly controlled. There are port authorities, airport authorities, the Army Corps of Engineers, and many other departments and committees of both government and quasi-government that are quick to stick their noses into any newly proposed event that even remotely concerns them.

Fire and Health Codes

The strongest of all the building codes are usually the fire and health codes of a community. Other building codes may be changed without the requirement of the change becoming retroactive to a building constructed under older codes. But fire and health codes are generally absolute, and it is rare for any building to be grandfathered in (allowed to remain as it is) if one of these codes gets changed. Meeting the new fire or health code can be very expensive. While it might be costly enough in a new building, tearing existing walls apart to install fire sprinklers is both a nightmare and a hunk of change out of your pocket. You will learn to pay careful attention to both fire and health codes.

Lack of Concurrency

This phrase can cause a property owner to shiver on a warm day. *Concurrency* is a term that was invented by a land planner. Having concurrency means that your property meets all the current requirements to enable you to develop the property more or less as the zoning might allow. If that sentence sounds vague, it is carefully meant to. Most zoning ordinances governing the use of a specific site or tract of land contain provisions that give the local governing body considerable control over the ultimate end product. However, one thing is absolute: If you do not meet concurrency, or if you lack concurrency, then your property may not be developable until you take steps to bring the property into concurrency.

The problem with this concept is it has grown into a many-armed monster that can eat developers alive. The simple fact is that to bring a property into concurrency may mean doing something to remedy the traffic congestion that is presently occurring two blocks away from the tract of land—like, for example, widen two or three miles of roadway from a two-lane to a four-lane traffic way. Ouch! An expensive remedy, but not as costly as many I have seen. Clearly, this is an important factor on which you can profit. How so? Well, if you have been following the events of a major new development and discover that the developer is going to have to build a new bridge over a canal to open up a new traffic route to reduce the flow elsewhere, then that new traffic way might be where you want to put your new trading post.

Land Use Changes

Land use is a part of the master plan of the community. This overall plan will designate where development can occur and in what form and density it can be approved. A change to this plan will suddenly change the overall outlook of the neighborhood and the anticipated growth of the market for certain businesses of that community. Any change in any kind of use in your neighborhood, and particularly where you own property, can either jeopardize the value of your property or make you a millionaire.

The sequence of land use plans and modifications to them usually starts at the state level. The state legislators pass an overall master plan for the state, and certain mandates are then passed down to the counties, which have some flexibility as to how they must then implement the plan. The cities within each county then are told, again with some flexibility, how they are to adopt the overall plan to their area. The use of the properties within the city or unincorporated area (county-controlled and not within a city) must fit to the overall land use which has been set by this chain of decision making.

If the ultimate land use plan allows flexibility, as often is the case, then it may not be necessary to actually request a change of the plan. However, if the intended or desired use is not allowed at all, then the owner or buyer must look elsewhere, or try to get a modification in the plan. An example of this would be where a property is classified as a retail commercial use. Along comes a buyer who wants to build apartments. If the land use plan allows apartments in the commercial area, then that is okay; however, if it does not (which is more often the case), then the buyer may have to go all the way to the state legislators to effect a change. This is costly and can take a long time—and ultimately it may not be approved anyway.

One of the key requirements in speculation in land is to pay very close attention to the land use plan and the options available for the use of the land you are thinking of buying. The greater the flexibility of the plan, the more options you might have. Keep in mind, however, that flexibility is not always a good thing. If the ultimate highest price a buyer would pay for a tract of land that you purchased 10 years ago turns out to be for a high-end retail use, and the surrounding land to your tract has become low-end industrial buildings (great flexibility), then you will lose out. The only way to overcome that potential is either to already know what and who your neighbors are, or to have a large enough tract to be able to buffer yourself from future development that is not up to your standards.

Condemnation and Eminent Domain Proceedings

There are two methods by which a governing body can acquire your property without your permission. The first is by condemnation, and the second is through eminent domain. Condemnation is generally the way a city or community redevelopment authority (CRA) will clear out a blighted area to make way for new development. However, there are certain legal requirements that must be followed, and some states require that the party that is initiating the condemnation or eminent domain proceeding pay for the cost incurred by the owner if the proceeding is contested. Eminent domain proceedings are the usual way that departments of transportation obtain rights-of-way for new or expanded traffic ways. Each proceeding has the same end result: You sell your property to the agency who wants it, and although you don't have to accept the price, you may end up having to take it unless a court rules in your favor at a higher price.

Building Moratoriums

When there is a rash of development going on, things might be progressing at such a fast pace that the level of services available to the people who live in the area is being outstripped. This happens most often when new roadways have opened up vast areas of vacant land for new housing development. Developers rush in and, before you know it, there are thousands of new residents living in the area, with thousands more likely to follow. Traffic can no longer be handled on the new road, and more are needed now.

Schools don't even exist yet, and forget about things like shopping, fire department and police services, water and sewer service, and so on.

When this kind of situation starts to get out of hand, there are two things the local government can do. It can make the determination that none of the undeveloped property meets concurrency, so it cannot be developed until something is done to remedy that situation; or it can impose a building moratorium. The building moratorium halts the issuance of a building permit in the area chosen until the city planners have been able to sort things out and, at the same time, to slow down the pressure on existing services. Building moratoriums and concurrency issues are difficult to predict, so it is essential that investors of developmental property take them into consideration in their acquisition proposals. The way you do this is to include provisions in your offers to purchase such properties that can protect you as much as possible against the potential delay or reduction of development you will ultimately be allowed on the tract of land. You will do this as a buyer and if you are a seller you will anticipate that a buyer will want to protect himself against such an imposition.

As a buyer interested in building apartments, you have to anticipate that just because the land is zoned for 50 units per acre does not mean you will be allowed that many, if any at all. You might cover yourself by putting a timetable in your offer for approval by the local authorities for your site plan, or even for the issuance of a building permit. If the seller will agree, you can also tie the price of the property to the number of units you will be allowed. This would be your best protection as to the maximum price you can pay, as the price per unit would remain the same if the city allowed you only half what the zoning allows. Of course, the seller would want to protect the minimum price by having a floor (the lowest price he would take) in the deal.

Economic Obsolescence

Eventually every real estate property will reach a time when the value of the actual use skids to a halt. That halt may be temporary or for a rather long time. For example, a roadway motel gets bypassed by a super highway and just is not economically viable anymore. It may continue to function, but the income stream drops and the value may go down for that reason. An office building becomes old and antiquated and tenants move out to newer and better functioning buildings. A fast-food restaurant that was viable 20 years ago is now too small and the operational costs too high for the volume of business it can sustain. These are all examples of economic obsolescence and can present opportunities to you as an investor if you can ascertain a new use for these properties.

The Rule of Small

Income-producing properties are valued by the amount of income they produce. This sounds logical, of course, but its interesting how the Rule of Small affects this concept. The Rule of Small is that small movements in the smallest increment of the income stream will have big impacts on the largest element of the income stream.

Here is an example of how this works: The smallest part of the income stream of a 10-unit apartment complex will be the monthly rent on each apartment. The largest element of the income stream of this same property will be the amount that someone will pay for this property based on the yield required by that buyer. Let's tie that to actual numbers. The monthly rent is $650 per apartment. That rent times 10 apartments generates a gross monthly collection of $6,500 and an annual gross revenue of $78,000. Assume that the expenses for last year totaled $20,000. This would give you a net operating income (income less expenses except for debt service) of $58,000. Ignore leverage for a moment. If a buyer needed to make 9 percent cash flow on his invested capital to purchase the property, he would pay up to $644,444. (I arrived at this by simply dividing $58,000 by the 9 percent: $58,000 ÷ .09 = $644,444).

Here's a recap of this 10-apartment example:

Monthly rent per apartment	$ 650
Gross rent per month from 10 apartments	$ 6,500

Annual revenue	$ 78,000	
Income less operating expenses	$ 58,000	(not including debt service)
An investor will buy at a 9 percent return	$644,444	(maximum price the investor would pay)

Let's assume the investor (perhaps you in another deal) understands the Rule of Small as it applies to real estate. It is clear that to increase the bottom-line return of this property, there are only certain things that can be done without changing its use:

- Increase rents. The best way to increase the bottom line is to provide for annual increases in rent. Some leases are tied to a cost of living index, or some other outside benchmark index. In these instances, any increase in that index will cause the rent to go up by the same percentage. If no such provision exists in the lease, you will have to wait until the tenant wants to renew or otherwise renegotiate the lease.

- Decrease expenses. Good management can accomplish a lot to attain this goal. The key is not just a reduction of expenses, but a reduction of the overall ratio of expense to the collected rent.

- Leverage the transaction. By obtaining financing that costs you less than the desired return on your investment, you will obtain positive leverage. The money you borrow will decrease the amount of capital you have invested, so your ultimate return is leveraged up.

- Do a combination of the above. A mix of more than one of these elements will generally be the target any new owner should seek to accomplish.

Let's look at these four strategies in action. In our 10-unit apartment example, say the investors can do a little of each of the value-enhancing techniques. The rents are bumped up to $675 a month, the expenses are cut by $300 a month, and 80 percent of the price can be OPM from a local savings and loan at an 8 percent total payment of principal and interest per year. Here is the new economics of the deal:

Gross rent	$ 81,000	
Less the new expenses	$ 16,400	($20,000 less $3,600 of reduction)

New net operating income (NOI) $ 64,600

Annual cost of debt $ 41,244   (principal and interest of the new
                                                 $515,555 mortgage)

New cash flow $ 23,356

Capital invested $128,889

The investors are going to borrow 80 percent of the purchase price needed before the changes, which was $644,444, so the loan will be $515,555. The cost of this debt is 8 percent of that amount per year, or $41,244. This leaves the investors with a cash flow at the end of the year of $23,356 (NOI of $64,600 less $41,244 of debt service equals $23,356 in cash flow). Here is the recap thus far into the deal:

Price $644,444

Loan $515,555

Cash invested $128,889

Cash flow $ 23,356

Return on cash   18 percent   (18 percent of the of $128,889 cash invested)

The investors purchased at $644,444 and borrowed $515,555 so they have only invested $128,889 of their own capital. On this they earn $23,356 in cash flow each year. That is a return equal to a touch over 18 percent. So the Rule of Small has done it again. The investors went from an anticipated return of 9 percent to 18 percent with some very modest changes in the economic structure of the deal.

Every rental deal you get into will have the same potential. Sometimes the move to a better leveraged investment does not occur overnight. However, it may occur the very next day after you close. How so? Well, what if you negotiated the above purchase, but the deal was that you would close in six months. In the meantime you would take some of the cash you were going to put down at the closing and use it to make some improvements to the property.

Improvements that can quickly show returns are interior and exterior paint (especially the front door), new landscaping, a nice new stone walkway, and similar sorts of things. You do this prior to closing—in fact, you do this prior to getting your mortgage commitment. Now the property looks different. You might even have rented out a vacant space or two at a higher monthly rent than the other tenants are paying, which shows the lender that higher rents are likely. Now, armed with a new proforma at higher rents, you borrow even more money than did the investor in the above example. Every deal will have the potential to allow you to increase rents and decrease the ratio of your expenses to your gross revenue. Remember, you don't even have to actually reduce expenses, only the proportion of expenses to the total revenue. Small wins every time. You will see a lot more of this in action throughout this book.

Six Primary Factors That Make Real Estate Value Go Up or Down

There are six primary factors that can cause the value of any real estate to rise or fall:

1. Supply and demand
2. Local zoning
3. Changes in infrastructure
4. Economic obsolescence
5. Maintenance procedures
6. Motivation to buy or sell

Each is discussed in detail here as to how and why it changes the value of real estate. You will quickly discover that the same property may be impacted in either direction by the same factor. A change in infrastructure, like the widening of the road in front of a strip store, can cause a sudden downturn in value as tenants move out or go out of business, but a year or two later that new roadway can cause the value to jump to a higher level than it originally was. The timing and duration of the factor can play an important role in how you time your acquisition or sale of the subject property. Let's look at each of these factors from the following angles:

- General comments
- Effect on value (increase or decrease)
- How to take advantage of the situation
- Pitfalls to watch out for

Supply and Demand

General Comments: The supply-and-demand effect tends to balance itself out in the long run. However, there is always a period at each end of the cycle when there is either a greater demand than supply or a greater supply than demand. It is important, when viewing a potential supply-and-demand situation, that you make sure you are looking at all apples, or all oranges, and not a mix of the two. For example, in a hot market there can be several things going on at the same time. All expensive homes in the million-dollar-and-up range can be in great demand with a moderate to low supply, while townhomes below that price might be overbuilt and the demand for such properties waning. This would suggest that an ideal time to buy a townhome is just around the corner and that it is likely a great time to sell a million-dollar house.

Effect on Value: Whenever there is a strong demand for a product, its value will go up. It is a good idea to examine the situation, however, to ascertain what has created the current demand that did not exist previously. If expensive high-rise condos are the hot ticket right now, what caused that? Have drug smugglers found this a great place to do business? Are people retiring to the area in greater numbers because the air above the ground floor is more healthful than at first-floor level? Or is it that no new high-rises have been built for a long time, and that newness of product has always been in demand but there were none available to buy?

Newton found out that what goes up also comes down, but when it comes to real estate, that fact may not have any real bearing on your future profit or loss. You have already seen that you can profit nicely even when you sell for less than you paid for a property, but it helps to make even more than you paid. Property values are relative, however, and the true test of value is what you can buy once you sell. Too many people overlook that factor and put a big profit in their pocket, only to find that there is nothing in the marketplace that they can purchase to replace what they just sold. Therefore I always caution investors when they get excited about a profit or despondent over a potential loss of value.

The supply-and-demand cycle is just that—a cycle. If the investment property is still throwing off a return you can live with, then hold on to a declining value if there is a good reason for the downturn, and if the light at the end of the tunnel—a change in the cycle—is just around the corner.

How to Take Advantage of the Situation: As I just mentioned, it might be a good idea to ride the down-cycle through its course if you find that you are well into it. If, however, you are just entering the cycle, you may want to consider making a move before the situation worsens, if you can. If you are in a really hot market, it is usually easy to see when the end is coming. All you have to do is to check out how much inventory is either available or being planned. If the product is flex-space (warehouse/office buildings), a quick review of industrial vacant or redevelopment land available can give you a good clue as to how long the rise in redevelopment will last. If there is a shortage of available land, the new development will come to a sudden halt and prices in the existing product will go even higher. This will occur because the demand will continue, until the high prices cause developers to open up other areas that are not too distant from the present area. Then local prices may stabilize or even drop as cheaper product comes available elsewhere. This concept can be applied to any kind of real estate use.

In almost any situation, there are opportunities to be had. A strong demand will eventually cause one of two events to happen. The first is that developers will run out of new sites to develop and the unspent demand will open up other areas. If you know that the current hot area will run out of development sites, then be the first (or one of the first, anyway) to find a new area that will offer opportunity for new product at a better buy. Keep in mind this new product will need to overcome the distance from the hot area by offering a similar or better product at a lower price.

The other possibility is that the demand will continue, and more and more supply will be developed in anticipation of the demand, until there is an overabundance of supply. Bam!—the hot market suddenly slows and things even out. You will have anticipated this and already be looking for an in-fill location and a new kind of product that will cater to the people who are occupying all these flex-space warehouse/offices. (In-fill locations are areas in the heart of existing communities or development where old buildings are torn down to make way for new product.)

Pitfalls to Watch Out For: The interplay of supply and demand is a factor that rarely exists by itself. There are almost always two or more factors occurring at the same time. One of the most critical outside influences to fuel the supply-and-demand cycle is the sudden loss or considerable reduction of the supply side of the equation. I say "sudden" because it may appear that way to the general public while not actually being sudden at all. For example, the city rezones a major area of land, currently zoned for industrial use that allows flex-space development and changes it into low-density office park zoning. This will not spur new office park development unless that was already a hot issue, but it sure will affect the flex-space market that is soon to be hot by decreasing the supply of that product. Be wary of well-intending government officials.

Local Zoning

General Comments: As I stress use over any other single determinant of the ultimate value of real estate, zoning becomes the critical factor that all investors must take into consideration. Zoning is an ever-changing element that goes through evolution within a city. When the city fathers are development-prone and embrace every new project with open arms, the codes and their interpretation may be relaxed; whereas when one or two of the city commissioners are voted out and new ones replace them, the mood changes and antidevelopment is the rule of the day. Because zoning is so important, be sure to pay close attention to the "pitfalls" section of this category.

Effect on Value: Zoning and the building codes that regulate what actually is buildable are far more critical to commercial real estate than to single family homes. Why? Because the codes are tougher and more comprehensive. A home owner can, in most areas of the country, install a well system for drinking water without being required to test the water quality. But if the property is a hotel or restaurant or any business operation, the well water would have to be tested, and if it were found unsuitable for consumption, another water source (bottled water or a water purification system designed for commercial use, for example) would need to be provided.

Zoning is in constant flux—that is, it is going through evolution and change. This means that what you were able to do with your property 15 years ago when you purchased it may not be the same today when you want to tear down your old motel and put up a brand new Hampton Inn. For this and many other reasons (specific to each unique combination of area, current zoning, and intended use), consider zoning to be a potential pitfall you must overcome. New interpretations of the code are made by zoning board members as well as city commissioners, none of whom may be experts in the field, and who may have no experience in investing, developing, or financing a project like the one they are nonetheless about to either turn down or approve.

Yet zoning is also a grand opportunity that awaits the investor who takes the time to study how it can be used. Those potentials for profit will come to anyone who can learn how to look beyond the fact that a neighborhood is made up of small frame homes that were built 70 years ago and realize that the underlying zoning allows multifamily homes with a mix of commercial areas in between. These are the places where dreams are formed, goals realized, and fortunes are made.

How to Take Advantage of the Situation: When you truly understand the zoning ordinances and building codes of your comfort zone, you will discover that it is the guidebook showing you where to look for your commercial investments. The example of old single family homes sitting on land that is zoned for high-density, multifamily properties is real. Many cities have these areas right in the more valuable parts of town—the center of town. Individual lots and building sites can be assembled, allowing a developer or investor to end up with entire blocks of high-density real estate. The creation of a large building site where only small lots existed before is not the result of rocket science. Mind you, the zoning was there all the time. The homes sat there for 40 years or more, but no one really paid attention to the situation—until you did.

Let this be a good example of why the steps to wealth are almost never seen by most people. The more you know about what is going on in your backyard, the greater the opportunity you will have to recognize where to dig for your gold.

Pitfalls to Watch Out For: There are many factors, however, that create difficulty when analyzing zoning. First of all, the terminology or classification of zoning differs greatly between communities. Cities within the same county may have similar zoning classifications but the interpretations of what they allow can differ greatly. An R-4 classification might mean four units per acre in one city, whereas RMM4 might be the counterpart zoning in the adjoining city. Some zoning classifications, such as a B-3 zoning, might be the most flexible commercial and business zoning in one city, but in an adjoining city it might be one of the least flexible. The key is to know the applicable zoning codes and what is allowed and not allowed.

Yet even when you think you've figured out what you can do, you may notice a small asterisk by the words "minimum setback" and 10 pages later discover that setback is tied to height, and that the higher you go, the greater the setback. These are what I call "gottcha" terms, and they can be hidden within the code—not entirely because the planners want to hide them, but because they get added years after the original code was drafted. When it comes to zoning (and anything else that is governed by the city or county commissioners or one or more of their departments), you must keep abreast of not only the codes and ordinances, but how they are applied to situations that parallel your own circumstance.

Be sure that any purchase agreement you present to a seller gives you the right to withdraw from the agreement if you are not able to use the property as you want to. Be sure that your intentions have been well documented in the purchase agreement so that there are not legal complications later if you need to withdraw from the deal, if you are turned down by the appropriate department. As a seller, make sure that a buyer does not lock you up for a period of time longer than you are willing to wait if problems arise in this or any issue where future approvals (building permits, occupational licenses, special exception approvals, and the like) are required.

Changes in Infrastructure

General Comments: A change in any infrastructure can have a rippling effect on the value of real estate. I have already used several examples of this kind of value-changing factor, such as new or expanded roadways, or bridges that bring traffic, good or bad, to an area. A new stadium, a playhouse, a new park—all these things will have an impact on the value of some real estate. Some will go up in value while others will decline.

Effect on Value: Because this factor is long in planning, the real estate insider will have ample time to consider how the change will affect the surrounding area, or to decide whether another, more distant area will benefit more from the change. The beauty of this factor is that the results from infrastructure changes are very predictable. What happens to the surrounding property when a mega shopping center is built? Where do the values go in any neighborhood that suddenly gets a university or a big expansion of the downtown government center? New roads, bridges, airports, schools and whatever else that has happened in the last few months, or has been announced as planned in the near future, will have an effect on property values. The key is to know which values will go up, which will go down, and why. To ascertain that, all you have to do is check out what happened elsewhere in similar circumstances. History will repeat itself—of that you can be sure.

How to Take Advantage of the Situation: You will be able to take advantage of a situation only if you have become aware of it. This is a dilemma with most of these factors. They can slip past you and by the time you know what is going on, it is too late to get the maximum benefit from the situation. You learn about changes of infrastructure at the same governmental offices where you find out about zoning and the city fathers' approach to future development. Remember, nothing happens with respect to changes in any infrastructure within a city that has not followed a process of public meetings. Anyone can keep informed by attaining these meetings. The most important of these meetings are city and county planning and zoning (P&Z) board meetings, city and county commission meetings, and new development workshop meetings (where the developer and the P&Z staff often try to satisfy the public and work out differences at the same time). There are other meetings that are noteworthy, but start with just your own city meetings first and go from there.

When you discover, at a P&Z board meeting, that a developer is planning a new amusement park on the north side of town where old man McDonald's farm is located, you might just want to take a ride out that way and start checking out property values. Remember that it is essential for you to be more than just observant at these meetings. Take the opportunity to meet the people—not just the commissioners and the board members, but the other important people in the room, and, most important, all those fellow real estate insiders who are already members of that exclusive club you are in the process of joining.

Pitfalls to Watch Out For: Government changes too. Appointed members of boards resign and the faces of everyone you ever saw sitting on the dais at one of these meetings will eventually be replaced. Not only are they gone, but there may be newcomers who have ideas and approaches different from those the former members had. This means you have to play it close, meet the new members, and learn which way they lean and how they are apt to vote when it is your turn to seek their approval for a project.

Economic Obsolescence

General Comments: I have touched on this factor earlier in words and concepts you need to know. It is one of the major factors that causes slums and brings about urban renewal. What is built and not maintained will deteriorate, just like the Roman Empire, and just like the housing project that is let go to ruin. But it is also more subtle. It can be an entire community that does not keep up with the times. Traffic flow goes to pot, the inner city starts to get run down, and people begin to move to the suburbs, leaving the downtown area even worse off than before as the spiral of devaluation increases. I've seen many cities where this has happened. Likely, so have you.

Effect on Value: Flip a coin, call it opportunity or chaos. Economic obsolescence is one of those natural events that allows for a renewal of thought and of use. The impact of this factor depends on how widespread the obsolescence is. If it is only one or two buildings then the problem is best seen as an opportunity. The value of the property affected by economic obsolescence will go down. This allows a buyer the chance to purchase it with room to improve the existing structure, or to buy it for the land value and start all over again. *Economic conversion*, a technique I discuss in Chapter 11, refers to the opportunity to transform an existing property when its current use has less economic viability than a new use for the same property. This is a good way to go with many properties.

How to Take Advantage of the Situation: I just gave you one answer. Economic conversion may be the best solution, but it is not the only one. In economic conversion you turn to our good friend, the zoning that is applied to the property, and review all the possible uses that can be put on that property. If none look promising, then visit with the head of planning and zoning and ask if the city staff would support an alternative zoning for that site. Remember, responsible government will not want to see economic obsolescence take hold, and the quicker they can introduce a more viable use, the better it is for everyone. They might actually agree with this statement and help you get a zoning that lets you be the one to make that introduction. As I have mentioned earlier, zoning is ever changing. Some of these changes are made by the city at staff recommendations. Other changes are made at the request of a property owner. Economic conversion may work best with a change in zoning to allow more flexibility in the future use.

Some examples of economic conversion include an old Victorian home that you can turn into several nice medical or legal offices; an old, single-story motel that becomes an antique mart; and a closed "big box" (any big building like an old supermarket, or department store—also called a "big black box") that becomes a multiscreen movie house, a mushroom farm, and so on.

Pitfalls to Watch Out For: I touched on the first pitfall earlier—that is anything to do with zoning and building codes must be approached very carefully. Some other pitfalls appear with closely related problems such as parking codes and fire codes. Both of these can be expensive to deal with if they become major issues in the remodeling. The word *remodeling* introduces something else, namely that the cost to remodel anything can get out of hand very fast. If you don't have detailed as-built plans, or if the building has been remodeled in the past and no reliable plans for that remodeling are available, every time you remove a wall you can be in for a big and very expensive surprise.

Maintenance Procedures

General Comments: Let it run down and pretty soon the whole neighborhood runs down with you. The approach you take to maintenance should fit with your goals of investing in the property.

Effect on Value: It's a downhill trip for the property that is not being well maintained, unless there is a good reason for the lack of maintenance. If the management posture is to just keep it producing for a little longer until you tear it down, then that strategy might be okay. For example, when you buy a property with the idea to remove the existing buildings in ten years or so, it might be easy to let the property deteriorate while getting every dime of rent you can. However, this may initiate a downward turn for the neighborhood, which will adversely affect your future development. Poor maintenance under any circumstance is not a good idea. I would recommend that you protect the surrounding values by at least keeping a good face on the property. If you don't, you may not be able to stop that downward spiral for the surrounding properties.

How to Take Advantage of the Situation: Whenever I see a property that is slipping down the maintenance hill, I make a point of checking with the owner to see if they want to sell and at what price. You will be surprised at the reasons people let well-located properties go into such a state: no money, out-of town or -state owners, so deep in debt and so out of shape that even the bank doesn't want the property, and so on. Often the property is owned by someone who just doesn't have the time or patience to deal with it. Interestingly, this same owner may not even want to deal with the process of selling the property. Root them out and you might get the buy of the year.

Pitfalls to Watch Out For: Today toxic mold is one of the worst nightmares you will ever face. A run-down property, especially one with roof leaks, may have that problem. It can be dealt with, but the remedy is expensive, so the new use for this property has to be a good one.

Motivation to Buy or Sell

General Comments: You have heard about the wolves being able to smell trouble, which is why they are suddenly at your door when you are down on your luck. That is part of the factor of motivation. When you are forced to sell is the very time that no one wants to come close to the price you need. It often doesn't matter how realistic your asking price is. On the other hand, when you are the most qualified buyer, the seller might try to hold you up for a price greater than what anyone else would pay.

Effect on Value: The answer to this is not so obvious as you might think. A seller who is highly motivated to sell may hide the reason for this motivation from the very person who is trying to help him—his broker. I have had many clients who were clearly so motivated to sell that you could smell it a mile away. Why were they so motivated? I heard dozens of the wrong reasons. Why the wrong ones? Many people are embarrassed to acknowledge they have failed at something. Also, they didn't want other people to know just how desperate things had become, either with a marriage, a health issue, job problems, debt up to their ears, or the bodies buried in the backyard. I have heard them all, but rarely the real reason.

Values go down when you show urgency, unless the market is so hot and your property so ripe that nothing will stop a buyer from paying a decent price. Buyers who are logical about the situation often do all they can to hide the fact that they actually want to buy. There are lots of ways to protect yourself in this situation. As a seller, try using an out-of-town lawyer or broker, as an example. But if word of your motivation gets out, then you might have to step up and accept the penalty in the form of a lower price.

How to Take Advantage of the Situation: Let's look at the two situations. Say you are a desperate, highly motivated seller, whatever the reason. What should you do? My advice is to take a step back from the property and the problem and look at the reality of the situation. Do you really need to sell at all? You see, most people believe that selling the property is their only way out. Divorcing, so gotta sell; moving to the other side of the world for a new job, gotta sell; wife is having triplets, so gotta sell. The dog dug up one of the bodies, gotta sell (okay, with this one, by all means, sell). All the reasons that exist should be reexamined. Perhaps the property should be rented out, or perhaps a joint venture with a local investor to do an economic conversion would prove interesting, or a real estate exchange for another property in the town where you are moving to. All of these are options that many people fail to look at.

The worst part of this situation is that many people let the real reason for this desperation fester to the point that someone else makes the decision for them. That is called foreclosure and it hurts. So look at all the options and talk out the real problem with your broker. If finances are part of the dilemma, then talk with the bank or the lender and see what can be done. Believe me, banks do not want to foreclose, but they will if a solution is not offered them.

For the potential buyer who might be faced with paying too much, there are some fine tactics that can help with that situation. One is called, "I'll pay your price if you accept my terms." This gives the seller the opportunity to brag about holding you up at the closing for big bucks, while at the same time you smile because you got terms that made it work for you. Sometimes the situation requires some hard negotiations to take the phantoms out of the picture. Who are the phantoms? They are all the other people the seller is telling you are out there trying to buy the property. If you know you are being asked to buy at a price that you think is too high, then put your lower offer on the table and give the seller a "take it or leave it" proposition.

You can always say, "I was only kidding."

Pitfalls to Watch Out For: The biggest pitfall for both sides of the motivation factor is to let emotion get in the way of a sound business deal, and to let it go to the point that you are not the one in control of the deal. I have sweated out many deals, both mine and my clients, where the motivation was so strong that all the other side of the deal had to do was get a hint at just how strong it was and the deal would go south. Buyers would not meet the asking price or anywhere near it, or sellers would hold out for price and terms that were not realistic. I don't have much sympathy for buyers or sellers who let that happen to themselves, so never let a deal die because you got too emotionally involved.

CHAPTER 4

How to Build an Effective Commercial Real Estate Comfort Zone

> The goals of this chapter are:
>
> **To Provide You with The Steps Necessary to Establish Your Comfort Zone**
>
> **To Illustrate How and Where to Locate Your Comfort Zone**

Your comfort zone is similar to a child's favorite blanket or stuffed animal. For a young child it provides comfort in the middle of a hectic day, as he cries himself to sleep. For you it is the relaxing realization that you are in your own territory, where no one can intimidate you, and where no one knows the terrain better than you do. In real estate investing, your comfort zone is that place you have chosen to be your farm of investment properties. It is where you will seek and find your fortune.

This chapter is dedicated to getting you started on the right foot. It is designed to give you all the steps you should take to pick the area, tips on what will make that area really work for you, and then a map of how to proceed to make that zone the single place you know like the back of your hand.

Key Words and Concepts to Build Your Insider Knowledge

Listing Services
FSBO
Active Listings
Tax Assessor
MapQuest
Zoning Maps

Listing Service

Your local board of realtors and other real estate groups have sources of their listed properties that you can freely access anytime you want. Check with any realtor about this, and look for those free magazines that advertise real estate for sale in your area. They are often found on curbside racks near full service restaurants and other businesses frequented by tourists. This information source will provide you with data that can be helpful to you when you start to review the local real estate market. Local newspapers often have a weekly section devoted to recent sales, with the names of both buyer and seller and the price of the property sold. Start clipping these out when you see property that is in your designated comfort zone.

FSBO

This is pronounced "fizz-boe" and means "for sale by owner." This is an invitation to meet the owner of a property that you might want to buy. Even if the property is not something you would like to own, if it is in your comfort zone, call the phone number on the sign or announcement anyway, and start meeting the people who own property in your comfort zone. The more inside information you get, the better it will be for you in the long run.

Active Listings

These are listings the local realtors are actively working. They are not sold, pending sale, expired, closed, or canceled (the other potential realtor listing classifications). Of the total list, the ones that are the most interesting are listed as active, closed, or expired. The active listings are those properties that are currently on the market. The closed listings are interesting because there will be information tied to them that tells you what, who, and how much the property actually sold for.

The expired listings can be a hidden gem. These are listings that didn't sell but eventually the original listing expired. They may have been relisted at a lower price, or they may now be free game for anyone who wants to track down the owner. Expired listings always raise the interesting question: Why didn't the property sell? If the seller was motivated before, he might be nearly desperate by now. Check these listings out when you come across them. If you are working with a realtor, then alert your realtor that you want to concentrate on the expired listings. Believe me, realtors will thank you for taking this tactic, because those listings do not belong to another real estate office so they won't have to split the fee with another sales team.

Tax Assessor

The tax assessor and his or her often very large staff maintains the property records of most communities. This is a county level position, so once you meet the tax assessor and get to know how their office works, and what a gold mine of information they are, you won't need to meet another until you go to another county. Slowly tax assessors' data is becoming available on the Internet and the information is getting easier to obtain. In most of the Florida areas where I prospect my investments and listings, I am able to sit at my computer and in seconds find out the names of the owners of a property, when they bought it, how much they paid, who the seller was, who the original owner was that took the vacant land and built the building, and a wealth of other information.

Keep in mind that every transaction that takes place where documents must be recorded—like property transfers, for example—is public information and will be available to you free, and usually without difficulty. In areas where the data is not yet available on the Internet, you may have to pay a visit to the tax assessor's office, but that is not a painful event. You will want to learn the ins and outs of this source of information as quickly as you can. There are people in these offices who will walk you through the computer programs (if they have them) or their card or microfilm files. When you are being shown the ropes of the system, be sure to make good notes of what you are learning so you don't become a pest who can never seem to remember what you did last time.

MapQuest

MapQuest is just one of many different mapping programs on the Internet. You reach their home page by going to www.mapquest.com. Once you are there, you might have to play around with it until you get the hang of it, but it is relatively simple. MapQuest will give you a detailed map of just about any place in the United States. You can zoom in to get a close-up, or expand out until you can see the entire state or states around the location you chose. There is also a section you can instantly switch to that will show you an aerial (if available) of the area. This simple and free source of data would have cost thousands of dollars a year to access a few years ago, but now it is free. Use these sources and make note of the ones that are most friendly and give you the best information for your area. While this information is generally accurate, any data network of this size can have glitches or improperly programmed information. If the data is critical, it is a good idea to double-check important information with more than one source. Search the Web for other "Map" web pages; there are several others that may provide better results for your specific need.

Zoning Maps

Each city and county has zoning maps of the real estate that is solely within its jurisdiction. The maps are usually not free but are never really costly. They are detailed enough that you should be able to find any property within the prescribed area without much difficulty, although sometimes you will need the help of a magnifying glass. These maps also include a section where the different zoning codes are scattered about on the map, with a brief description of what each code represents. Remember that these descriptions are basic and will never tell you the whole story.

For example, under a general heading of "Residential Zoning" you might find a list that starts with R-1, then R-1a, R-2, R-4, and so on. Next to each of these will be a brief description, like "R-1—single family low density;" "R-1a—single family cluster;" "R-2—duplex" (two units), and so on. Believe me, you don't know much yet, and to learn more you will have to get the building and zoning code book for that specific city or, if it's an unincorporated area (not within a city limit), for the county. Unfortunately for the computer illiterate, these codes have been brought up to high-tech levels and might be available only on the Internet.

The bad news even for the computer literate is that these codes are usually cumbersome to deal with because of the amount of information you have to absorb. Worse, however, is the fact that the full scope of rules that govern any single property is almost never found in one section. An example of this is where a zoning code indicates that in a B-2 zoning you can also build anything allowed in B-1 zoning. Okay, so you look at B-1 zoning, and it tells you that B-1 will allow anything which is also allowed in C-3 zoning, and so on.

The best way to deal with city ordinances and building codes is to have a printed version of the building and zoning codes—buy it, or get a computer friend of yours to print out the one on the Internet. Only with this book, and frequent updates that contain changes to the printed or Internet versions, will you be able to get the whole of the *printed* story. In other words, all you can get is what is printed. How it is interpreted by those who regulate and control these ordinances and codes may be another story in itself. I won't get into that right now, but as you read this book you will see examples where what the code says is not entirely what the city fathers will allow. That is one of the major issues with building and zoning codes that frustrates many investors as well as professional land planners.

I advise you to make several copies of the zoning maps of your area (maybe more than one page), as you will eventually need more than one copy. Copies of large zoning maps can be obtained at a blueprint facility, which is where architects and engineers obtain copies of large plans and drawings. This will generally be less expensive than purchasing several copies from the original source.

Elements Common to All Initial Comfort Zones

The specific elements of your comfort zone will have to be defined by you. These elements will be the categories of property you most want to include in your investment portfolio, the general price range of those properties, and their level of rental potential (already at the top, needing some improvement, or real fixer-uppers). I will, however, illustrate what makes up a good zone and how you can establish the boundaries of that zone to maximize its benefits to you.

Some elements are universal to all comfort zones. I will list these as they apply to your first comfort zone, as the first such zone is the most important. Later you can relax some of the criteria about to be listed, but for now, stick to the following four:

1. Close proximity
2. Limited number of opportunities
3. Within one governing area
4. Well-defined area

Close Proximity

Choose an area close to where you live and work. This proximity will let you drive through the area every time you travel to and from work. Vary your routes as much as you can, and you will begin to see things about the area you have overlooked before. These things will be opportunities that will soon begin to stick out like sore thumbs.

Limited Number of Opportunities

Design each comfort zone so that it does not contain so many properties that it overwhelms your ability to learn about them. As your knowledge in zoning and other codes grows, you will be able to expand the area.

Initially the zone should contain a minimum of several hundred of the category of investment properties you believe you would like to own. Keep in mind that you don't have to narrow your investments down to one single kind of property. Be a bit flexible, particularly in the beginning. Later on, as you find you are more comfortable with one niche of property over another, you can begin to specialize. I know people who consider themselves to be "Mr. Gas Station" or "The Fast Food Brothers" or "Rental Apartment King." Other investors branch out into different kinds of real estate. Let your natural feel for the property tell you what best suits your talents and abilities.

Within One Governing Area

Your first comfort zone should be totally within one governing area. By keeping the properties within the same city or county unincorporated area, your research and study will be confined to one set of rules and regulations. You want to limit the number of meetings you go to and zoning ordinances and building codes you need to learn.

Once you master this zone then expand it, staying, if possible, in the same city until you run out of properties to buy and need to branch out into another area.

When you do expand, try to first expand the existing zone by simply adding area that is adjoining. If that is not possible or beneficial, due to the lack of the category of property you are interested in, then try to stay within the same governing area.

Well-Defined Area

Mark your comfort zone on the city zoning maps so you always know when you are there. It will be tempting to constantly expand the zone, but you must resist expanding it too quickly. Let that happen slowly until you come to a natural boundary. This might be a main street or the end of a specific subdivision. Keep the areas small at first, and work them until you know everything possible about the history of the area, the current market values of the properties it contains, and the potential for the area or parts of to improve in the future.

Key Factors to Becoming an Expert in Your Own Backyard

The following five key factors will aid you in becoming an expert in your comfort zone:

1. Learn the simple things.
2. Get the right tools.
3. Keep records of important data.
4. Research what happened in success stories.
5. Build walls around your comfort zone.

Learn the Simple Things

Remember, your goal is to get to know everything about the zone you will chose. This is 90 percent becoming aware of what is going on—meeting the people in the zone, getting to know what factors can affect the value of the real estate in that zone—and 10 percent relating what you learn to a specific area of your zone.

As you begin to absorb everything you can about the value of the property in the zone you will, slowly at first, begin to see opportunities where previously you only saw a run-down building. The actual learning process will occur as you make the commitment to start attending the planning and zoning board meetings. This is where new development projects are first introduced to the public. After one or two P&Z meetings you will want to begin to attend the City Commission meetings, as this is where those projects might get discussed and voted in or out.

The people you meet at those meetings are the present members of the unofficial real estate insiders club. Get to know them, just as you will get to know the mayor, the staff members of the city planning and zoning departments, the building department officials, and the other members of the city commission. All the members of the planning and zoning board—volunteers appointed by the commissioners—are the first line of attack (or defense, depending on your point of view of any project) and can have an important effect on what goes on.

The people who make presentations at these meetings or speak for or against any of these projects will be the developers, their lawyers and experts, and those who are against the projects, along with their lawyers and experts. All these people will become your teachers as to the elements that govern your comfort zone.

Get the Right Tools

Prior to attending any meetings, it is a good idea to obtain the initial tools you will need. You can obtain most of the items or information from the area building department, the city hall, or other departments within the city. The tools to start are few. Here is the initial list:

- The city zoning map and the book of the building and zoning ordinances and codes which you will get from the city building and zoning department.
- A list of principal characters, with full names and phone numbers, which include all the city commissioners, and the city manager, and city attorney; head of the building department; head of the planning and zoning department; head and members of the planning and zoning board; county commissioners.

You will be able to get this list from the appropriate departments. If you run into any snag, my best suggestion is to call the office of the mayor, ask for his or her secretary, and introduce yourself as a real estate investor new to the area. Explain the list of characters you need to obtain addresses and phone numbers for, and ask the secretary or assistant who might be the best person to help you. You will get help.

Once you have these tools and information, you are ready to start meeting the principal players. As you begin to narrow down your comfort zone, you will find the zoning map and codes essential to the ultimate selection of the area.

Keep Records of Important Data

Your record system can be as elaborate or as simple as will work for you. The key in the early stages is to meet people and let them get to know you as a real estate investor. They will later assume (rightly so, by then) that you are, in fact, a local real estate insider. However, you will need to make note of important people you meet or see in action at the city and county meetings. As you drive around your potential comfort zone, make note of what you encounter. What is for sale, whom to contact, and so on will all become important later on.

As you discover phone numbers and names of owners or brokers, make contact with those people. Do not worry if the property in question is not what you want to invest in. This is your fact-finding stage, and you need to learn about all the property in your zone.

You should become an avid reader of the business and real estate sections of the local newspaper. These will be filled with information that at first won't appear to be important to you. Then one day you meet one of the people interviewed, and it turns out they own a property in your area. Start programming your onboard computer (your brain) to track the events of your community

A good source of information for years to come will be your photographic record of the events in the zone. If you don't currently own a simple 35 mm camera, or a digital camera, then buy one or the other. Whatever it is, it should be easy to operate and small enough to fit in your coat pocket. As you see properties that are for sale or have recently sold, take a photo of them. On the back of the photo be sure to note the date, the property address, the legal description, the property owner at that date, the asking price, and the sold price. All this information will be easily obtained and will create a historic record of what has been going on in your zone. In just a few years you will have visual proof of what kind of trend is occurring in your area.

Always take photographs of property you own at regular intervals, say at least once a year. You will be surprised how fast time flies and how differently a well-maintained property matures compared to those that are just barely kept in operation.

Research What Happened in Success Stories

You will often hear or read about how someone developed a new shopping center on the other side of town, or filed for a permit to build a high-rise office building in the center of town. These are success stories you should pay close attention to.

How did they come about? Who were the players? Be curious about these events because you will probably cross paths with these people at some time in your investing future.

Build Walls around Your Comfort Zone

You want to keep the area small enough that you can effectively become an expert in that area. Nothing that goes on in the zone should be excluded. In the box is a list of factors that you should get to know. Although some of these factors may appear to have little to do with your investing in any category of real estate in the area, I can assure you that each and every one will play some role, no matter how minor. While this list is rather comprehensive, it may not include certain elements that are particular to your community or your comfort zone. You must remember that the success of any commercial real estate venture is dependent on the acceptance of the project by the local area, the attitudes of the people who work in the venture, and the patrons of the businesses, or those who rent the apartments or facilities.

Review this list and type or write it out as a checklist of the things you need to be aware of to insure that you are learning everything possible within the walls of your comfort zone. Consider each item on this checklist as it would apply to any property in your zone. Remember that different zoning codes may have different applications of these items. Be sure to learn each variation, or at least know where to quickly find the answers. Most of the answers will be found in the zoning or building code books, or by calling the appropriate city department.

Learn How to Let Your Computer Lead the Way to Your Success

If you are not computer literate right now, then after you read this paragraph, stop and make your next goal to learn how to surf the Web for information. You don't have to

> **Your Comfort Zone Checklist**
>
> Building setback minimum allowed by zoning code
> Building heights allowed by zoning code
> Commissioners (city and county) for the zone
> Emergency plans for storms or other emergencies
> Fire codes
> Fire stations serving the zone
> Libraries serving the area
> Master plan for transportation and traffic ways for the zone
> Nearest emergency room and hospital
> Public transportation
> Public parks in the zone
> Residential density per acre allowed by zoning code
> School districts
> School locations
> Shopping areas for the zone
> Storm or emergency shelters
> Utility upgrade plans for the zone
> Zoning codes

own a computer, but even a used one will be worth the investment, and it does not have to be loaded with bells and whistles either. There are computers available for public use at libraries and satellite libraries around town, so get with it. You will be very glad you did.

There are many ways to start to build an address book for Internet information sources. The best way is to start with the most effective source you will use, the tax assessor's web page. This source is full of data you will need in order to be on the top of your real estate investment game.

Almost every developer who has a reputation to protect has a web page. Usually, in the local real estate section of the newspaper, somewhere down at the bottom of their advertisements, they will print their web or e-mail address. (Mine, by the way, is a simple e-mail address, CummingsRealty@aol.com.)

You can start to search for other sources by going to the "search" line of your Internet browser. Ask for almost anything and you will generally get many potential sources. Spend a moment looking for what appear to be the best sources, those that are governmental or institutional and not just advertisements. Check out only the important-looking ones, and save the advertisements for a day when you have absolutely nothing better to do.

When you find a source that proves to be valuable to you, mark it as a favorite (that little red heart in AOL, or just "favorite" in most other Internet browsers) so you can get back to that site easily. If you can, form a file—say, "Real Estate Data"—and save those web sites as favorites in that file on your computer.

How to Choose Your Comfort Zone

The actual process of choosing your comfort zone is depicted in the following nine stages. These nine steps should be treated as an overall process that takes place simultaneously, rather than as a series of individual steps that must each be accomplished prior to moving on to the next one. The following list outlines the stages, each of which is then discussed in detail.

1. Pick two categories of real estate you want to own.
2. Discover what kind of zoning allows that use.
3. Review the city zoning maps for that zoning code.
4. Highlight the areas of town with that zoning.
5. Drive around town and decide what areas appeal to you.

6. Combine one or more areas until you have a minimum of 100 properties.

7. Mark the boundaries of these areas.

8. Watch for notices of public meetings or homeowner meetings pertaining to your zones.

9. Begin to become an expert in each area.

Pick Two Categories of Real Estate You Want to Own

It doesn't matter if these are the two categories you ultimately end up with. The key here is to get started with something. My suggestion is that one of the two categories should be tied to a need you have right now. Are you renting? If so, then why not include small apartment buildings as one of those categories? Many real estate investors have started out owning and living in their own rental apartment building. I know from experience that it was a great way for me to start. If you are in business for yourself or with others and rent your place of business, then a strip store or industrial complex might fit the bill to satisfy that need. Whenever you can stop paying rent and apply that capital to your real estate, you are ahead of the game.

Discover What Kind of Zoning Allows That Use

Once you have chosen two categories of real estate, dig into the building and zoning code books and find out which zoning categories will allow that use. You are likely to find more than one zoning category that will work, as it is usual for some uses to be progressive in a specific zoning. In other words, you can build a house in single family zoning but also in multifamily zoning. Going up the line, you can build a low-density apartment building in medium-density zoning, and a medium-density apartment building in high-density zoning. So cover all bases. By the way, when you are driving around and you see a small, single family home, do not *assume* that the zoning is limited to small, single family homes. Check it out—it might also allow a high-rise office building.

Review the City Zoning Maps for That Zoning Code

Once you know the different zoning categories or codes that you will need for the real estate you want to own, carefully go over the zoning map and make note of where these zoning categories can be found. It is likely that you will recognize some of the parts of town where you see these zoning codes, so you might rule out some of the areas you don't want to start with right away. But I caution you about doing this too early. If we are talking about investments and not personal residences, then do not be too particular early in the game. Great investments are often those that cater to the middle-range tenant, as there tend to be more of them than the super-rich tenants.

On the other hand, if you want to start out with the high end of whatever the real estate is, that is fine—however, it will narrow your selections.

Highlight the Areas of Town with That Zoning

Using a yellow highlighter, mark on the map the areas you want to scout out. Then drive around to review the neighborhoods. This is your chance to see what is going on in parts of town you may have never been to. Remember, this is a scouting expedition and needs to be given time and effort. A fast drive around town will not do. You should make note of any property that is for sale, for rent, or marked "sold." Check out the ownership and sales history of those properties. The ones that are for rent are especially important because they will give you an insight as to the income potential for the area.

As you begin to travel into other parts of town, you will find that the rental market and prices of properties that have sold have gone through some changes almost every time you visit the area. Ask yourself why. What is it about one area that makes the obtainable rents different from other areas of town? Don't try to rack your brain for the answer; ask the owner or a realtor who has a property for sale in that area or another area. Use their already loaded brain cells and save time.

Drive around Town and Decide What Areas Appeal to You

After you have made some preliminary scouting expeditions into different parts of town that fit the required zoning for your chosen real estate venture, then begin to narrow down the area or areas to create your first comfort zone. Be sure to mark each area clearly on your zoning maps. Remember to make several copies of the blank maps, as you will need many along the way.

Combine One or More Areas Until You Have a Maximum of 200 Properties

These will be separate properties made up of the two or more categories of real estate you have selected, plus properties that may not fit the category but are located on properly zoned lots. For example, if your choices are small professional buildings and mid-range apartment buildings, you might luck out and discover that in some areas the same zoning works for both uses. As you drive around, with the zoning map on the seat next to you (or in the hands of your trusty spouse, who can become a very important assistant in this process), you can start to make note of the older, need-to-be-torn-down properties that would be good locations for exactly what you want to own.

Mark the Boundaries of These Areas

Once you have made the selection of the initial comfort zone, mark the boundaries on the zoning map, and make several copies of the section you are going to turn into your investment gold mine. Enlarge the sections to a scale where you can make notations on the map. Your notations could be as simple as small numbers that refer back to a master sheet of information.

Watch for Notices of Public Meetings or Homeowner Meetings Pertaining to Your Zones

One way to do this is to be sure you get copies of the agendas of appropriate public meetings sent to you. Again, turn to the secretary of the mayor and ask him or her how you would do that. If you have an e-mail address (get one if you don't), they might be able to e-mail you the dates and agendas for every meeting. With the agenda in your hand, you can pick and choose which meetings to attend and which ones to skip. There will be meetings where absolutely nothing will seem to be of interest. However, I have never failed to benefit somehow from attending a public meeting.

The local homeowners' associations (HOAs) might be a little more difficult to locate, but they are listed somewhere, and the mayor's secretary will know where. Those associations are made up of homeowners or property owners in the area or people who have an interest in the area. They discuss what is going on and frequently have the developers of a pending project come and make presentations to them. This is so important, in fact, that most planning and zoning boards and commission meetings insist that the developers conduct such meetings to make sure that the local property owners are aware of what is happening. The voice of the neighborhood has been able to stop many projects cold in their tracks.

Begin to Become an Expert in Each Area

The process will move much faster than you think. Let me explain why. Take a look at the neighborhood where you presently live or work, or both. What do you know about what is going on there? Do you know the names of your neighbors? How about what they paid when they bought their properties? Or what they pay in real estate tax? Or the direct phone line to the nearest emergency room? Or where your employees would catch the bus to get to where they live? Odds are you struck out on most if not all of these questions. But you would not be alone.

The beauty of this process is that you will know more than the property owners and those who live there. This is a big boost to your confidence in learning about any specific real estate market area. And never underestimate the effect that eyeballing an area during your scouting expeditions has in building your knowledge of these areas. Real estate is a must-see, must-feel commodity. You can not get the true picture from a photograph—it is impossible. It takes a physical visit to a property to get to know it. Its value is based not just on what it looks like, but how the whole neighborhood shapes up, what kind of traffic flows through the area, who works there, and who comes there on business. Spend time in your comfort zone and it will treat you very well indeed.

CHAPTER 5

How to Accomplish Effective Due Diligence

The goals of this chapter are:

To Illustrate What You Must Know Before You Buy, Build or Lease

To Show You the Easy Steps to Ascertain This Data and What to Look For

To Give You Directions to Turn to When Things Turn Up Less Than Sweet

Due diligence is a term that few people used 20 years ago. Back then it was simple: You were allowed to make inspections, and if everything looked okay, you'd go ahead with your plans. But times change, and prices are getting higher and legal problems more costly to deal with, no matter if you are the buyer or the seller. The word of the day is *caveat emptor* (let the buyer beware). This applies no matter what kind of real estate you are buying, and especially with commercial real estate, because consumer protection laws that give home buyers some legal rights against sellers who violate those laws generally do not apply to investment property of any nature. You must be cautious and assume that the worst can happen even when dealing with noncommercial property.

In one recent Florida court case, the judge ruled that a residential condominium was a commercial property because the buyer planned to rent out the apartment. Because it was now a commercial transaction the buyer could not claim protection under laws of willful misrepresentation by the seller, even though the seller had lied about certain violations. The decision was based on the fact that as a commercial transaction, the buyer had been given ample time to make any and all inspections possible, and he had signed a contract that indicated the property was to be purchased "as is."

In this chapter I show you what you need to know before you buy, build, or lease; what you should do to go about getting the information; what problems you might find and where they can hide from you; and what to do once you are faced with those problems. It is essential for you to understand that commercial real estate presents far more problems when it comes to due diligence than does residential real estate. First of all, the laws of most states are very strict as to disclosure of known problems with residential real estate but much less strict in the area of commercial or investment real estate. Also, because you are apt to be dealing with leases and other contracts that are going to be a part of the investment package you are buying, these elements increase the amount of time required and the number of experts you may need to add to your due diligence team.

I want to caution you about the legal responsibilities that you think the buyer or seller or their brokers might have in any real estate transaction. Laws that deal with fraud, misrepresentation, outright lying, theft, and that sort of thing will vary from state to state. But no matter what wrong is done to you, the ultimate problem may not be who is in the right but how much it will cost you to try to get a remedy. Legal actions of almost any kind can be long, expensive, and stomach acid–forming, to say the least.

The best thing you can do is to keep your eyes wide open and learn to do your due diligence with a fine-tooth comb. If you can walk away from buying a property that even hints at having problems, then either make sure the problems are cleaned up, paid for, or dealt with to your satisfaction, or walk from the deal. Life is too short to walk into a deal where you know something smells wrong and you try to tough it out. So what about deals that people close on every day without ever having done one tenth of the due diligence this chapter stresses as essential? Well, fortunately, most people are honest, and most deals don't have problems, but why take that chance? Do your due diligence, with gusto.

But another word of caution: Avoid making the mistake of doing extensive and expensive due diligence without having a signed agreement that ties up the property. The reason should be obvious, but if you don't see it, take note: There are many sellers who don't want to give prospective buyers sufficient time to make these important investigations. Unless you feel you know so much about the property that you don't need to do such inspections, then pass on properties where sellers balk at reasonable due diligence periods in purchase contracts.

Key Words and Concepts to Build Your Insider Knowledge

Due Diligence by Definition
Letter of Intent
Formal Agreement
Inspection and Review Period
Environmental Inspections
Easements
Encroachments
Code Violations
Zoning Use
Allowed Use

Due Diligence by Definition

Due diligence is the process you perform prior to having your purchase contract go "hard." It goes "hard" when you reach a point where you have something other than your time and inspection fees at risk—perhaps a deposit, or a promise to close on the property without further inspections. Until then, in essence, you are asking the seller to take his property off the market with nothing more than a contract and perhaps a deposit that would be refundable if you decided to walk from the deal.

The amount and extent of the inspections and reviews you do to satisfy yourself of the condition of the property, buildings, and title will depend on what you are buying and what you intend to do with the real estate after you buy it. If it is a vacant tract of land that you don't have a clue what you will do with other than sit on it and hope it goes up in value, then your amount of due diligence will not be very extensive nor time consuming. On the other hand, if the property is an old shopping center you plan to tear down in the hope of getting apartment zoning to build affordable housing, you will have a lot of issues to investigate. The word *extensive* can be misleading. In fact, everything you inspect or review will be extensive. There is no such thing as inspecting for lead and only looking in half of the rooms of the building. The same is true for asbestos or other hazardous elements.

Do not be afraid of due diligence. All of the detail work can be done by firms that specialize in the different areas of due diligence that I cover in this chapter. I provide a detailed list of things that need to be inspected and reviewed, but a lot of the items on this list will not apply to your intended investment at all, whereas, some items on the list will apply to all properties that have buildings or other improvements on the land. The snake that can bite you is not the inspections and reviews that are done by the inspection teams you hire, but what they tell you they *don't* inspect. Pay very close attention to this aspect of due diligence. Know what you need, and know what you are getting. If those two lists don't match, then get the missing elements taken care of before you move forward.

Letter of Intent

This is the form that begins most negotiations on commercial properties (on many homes, too). It is exactly what the term indicates: a letter that shows the intentions of the buyer. The sample letter given here covers the important bases.

A Simple Letter of Intent

Dear Property Owner,

My name is Jack Cummings and I am a real estate investor from Fort Lauderdale, Florida. In a recent visit to your area I became aware that you may consider selling a shopping center you own. I would like to purchase that center and I will pay you $10,000,000 cash at closing. The closing will occur 60 days following my approval of my due diligence, and I will have a reasonable time to complete the necessary inspections. This time will be detailed in the formal agreement once the seller has supplied the buyer with property data.

If I do not approve of my due diligence inspections and review for any reason whatsoever, then I may withdraw from the contract, and any deposits placed in escrow by me, as indicated by the terms of the contract, will promptly be refunded to me. If this is acceptable to you (the seller), then so indicate below and I will have my lawyer draft the formal agreement for your review. That document will be in your hands within five working days from your notice to me that these or any other mutually acceptable terms are accepted by both parties.

As this is a letter of intent and not a formal contract, no binding agreement to purchase and sell will be in effect until the parties have executed a formal agreement. However, both parties agree that they will act in good faith in the negotiations of this agreement, and if this or a subsequent letter of intent is acceptable to both parties, the seller agrees not to negotiate with any other party for the sale of this property for a period of 30 days so that the formal agreement can be drafted, reviewed, and, if acceptable, executed.

If I don't hear from you on this matter by noon this coming Friday, then this letter of intent shall be considered null and void.

Sincerely,

Jack Cummings

Letters of intent can be as simple as this, or much more detailed. The point is to nail down the most important business decisions right up front. If you don't like my price or terms, say so or make changes to see if I will go along with them, or forget it. The letter of intent should not attempt to illustrate more than price and terms and one or two other important issues. The details of an agreement will be outlined in a more formal state after this business end of the deal has been agreed to. At that time the agreement will be expanded to include the legal issues of the sale and the specifics of arriving at a closing.

Formal Agreement

This is the legally binding document. It is the purchase agreement, the final contract between the parties to accomplish what the letter of intent started. I use the term *legally binding* but that is only partially true. The buyer generally has certain provisions and a timetable to conduct the due diligence portion of the contract. Those elements will contain *out provisions* or *escape clauses* that will allow the buyer to withdraw from the agreement in the event that some problems with certain aspects of the property turn up during the inspections and reviews. Even if no problems turn up, those provisions usually allow the buyer to walk for any reason, provided that notice of that decision to do so comes within the time provisions of the due diligence period.

Sometimes the seller has an opportunity to terminate the agreement if the buyer fails to timely accomplish certain elements of the due diligence, or the seller doesn't like the results of a credit report on the buyer (usually this is requested if the seller is holding a mortgage or note from the buyer). Remember, whatever the contract says, provided the terms are legal, establishes the obligations and penalties to which each party must adhere. A word of caution: Do not expect the other side of any negotiation (buyer or seller) to "do the right thing" or have sound business ethics. You may hope for this, but there *are* people who have no scruples and until you get their signature on the contract, you do not have a deal (unfortunately, not even then in some situations).

Inspection and Review Period

This is the due diligence period or timetable. Its length depends on the nature of the property and the ease with which inspections can be scheduled. A complex due diligence may take a much longer time if the property is remote (say in the islands somewhere, or in a small town where everything has to come from a larger city a great distance away). Environmental inspection provisions, discussed in the next section, are often drafted to allow for extensions of the due diligence timetable in the event an initial inspection uncovers a potential problem that can only be researched properly with additional inspections.

Environmental Inspections

Environmental inspections are exactly what the term suggests: inspections to ascertain if there are any environmental issues that need to be addressed. Some of these potential problems are deal killers, as it can get very expensive to remedy an environmental problem. This would be the case with discovery of a hazardous issue.

There are many facets to environmental inspections. Some deal with protected areas, wetlands, areas that are off-limits due to the presence of certain plant and/or animal life, dangerous conditions that either exist currently, or might come to exist if you tear down a building (such as one that is full of asbestos that will become airborne), and so on. Rather than attempt to list all these problems and perhaps miss the most important one for your area of the world, let me suggest that you contact any of your local environmental inspection companies and discuss the situation with them. This tip goes for any inspection you might choose or need to make.

Easements

Easements are rights that others have to access, pass, or use property, and in other ways possibly make it difficult or impossible for you to use land you thought was yours. They should show up on a good recent survey, but they don't always get picked up by even the best of surveyors. Some of these easements are classified simply as *utility easements* which are designed as passages through or across a property for the placement of any of the usual utilities, such as water, electric, gas, telephone, cable services, and so on. There can be other public easements prescribed by law or city ordinance that can get skipped in a cursory investigation either by a lawyer or a surveyor, so it is a good idea to check with the city building department and public works to make sure there is not something unforeseen that could blow your project out of the water.

Encroachments

An encroachment is where something protrudes from another property into your property. Usually the encroachment is a building that a survey should clearly show. However, you can have a hidden encroachment that is underground. This happened to me once when a property adjoining one I own was occupied by a local fire department. When I purchased the property, the surveyor made a mistake and placed the south border line 20 feet north of where it should have been. The problem got worse because, prior to my buying the property, the fire department had built a building and installed a septic tank that had a drain field on what they thought was their property but which was actually mine. They had relied on information given to them by the same surveyor. When I wanted to build on this tract of land I discovered the error in the survey, and later my contractor discovered the septic tank. The fire department was expecting the county to take the south 20 feet of my property to resolve the problem, but the county didn't like the prospect of getting into a lawsuit over such an issue.

In any event, it still took me nearly a year and several thousand dollars of legal expenses dealing with the city, county, and, of course, the fire department. All worked out in the end, and it was all over something that would never have been found by anyone had we not discovered the survey error.

Code Violations

When some aspect of a building does not meet the current building and fire codes, as well as any other city ordinance or zoning code, you may be in violation of that code. I say *violation* because it is possible that you may not meet the code but may still be allowed to maintain the building as it is because you met the code at the time the building was constructed. This works for zoning and some (but not all) building codes. This situation is called a *nonconforming use*.

Code violations are usually a matter of record, but the difficulty is, whose record? Not all cities function the same, and fire code violations might be dealt with in one department (I would try the fire department first) whereas a building code would likely show up in the building and zoning departments. Any code violation can be a problem but the worst are usually the fire codes, because there is no grandfathering in on those codes in most parts of the country.

When you hire a general building inspection company, they may or may not also check for code violations. Be sure to ask, because if they don't, you may have to farm that task out to someone else. I recently had a good lesson in how this can lead to lots of problems after the closing. I brokered a sale to a long-time client of mine and it turned into a mini nightmare. It was a well-located office building, and the seller indicated he had partners and wanted to sell because he could not work with his partner friends any longer. (This happens sometimes when you have great social friends and you bring them into a business deal and the friendship goes down the toilet.)

Not long after we closed on the office building, I suggested that we put the building right back on the market. A quick profit was the motive, if I could produce one. Along came doctor whats-his-name and bought the building, paying my client a clear $100,000 profit after all costs and fees. All was fine for about a year, and then suddenly there were threats of fraud, accusing my client of not disclosing certain elements of the building to the doctor. A foreclosure suit was filed by my client, who was holding a second mortgage on the building, which the good doctor had not paid. Then, countersuits were filed, and so on.

It turned out there were some outstanding code violations from the fire department. These violations had been filed on the former owner, and when they turned up, the cost to remedy was, according to the doctor, so high that, had he known about them, he would never have purchased the building.

I won't get into all the details, as the case has yet to be settled. All I can say is that in Florida and many other states, when it comes to commercial and investment real estate, the buyer had better beware. In essence, if you have the time to make your inspections, do so—especially if the contract has an "as is" provision, which warns you, "Hey, you are buying this just as you see it. Make your inspections, then take it or leave it." This is not as harsh as it sounds. Almost all investment real estate is sold on this basis, just as most used cars are. However, unlike with most used cars, you as buyer can have considerable time to make inspections and review everything prior to purchase.

The good doctor had these opportunities and hired two inspection teams to give him a report on the property. He could have hired a dozen, as he had ample time to do so. The contract said "as is," and on top of that, the seller gave him a credit of around $18,000 to handle any problems that might occur with the building. This was the seller's insurance that if there were problems they should be covered.

Well, those code violations surfaced the next time the fire department inspected the building and, like a bear to honey, they were after the good doctor to make the necessary repairs.

The point is, no matter where your legal rights are, no matter how much you try to satisfy either the buyer or the seller, depending on your position in the deal, legalities can be the end result. My suggestion, following this experience, is this: If you are a seller, give a letter to the buyer, listing all the items that you think the buyer should inspect. If you have any hint of a problem, make sure you have that category listed. Always list code violations that you are aware of.

Zoning Use

Every zoning classification has a list of possible uses that would normally be permitted within that zoning. It is important to read the zoning codes very carefully, because many of them allow uses permitted in lesser zonings. For example, in a high-density multifamily zoning category, which is one of the most unrestrictive multifamily zoning categories, you may also be allowed to build a mid-rise low-density building. On the other hand, if a property is zoned low-density multifamily, you could not build a high-rise without going through a change in the zoning or obtaining some other permission. While some commercial zoning also allows multifamily use, multifamily zoning may not allow commercial uses but may allow professional offices. The more you know about the exact zoning and what it will allow, the better your chances of spotting a windfall in the form of an allowed use that will give you added income, and therefore increased value.

Allowed Use

The use the city will allow for a specific property may differ from the use the zoning says is allowed. Why? Because it can exercise one of the "gottcha" clauses in the zoning or building codes. The key is to find out what potential gottcha clauses might exist and then explore them until you are satisfied with your findings. In all developmental property, I recommend that a buyer condition his actual purchase on the approval of a site plan (and, in some large projects, the building plans), which includes the use approval by the planning and zoning boards and the city commission. If the use they approve is more limited than you thought you would get, then you have several choices: Take what they gave you, fight for what you want, renegotiate the contract, or walk from the deal. I say more about this later in this chapter.

The Eight Most Important Elements of Due Diligence

1. Assume nothing told to you by the seller is correct.
2. Hire qualified building and land inspectors.
3. Audit all leases.
4. Obtain inventory list and double-check it.
5. Review all contracts.
6. Get a recent certified property survey.
7. Make sure title is valid and all liens and debt are verified.
8. Properly set the due diligence timetable.

Assume Nothing Told to You by the Seller Is Correct

If this sounds cynical, it is. I'm not talking about factors of trust and honesty. Many sellers do not know what problems exist, so they will say that none do. That is not sufficient information on which to base the decision to proceed with a multithousand- or multimillion-dollar investment. The safest thing you can do is to ask if the seller has any documentation, such as prior inspection reports or recent surveys, that would show the status of the property.

Hire Qualified Building and Land Inspectors

Getting good inspections might be difficult. Some inspection companies are great for homes but not so great for shopping centers and absolutely horrible for large apartment complexes. Look at their references. Check with past clients. Go back several years, because that will be where unknown problems surface. If you get marginal responses from past clientele, forget that company and move on to another inspection team.

Audit All Leases

This is something that you may not be qualified to do or want to spend the time doing. You should hire a property manager or accountant versed in commercial leases of the same category of real estate as that being inspected. If all the leases follow a standard format, you may want to have a real estate lawyer review one of the leases to make sure there are not some potential problems with the terminology that was used. It is possible that a former owner came from another state and used a lease that was okay in his home state, but for your state the lease violates tenant rights. Do not attempt to audit a lease unless you have special knowledge in lease terms and conditions.

Have the leases audited and then verified as current. Verification is done through an *estoppel letter*, which the seller must obtain from all the tenants and which is attached to a copy of the current lease. This letter simply states that the attached lease is a true and accurate copy of the existing lease and that no other agreements have been made between the tenant and the owner. The letter will also spell out the status of the lease and when the last payment was made. If you discover later that the estoppel letter was not correct, you will have a claim against either the tenant, the former owner, or both.

Obtain Inventory List and Double-check It

This is the real drudgery of many large commercial closings. I especially hate having to go through a 400-room hotel, room by room, to verify that each item is actually in the room and is in good condition. But you or someone you hire should be responsible to do this. I recommend that in addition to a visual inspection of this kind of inventory, someone makes videotape of it as well. That is one of the best bits of evidence to fall back on, if done properly.

What is the proper way to do a videotaped inventory? I start the tape by verifying the date and location of the inventory inspection and introducing the parties who will accompany the inspection. At least one of these persons will be from the seller's team. As

I approach a location, I announce it so that the tape picks up the verbal introduction to the room. If it is a hotel room, I videotape the entry of the room with the room number clearly showing. Several of the inspection chaperones will be inside the room and will show up on the film as the room is slowly scanned so that every item is seen while also being called out. If any of the items that should be there are missing, they are mentioned. If anything is not working or is in need of repair, that is shown and stated.

So far, none of the inventories that I have conducted in this way have led to any dispute over what was missing later on. Be cautious with any kind of investment that has a major inventory, as it is easy for thousands of dollars to slip through the cracks of the deal with sloppy inventory taking.

Review All Contracts

Contracts will include leased goods or fixtures, repair contracts, employment contracts, service contracts, insurance agreements and contracts, legal representation, obligations on municipal bonds pledged to cover local tax assessments, and so on. If the property is part of a condominium (a condo office building, for example) there will be obligations that come with the property, such as assessments imposed by the homeowners' or property owners' association, or other maintenance agreements. If you, as buyer, have the risk of becoming responsible for any of these agreements or contracts, you need to know what they are. If you disagree with them, you must do so within the due diligence period and seek a remedy from the seller. This is not something you can do after the closing and still expect to get full satisfaction.

Get a Recent Certified Property Survey

A proper survey should show the legal address of the property—its lot, block, and subdivision, or metes and bounds description, in addition to the street address. All the property dimensions should be clearly noted, together with the exact location of any buildings and their outside dimensions. All utility easements and any other possible easement should be noted. If the property has any recorded deed restrictions, those should also be noted.

Of these items, the one that is rarely shown is a deed restriction. If any exist, they are imposed by a previous owner, often the developer of the property. Sometimes, by local laws, deed restrictions expire after a certain period of time, but in some cases they never expire. Deed restrictions are important because they can contain any whim a previous owner decided to impose on the buyer of that property. This can include things such as greater setbacks than the city ordinances require, no buildings less than a minimum square footage (which may also be greater than what the city requires as a minimum), and a multitude of sometimes silly things. If there is a recorded deed restriction, be sure the surveyor includes notation to it on the survey.

The real danger with a survey is that a problem may be there right in front of you and no one catches it. Why? Because most closing agents (lawyers, title companies, banks, and the like) do not compare the survey to the property. Consider that a surveyor is hired to do a survey of a specific property. The surveyors aren't aware of what you know or don't know about the property, so they go out and correctly and accurately perform their job. The survey is passed on to the title company, which reviews it for things that may affect title—encroachments, easements, violations (such as improper setbacks of buildings on the property), and that sort of thing. The title company may elect to exclude certain elements from their title coverage, in which case you and your lawyer may seek a renegotiation of the deal. But beyond the normal things that a title company can check with their computer, they (and most all closing agents) will assume that all else is okay. Lawyers then look at the survey and, just as with the title company, they may pass it on as proper because the title policy shows no problems.

So far no one has taken the survey out to the property and asked, "Is what I see when I am at the property what is shown on the survey?" Often that is not the case, and yet the problem was there to see all the time, if you knew what to look for. Let me give you two examples of how serious this can be.

I wanted to buy a lot in Fort Lauderdale on which to build a new home. One criterion I wanted to fill was the lot had to be within a couple of blocks of the beach, and it had to have a deepwater boat dock (ocean access without fixed bridges) so I could dock my 40-foot sports fisher behind the house. I liked one lot because of its location, but I had ruled it out when I walked the lot with a measuring tape. Measuring along the seawall, I found that there was only 25 feet of frontage along the canal, which was too short to allow a dock for my boat.

The lot was odd-shaped, mostly rectangular, with a piece that extended down to the water of the canal. Two surveyor nails had been driven into the concrete header of the seawall, and each had a faded yellow circle around it. Landscape hedges from the two neighbors came down to the seawall just outside those marks. My assumption that those nail markings showed the actual water frontage was the same as perhaps thousands of other people who had walked down to the canal and then ruled out that lot.

A year went by, and one day I was at the county tax assessor's office and happened to look up that specific lot. I had the clerk pull up the plat of the subdivision and made a copy of the lot, blown up several times its published size. Later that afternoon I took a walk around the lot and paced off the boundaries as the plat showed them to be. Lo and behold, if the plat was right, a large amount of the landscaped area used by the neighbor to the north, plus another 25 feet of seawall, actually belonged to this vacant lot.

I researched the history of the sales of the property to the north and discovered that in the past 7 years the house north of the lot had sold three times. That seemed strange yet logical when everything came together. People had been buying the house to the north thinking it was on a larger lot and had a much greater frontage on the seawall than it actually did. How had the landscaping come about? The original builder of the house, who had landscaped the lot, had also owned the vacant lot at the time. What happened after that was failure on the part of at least those three succeeding owners to properly check the legal description of the lot with the actual "what do I see" version.

I purchased the lot, then sent the neighbor a case of what his wife said was his favorite beverage, prior to having my surveyor drive little wooden stakes down the real property line. Gone was his beautiful hedge, outdoor stone barbeque grill, and 25 feet of his seawall and dock. I was the beneficiary of doing my homework.

The other example was what happened to Mr. L, a well-known apartment builder in the South Florida area, who purchased a lot on which he planned to build an apartment complex. The seller owned several lots in the area, and Mr. L chose one that suited his dream apartment complex. A survey was made, and everything seemed to check out. The legal description that showed up in the contract and title policy matched the survey, the dimensions were exact, and everyone, including the seller, signed off on the deal.

A couple of years later Mr. L, who was living up north at the time, had a set of plans drawn up and spent several thousand dollars getting the lot ready for construction. Trees had to be cleared and the lot needed fill, so tons of that were ordered and delivered—and the small building in the rear was torn down.

"Wait!" Mr. L must have screamed when he saw the bill for that item. There had been no small building in the rear of the lot. "Oh no!" the seller must have screamed when he drove by his lot and noticed all the action going on, and the demolition of the artist cottage that he used when he was in the mood to paint. Where was Mr. L's lot? A block away. The seller's lawyer had sent the closing agent a legal description and survey on another property the seller owned, and no one ever checked it out.

Make Sure the Title Is Valid and All Liens and Debts Are Verified

Not every document is absolutely correct, no matter how legal it looks and how genuine it appears. You may have heard the saying, "Don't buy the Brooklyn Bridge," which stems from an early con game in which a company was set up to sell shares in the Brooklyn Bridge that links Manhattan to Brooklyn. People who bought such shares ended up owning a worthless document.

There are many things that can affect the value of title to a property and not be part of a con game, so it is critical that you have a title company or your lawyer search the title for anything that might hint at a problem or, worse, show a cloud on the title. A *cloud on the title*, as it is called, is evidence of an outstanding issue that does not appear to have been closed. Such an issue could be the death of an owner without legal notice of that effect, or a prior sale that indicates there was a mortgage taken back by the previous owner in a foreclosure suit, but there was no satisfaction of that mortgage in the records. Some of these matters are errors, misfiled documents, or documents that were lost somewhere between the delivery to the clerk of circuit court and the actual recording of the document. Sometimes a party shows up as an owner, but no one has gotten that person's signature on the contract you are holding.

Get these things straight. Often the title work is done only at the last minute. However, in commercial transactions many of the inspections and other due diligence work is far more time consuming and expensive than the title search. Because of this, I recommend you have all the title work done early. If problems do show up, the seller will have additional time to get things straight prior to the actual passing of a clear title to you. Title searches are an essential method of checking for any recorded easements across the property too. It's a nasty surprise if you find out at closing that there is a subway under the building you intended to tear down.

Properly Set the Due Diligence Timetable

Timetables for due diligence are generally referenced in the formal contract as 45 days, 60 days, or some longer period of time. They may also have extensions, as I have mentioned earlier, that provide for more time if certain inspections are required, or if the seller drags his or her feet in making certain disclosures or delivery of certain documents necessary to accomplish the inspection. Then, somewhere else in the contract, in a paragraph that is unrelated to the due diligence issue, is a sentence something like this: "In this agreement all days referenced will be construed as business days, which exclude weekends as well as nationally recognized holidays when the majority of banks would be closed."

That simple sentence now turns calendar days into a much longer period of time. That is okay, if you understand it that way and agree to it as the seller. As a buyer, the longer you have to do your due diligence the better it is. Make sure that the contract is very clear on that point. Often a buyer will put in a sentence that makes the change from calendar days to business days in the hope the seller doesn't catch it, so look for some provision that does exactly that, often in the most unlikely place of the contract.

The Four Elements to Prepare for Due Diligence

1. Ascertain what to inspect and/or review.
2. Select the inspection team(s).
3. Make sure all aspects are covered.
4. Carefully debrief the inspectors.

By now you are pretty well primed on what you need to look for in your due diligence and you are ready to set the process in motion. I have broken this procedure into the following four steps.

Ascertain What to Inspect and/or Review

Make a note of the critical elements of the property that first caused you to select it—size of seawall, how many units you want to build, how many floors, and so on. Those factors should be absolute to you. If those criteria aren't satisfied, then nothing else matters. But how well will your plan for the property fit, and what costly elements will you face? Those issues must be covered in the balance of the inspection. Discuss this matter with two or more inspection teams if this is your first time up at bat in this part of the world or with this category of real estate. Ask what unique things should be inspected. Be sure that code violations, deed restrictions, and other easements are on the list.

Select the Inspection Team(s)

Based on what you need to accomplish, choose the inspection team or teams you will need. They will include the property and building inspectors as well as a title insurance company or lawyer to review the title of the property. Make sure that you understand the limits to which any of these members will inspect. If they leave out something, then find another inspector who can do that part, or do it yourself if you feel able to.

Make Sure All Aspects Are Covered

Remember the data on the survey problems. This is the most overlooked aspect of all. Don't wait until you get past your due diligence period to make this kind of a comparison. It is easy for you to miss out on something if you let all the inspections go on separately without some coordination. Your lawyer is checking the contract, the title, and that sort of thing. But if you are not aware of the problems that he or she has uncovered, there may be another complication that should have been double-checked but wasn't. Be sure that all the inspectors have actually seen the property. That is the only time they may notice that something is missing—like where is the lease for the supermarket on the site.

"Oh," says the seller, "that is on an out-parcel," which means it is not included in your deal. And all the time you thought it came with the property. Or it might be something less obvious, such as, did you know there was a land lease under part of the real estate? Worse still can be a long legal description that is difficult to read due to its metes and bounds descriptions. In the end the title turns out fine, but it did not cover all the property you thought you were buying. This could be similar to a missing out-parcel, or several buildings that you also thought went along with the center.

What happened? Well, someone forget to give you the lease, and your lawyer or the title company didn't know about it. They assumed that the legal description on the contract covered the total property.

Carefully Debrief the Inspectors

Carefully read the report, then go over it with the inspector or head of the inspection team. Make sure you understand everything stated, and ask about the consequences to any potential problems the report might raise. Later on, be sure to have each member of the team read the summary of the results of other inspectors. Ask them this question: "Based on those other reports, is there anything you would like to reinspect or anything in your report that you need to change or modify, or anything that you think the other inspectors should reinspect or change or modify based on what you have found?" Do this with all of them, including your lawyer, and your accountant (if a review of financials and or leases and contracts were a part of the inspections). Make sure that each member of the inspection team knows the timetable in which you have to give a "go forward" approval to the seller, or stop the deal right then and there.

Eight Things You Can Do When You Find Problems

The following list gives you eight options to consider when you find problems. Perhaps your initial assumption of the problem was an overstatement and it will work itself out relatively easily. Or the initial problem you uncover could turn into a nightmarish quagmire of one problem growing into another. Review this list of options—it might take you all eight to discover that the last one should have been the first.

1. Double-check the extent of the problem.
2. Ascertain if there is a dollar amount to fix the problem.
3. Check with previous owners.
4. Go over the problems with the seller.
5. Do a soft renegotiation.
6. If that fails, "take a way."
7. Consider legal action.
8. Move on.

Double-check the Extent of the Problem

All older properties will have something that gives away their age. Even the best-maintained property has something that may need fixing, painting, or simple repair. Aesthetic elements are simply a matter of opinion. Are you going to paint the building another color anyway? Are you planning on replacing all the AC units next year when you redo the roof? These are elements you may have already taken into consideration when you made your offer. If so, either attempt to improve the deal or move forward. But real problems that you didn't expect need to be rechecked and dealt with as I suggest in the following sections.

Ascertain If There Is a Dollar Amount to Fix the Problem

Most problems will have a dollar amount attached to them. The catch is that the final dollar amount may not be known until the job is actually finished. What looks like a simple job to replace some rotten wood might turn out to be a complete roof removal and a full roof replacement. Many residential purchase contracts have a provision for repairs. It is not uncommon for the seller to agree to a buffer of 2 percent of the purchase price to cover needed repairs. In commercial transactions in the multimillions of dollars, that might seem like a lot of money, but repairs can be very expensive.

You need to find the problem, then find out what it will cost to remedy it. Keep in mind the time it will take to make those repairs, too. On whose clock does the repair fall? If you are the buyer and don't mind being shut down for a couple of months following the closing, then let it be on your clock.

Check with Previous Owners

If the previous owners (prior to the owner you have a contract with) are still around and the time period between ownership was relatively short (two to three years), you might call or have your broker call them and discuss the current problem. If it turns out that the problem was around when they owned the property and a settlement was made when they sold it to cover its remedy, but the current owner did nothing to fix the problem, then you know what kind of seller you are dealing with. This might do nothing for you in the end, but you will have an issue to pick with the owner and a good reason to ask that the problem get fixed prior to your closing on the property.

Go over the Problems with the Seller

If the past owners give no hint at the problem or its existence in the past, then sit down with the seller and discuss the situation. Ask questions like "Did you know about this problem? Have you priced out the cost to fix it? Has any tenant complained about this problem? (If the problem has been around for a long time, then the tenant may have put the seller on notice, and this is something you might find out.) If so, what did you do about those complaints?" All this puts the seller in the "is there going to be legal action" mode, and this will either loosen the seller up for a realistic remedy, or cause the seller to simply clam up altogether and refuse to meet with you in the future. Either way, you are moving in a positive direction to decide either to buy or to walk away.

Do a Soft Renegotiation

Attempt to reconcile the deal. This is best done through your broker or lawyer. Simply send over a *contract modification* agreement that states that a problem exists and that the seller will agree to (1) fix the problem to certain specifications that you spell out, or (2) reduce the down payment or price or both by an amount of money that is either shown in the agreement or follows a formula or is based on a firm estimate from a bonded contractor. You can add to this other provisions, too, as you see fit, and then present it.

It is a good idea to do this well within the due diligence period so that you have time to attempt this and any other renegotiations, rather than running out of time and having to either go hard or walk away from the deal.

If that Fails, *Take-a-Way*

The *take-a-way* is a contract negotiation tactic. It works best when it occurs within the due diligence period because of its finality. Here is how it works. You have tried to do everything possible to remedy the problem or to bring the price to a level where you can satisfactorily accept the property as it is. But there is still a gap of value or time or both that you need to obtain out of the deal. So your lawyer writes a letter to the seller or the seller's lawyer that says something like this:

> ". . . which describes the problems that have been uncovered in the present due diligence that my client has undertaken. I have been asked to propose a drop in the price by $250,000 and an extension on the closing for another 90 days from the contract date of two months from now. Based on the current findings my client has informed me that unless the remedy which this letter proposes is acceptable to you then my client may be forced to withdraw from this agreement as the contract allows."

This does not say you *will* withdraw, it only hints that you *might*. If the seller is motivated and there are no other buyers in the wings waiting for you to drop out of the picture, this sometimes works.

Consider Legal Action

The subject of legal action might be the next step. Assume that your lawyer tried the take-a-way and there was no response. (That would likely be my reaction as a seller.) Bring the negotiations right up to the brink, but always leave a reasonable time for a decision to be made (not "I need to know within two hours"). Or, if there was a response that you don't like, then your lawyer can move to the next step:

> "My client has asked me to make one more attempt to resolve this matter prior to his review of what legal actions he must take in court. If you have any thoughts about how we can solve this problem, please call me or have your lawyer give me a call so we can discuss how to bring about a speedy closing. My client has informed me that if the terms of the modification are agreeable he will increase his deposit by $500,000 and close within 30 days."

You can see that this letter hints at a potential legal action, and then goes on to hold out a carrot for a larger deposit and a quick closing if the matter is resolved right away. It is always good to make your last or even next to last overture with some positive benefit that is not in the contract.

Move On

If you cannot become satisfied with the situation and your lawyer says you don't have much of a case to go to court over, or you just don't want to deal with that issue in that way, then move on. There is always another property to buy, and as long as you have not fallen in love with the property, the breakup will be next to painless. Move on.

CHAPTER 6

The Effects of Leverage

> The goal of this chapter is:
>
> **To Show You the Benefits of Leverage**

Leverage is an easy to understand tool that gives you the added edge in your real estate investments. When used properly it will boost the return you receive from your invested capital and shorten the doubling effect of your investment. (*Doubling effect* is the number of years it will take for the income from the property to equal double the cash investment.) We have already looked at several examples of how leverage works.

The principle of obtaining positive leverage is to reduce the amount of capital you invest and increase the yield possible from the property. Naturally, you reduce your invested capital through price reduction and/or borrowing money from other people (the seller, a bank, or other third party lenders). You may begin with a goal of making 9 percent on your investment and end up making 18 percent. You start this process with negotiation on the price, and once you are comfortable that you have gotten the best price, then you work on the financing. Maximum leverage will now occur at the financing level. This happens because of one important factor: long-term financing that is available at interest rates that are lower than the yield on the investment.

This chapter is designed to show you the positive elements of leverage and some new twists on how you can maximize its benefits. However, leverage has a dark side as well, and when improperly used can create a negative result with the investment, both as to return on your capital invested and to a future sale.

Key Words and Concepts to Build Your Insider Knowledge

How Positive Leverage Works to Your Benefit

Cheap Money + Cash Flowing Investments = Opportunities

How Positive Leverage Works to Your Benefit

If you are able to borrow $100,000 at 8 percent interest, invest it, and make 10 percent return on it, you will earn $10,000. Now deduct the $8,000 in interest you have to pay on the $100,000 you borrowed. Your net gain is a $2,000 positive cash flow at the end of the year. This is the basic principle of how leverage works. You can see that if the interest rates were reversed and you had to pay 10 percent and only earned 8 percent, you would be out-of-pocket $2,000 at the end of the year and have just experienced a negative cash flow.

If the situation was the purchase of a $150,000 commercial building, with gross rents of $25,000 and all operational expenses totaling $10,000 (maintenance, real estate tax, insurance, professional and collection fees, etc.), net operating income

(NOI) would be $15,000 and your return would be 10 percent on the invested capital of $150,000.

Now if, instead of investing your own $150,000, you borrow $100,000 at an interest rate somewhat less than 8 percent, so that over 25 years you have an annual debt payment of principal and interest (P&I) of only $8,000, your investment is starting to look a lot better. Now your cash-out-of-pocket is only $50,000. Your NOI is still $15,000 (the first year); deduct the debt payment of $8,000 and your cash flow is $7,000. This represents a 14 percent yield on your invested cash (14 percent x $50,000 = $7,000). This is a strong example of how positive leverage functions. Look at the recap of this example below.

The Deal at 100 Percent Cash Invested

Purchase price	$150,000	(Also your cash investment)
Gross rents	25,000	
Less operational expenses	– 10,000	
NOI	$ 15,000	
Return on cash invested	10 percent	

Introducing Leveraged Debt

Purchase price	$150,000	
New mortgage	100,000	(At a total annual payment of $8,000 P&I)
Cash invested	$ 50,000	
NOI	$ 15,000	(No change from the previous mortgage example)
Deduct mortgage payment	8,000	
Cash flow due to leverage	$7,000	
Return on cash invested	14 percent	

Cheap Money + Cash-Flowing
Investments = Opportunities

Forget, for a moment, the magic of OPM that was discussed in earlier chapters. What you create by borrowing at a lower cost than you can make is the whole essence of free enterprise. However, the ability to gain positive leverage only works when there are two necessary ingredients available: money you can borrow at lower rates than you can earn, and investments you can make that will give you a higher rate of return than the cost of the money. That might sound like chicken-and-egg logic, but it is essential for you to realize that these circumstances are not always available. There are times when the interest spread between the borrow rate and the return on other investments is so narrow, or the risk of those investments so high, that positive leverage is a hit-or-miss endeavor. But in general, real estate maintains its edge over the borrowing rate because historically, in the more developed parts of the world, loans that are secured by real estate are tied to a long-term repayment schedule and are available on a fixed rate of interest. These loans are also set on a payment schedule that is amortized over the term.

Three Magical Factors to High Positive Leverage

Many people take these three factors for granted: long repayment terms, fixed interest rate, and amortized payment of equal payments of principal and interest combined. However, without the combination of all three things, it would not be easy for the real estate investor to obtain high leverage, or any leverage at all, for that matter.

When a long-term mortgage with a fixed interest rate is repaid by amortized payment schedule, each payment will remain the same for the full term of the mortgage. For example, a $100,000 loan at 8 percent annual interest to be repaid over 20 years will have a monthly payment of $836.42 or a total of $10,037 for the year. On the average then, for the first year you have paid a little less than $8,000 of interest, and the balance of the payment ($2,037) applies to the reduction of the principal owed. As your total annual payment of $10,037 will remain the same for the entire 20 years, the annual amount that is applied to the principal reduction of the loan will increase each year, while the amount of interest charged is being reduced. The function of this kind of math is really magical if you think about it.

On an annualized basis, at the end of the first year you no longer owe $100,000. You owe $97,963 ($100,000 less the $2,037 of principal you paid during the first year). The second year the same circumstance occurs, only this time the amount of interest you pay is now based on $97,963 owed. At the same 8 percent rate, the interest charge for the second year would be reduced to $7,837.04. Because your total payment has not changed, the amount of principal reduction for the second year would now be $2,199.96 and at the start of the second year your principal outstanding (what you still owe) is $95,763.04. Look at a recap of this example below.

Principal and Interest Payments on a Fixed Rate Mortgage

Loan amount	$100,000	
Interest rate	8 percent	(also called *contract rate*)
Term of loan	20 years	
Constant yearly payment	$ 10,037	(total of 12 monthly payments of $836.42)

Year	Principal Owed	Annual Payment	Principal	Interest
Start of first year	$100,000	$10,037	$2,037	$8,000
End of first year	$ 97,963	$10,037	$2,199.96	$7,837.04
End of second year	$ 95,763.04	$10,037		

These numbers are actually shifting each month, so the numbers I have given you are not entirely accurate, as the principal is being paid down bit by bit each month. But you see how this amortized situation works. In all fixed-rate mortgages, the interest rate, which is also called the *contract rate*, does not change during the life of the mortgage.

Other forms of mortgages may have variable or adjustable interest rates, which can change according to a benchmark or other factor, such as the rate of a treasury bond, or another identifiable financial rate like the average prime rate set by the major New York banks on February 1 each year. (It's up to the lender to select a benchmark, and often you can negotiate each part of it.)

In any loan, the positive leverage factor remains in your favor as long as you can earn a greater return (interest) on your invested cash than you pay. But let's stay with the fixed loan for a moment. Because it is generally available over a long term, say 15 to 40 years, you can plan your investment with certain assurances that you can manage your risk factor within the income-producing capabilities of the investment. You do not have to worry about the prime rate or other benchmark jumping from 4 percent to 20 percent and quickly pushing your positive leverage into a losing negative leverage situation.

But in many parts of the world the combination of these three elements of OPM (in this instance, mortgages) do not exist. Loans are not long-term, rates are often not fixed, and they are not amortized with constant equal payments of principal and interest combined. That same $100,000 loan might be a five-year loan payable with one fifth of the principal each year, together with interest that is adjusted each month to a rate that is set at 3 percent annualized above the prime rate as set in the top three banks in Cairo, Egypt (or whatever the lender wants and you agree to). If the rate was initially 8 percent, and assuming no change in the rates, either up or down, for the year, your annual payment for the first year would be $28,000 in the form of a combination of principal and interest ($20,000 is 1/5 of the total loan, plus $8,000 as the first year's interest on the total loan). This is quite a change from the $10,037 with the long-term loan with fixed and equal annual payments of principal and interest combined.

The kind of mortgages that are easily available in the United States are long-term loans with reasonable interest rates, often with fixed interest for the entire term. The situation of the fixed rates gives rise to another important term: *constant rate*.

How Constant Rates in Mortgages Work

A mortgage constant rate is the blended rate that takes into consideration both the payment of the interest portion due at the time of the payment and a reduction of part of the principal. This is done through a rather complicated mathematical formula, which you need not learn, as the resulting payments for practically any mortgage combination of term and interest is found by use of tables or inexpensive handheld financial calculators. In the example shown earlier, the $100,000 loan has an interest rate of 8 percent, with an annual payment of $10,037. At the time the loan is made, the borrower agrees to pay back that loan at 10.037 percent of the original loan amount until fully repaid (in 20 years). This constant rate is quickly found by dividing the annual payment by the loan amount ($10,037 divided by $100,000 = 10.037).

This 10.037 percent is the constant rate of this mortgage as seen at the time of the origination of the loan. In essence, the constant rate is your shortcut to what that loan is going to do for you at the end of the year from a cash flow point of view. This percentage rate, although called a *constant rate*, is so only as it relates to the original loan amount and to the steady, fixed payment throughout the loan. Every year, the loan principal is reduced, so there will be a new constant rate for the next year. Its percentage will be based on the amount of principal still owed. In essence, as the loan is paid off, the monthly (and therefore annual) payment made remains the same, but the relationship between the payment and the principal owed changes each year. This causes the constant rate to increase each year.

The quickest way to understand this is to consider what happens the last year of the 20 year payout of the loan. In the case of this $100,000 loan, the final year will still have a payment of $10,037 dollars, which has remained the same for 20 years. Of that amount, however, slightly over $9,200 is the principal outstanding, so the constant rate for the last year would be based on the principal remaining. A payment of $10,037 is approximately 108 percent of the loan at that point in time.

This relationship will be useful to you in making quick mortgage calculations. The Annual Constant Rate Chart Based on Monthly Repayment Terms gives a number of constant rates to consider. Based on what the current loan rates are (as quoted by lenders in your area at any given time), memorize the constants that you are most likely to use in any investment situation. By using this table you can easily calculate what the annual debt service will be for any loan amount by multiplying the constant rate by that loan amount. To approximate the monthly payment, divide the annual payment by 12.

How to Use the Annual Constant Rate Chart

With this chart, or with a few of those constant rates imbedded in your mind, you can easily multiply a loan amount by the constant rate to get the total payment for a year. For example, a 9 percent loan for 30 years has a constant rate of 9.66 percent. A $1,000,000 loan will have an annual debt service of $96,600 a year. Divide that amount by 12 to get the monthly payment of $8,050.

One note of caution: If you check this payment by using a mortgage calculator or a computer program designed to arrive at mortgage amounts, you may come up with a number slightly higher or slightly lower. This is because different computers round off with more or fewer digits to the right of the decimal point. Of course, the farther you carry out a fraction, the more accurate will be the answer when using the fraction in a mathematical equation.

The first of the three examples of negative leverage in the following section demonstrates how this chart can be used to find answers to other mortgage problems.

How to Determine If Negative Leverage Is Bad

Negative leverage isn't necessarily a bad situation. While positive leverage is certainly a bonus in any real estate deal, there are many situations where it is not the end of the

Annual Constant Rate Chart
Based on Monthly Repayment Terms

Interest Rate	Years	Constant Rate
5.5	15 years	9.81
5.5	20 years	8.26
5.5	30 years	6.81
6.0	15 years	10.13
6.0	20 years	8.60
6.0	30 years	7.20
6.5	15 years	10.45
6.5	20 years	8.95
6.5	30 years	7.59
7.0	15 years	10.79
7.0	20 years	9.30
7.0	30 years	7.98
7.5	15 years	11.12
7.5	20 years	9.67
7.5	30 years	8.39
8.0	15 years	11.47
8.0	20 years	10.04
8.0	30 years	8.81
8.5	15 years	11.82
8.5	20 years	10.41
8.5	30 years	9.23
9.0	15 years	12.17
9.0	20 years	10.80
9.0	30 years	9.66
9.5	15 years	12.53
9.5	20 years	11.19
9.5	30 years	10.09
10.0	15 years	12.90
10.0	20 years	11.58
10.0	30 years	10.53

world if you have a negative leverage situation. Many real estate investments, such as speculation in land or a purchase of a vacant lot on which you plan to build someday, do not have any cash flow at all. Without cash flow there is no income to offset any debt service you incurred when you purchased the property. This automatically creates a hefty negative leverage situation. To make sure you understand what leverage can do, either positive or negative, let's look at three examples. Each occurs for a different reason, and we can examine the result and the merit, if any, of the transaction.

Sylvia's Purchase of a Duplex

Sylvia is a single mother and decided that paying $860 a month rent was not getting her anywhere. So she looked around and found a nice duplex apartment building that was in a neighborhood she liked. The building contained two apartments, each of which had two bedrooms and two baths, a full garage with room for one car, and a clothes washer and dryer. The asking price was $165,000. The seller was anxious to sell, as he had been transferred to a new position out of the state. With her parents cosigning on the mortgage, Sylvia was able to borrow 90 percent of the price, which she negotiated down to $160,000. This resulted in a debt of $144,000 which, together with the $16,000 she had saved, was just right for the deal. The loan was for 30 years with a call (the term *balloon* could also be used) at the end of 15 years, at a fixed rate of 7.5 percent. This meant that the amortization would be set at a schedule of 30 years, but the balance owing at the end of 15 years had to be paid off or a new loan at new terms placed on the property. A quick look at the Constant Rate Chart for an interest rate of 7.5 percent will show you that for a 30-year loan the constant rate is 8.39 percent, and the 15-year term has a constant rate of 11.12 percent. This loan then would have a total annual debt service of $12,081.60 ($144,000 x .0839 = $12,081.60) based on the 30-year constant rate. Divide that by 12 and you get the monthly principal and interest of $1,006.80.

To quickly calculate the outstanding principal at the end of 15 years, you would first ascertain how many years remain. As this was originally a 30-year loan, the remaining years at the end of 15 years would be 15 years. Now divide the annual payment of $12,081.60 by the (remaining) 15-year constant rate shown on the Constant Rate Chart for a 7.5 percent loan with 15 years term (11.12 percent): $12,081.60 ÷ .1112 = $108,647.48. In essence, as you know the annual payment, the question is this: What is the amount of a mortgage (the principal owed) that has a term of 15 years at a contract rate of 7.5 percent?

Sylvia knew she could rent one side of the duplex for $975.00 per month. The annual taxes on the property were $1,750 per year, and she estimated that general upkeep of the yard and building would be another $2,000 a year. Her income was $11,700 a year, and her expenses (not including the debt service) totaled $3,750. This gave her a net operating income of $7,950 a year. But her mortgage payment was $12,081.60, which meant she was not getting any positive leverage out of this deal. Sylvia was out-of-pocket $4,131.60 a year.

However, the reason for negative leverage is that she is collecting rent on only part of the property, and she is living in the other part of the property. Is this negative leverage bad? In this situation it is absolutely not. She has improved her situation, as she was paying $860 a month in rent and she has reduced that expense by more than half. She is building up equity and, with her care, the property will appreciate in value as well. Look at the recap of this example below.

Sylvia's Deal

Renegotiated price of the duplex	$160,000	
Mortgage obtained	144,000	(90 percent loan @ 7.5% for 30 years)
Cash invested	$ 16,000	

Note: The loan was amortized over 30 years but would have a balloon at the end of 15 years with annual payments totaling $12,081.60. The principal that would still be owed at the end of 15 years would be $108,647.48. If the loan were to continue for the full 30 years it would fully amortize. The initial 15 years total payments made by Sylvia would be $181,224 and all but $35,352.52 of that is interest.

What does Sylvia's cash flow look like? She will collect rent from half the duplex at an annual rate of $11,700. Subtract her expected operating expenses of 3,750 and Sylvia will have the balance to apply to her debt service: $7,950. However, her mortgage is $12,081 per year. Sylvia will have to dig into her pocket to the extent of $344.00 per month to make up the difference. This is still a good deal for Sylvia, as she has cut her overall expenses to less than half of what she had been paying for rent. Now she gets tax shelter, housing at a bargain, and equity buildup, plus potential appreciation.

Robert's 10-Unit Deal

Robert came to the same conclusion as did Sylvia and wanted to stop paying the $1,400 per month rent to shelter himself and his family. He had $35,000 to invest and found a 10-unit apartment complex that had a nice owner's apartment as one of the units. As he had 9 units to support the expenses and the debt, he was almost able to break even at the end of the year. His loan debt service was just barely covered by his net operating income so, although he had a negative leverage with no cash flow to start out with, he anticipated that over a couple of years he could increase the revenue of the property to move him into a positive leverage position. And from the first day, he was saving all the rent he had been giving to some other landlord.

Jose's Strip Store Transaction

Jose negotiated a deal to purchase a small commercial building that contained seven shops with an annual net operating income of $92,500. The price was $875,000 and at closing there were three loans: an assumable first at 7 percent interest, a seller-held second at 8 percent interest, and a private unsecured loan at 9 percent interest. Jose had $120,000 cash to invest, so the total debt was $755,000. All of the loans were at an interest rate less than the yield of the property (10.57 percent), but the combined annual payment for the three mortgages was $96,570, which exceeded the NOI. Although the first and second mortgages totaled only $76,570 per year, the private loan Jose needed cost $20,000 per year in payments on the amount of $52,411 that he had borrowed to close.

Jose had a negative leverage at the cash flow position in the deal, but he was getting positive leverage on the interest rates he was paying. This happened because the term of one of the loans had jumped the total constant rate to 12.79 percent. It turned out the problem was with just one of the loans and was for a short period. As it was only a three-year at $20,000 (including interest), once it was paid off, his return (even without increases in rent) would be excellent. Jose's investment in the property will be $120,000 plus the shortage for three years to cover the debt shortage of $4,070 per year, a total of $12,210 for the three years. Therefore the total capital out would be $132,210 and his cash flow at the end of three years will be $15,930—a 12.05 percent yield on that investment. His loan situation has then shifted into a positive leverage situation. Look at the recap of this example below.

Jose's Strip Store Transaction

Price	$875,000	
NOI	92,500	(10.57 percent of the price)
Yield	10.57 percent	(Jose's return if he had paid all cash)
Cash invested	$120,000	
Debt	$755,000	(made up of a first mortgage at 7 percent, a second mortgage at 8 percent, and a private loan at 9 percent)
Total debt service	$96,570	(unless income increases, Jose is short $4,070 per year, due to the $20,000/year private loan payment on $52,411)

Jose's Situation after Three Years

Debt service	$ 76,570	(the short term private loan is paid off)
Cash flow increases	$ 15,930	(NOI of $92,500 less debt service of $76,570)
Jose's cash invested	$132,210	(includes debt service shortage for three years)
Yield	12.05 percent	

In each of these three situations, the leverage was either negative or just marginally positive in the beginning. Jose's deal turned out real sweet once he paid off the unsecured loan. However, in all instances, the investment strategy was sound. Had each party had more cash to invest they might have started with a stronger leverage position, but in the end their goals were met with the amount of capital they had to start with.

Cash flow is something that comes from real estate—it is not inherent with all investments. If you buy a stock that does not give a dividend (which is the way most of them are), you get zero cash flow. Yet billions of dollars are invested in something that has to go up in value for you to profit. Never forget that cash flow is the excess of the OPM (your tenants) that is left over after you pay off the other OPM (your debt). Whenever you are down in the dumps because your cash flow isn't as high as it should be, just think of all those monthly installments you are putting in the bank every time you pay down the principal of the mortgage.

Six Elements for Maximum Leverage

1. Stay within your comfort zone.
2. Understand the power of using other people's money.
3. Get to know the money market in your area.

4. Follow the lender's dream.

5. Fill a void.

6. Get the facts right.

Stay within Your Comfort Zone

Your comfort zone is one of the keys to your success. The moment you are enticed to a property that is out of the zone and you feel that what you know about the property and the area where it is located is sufficient for you, then step back. Make a commitment to yourself that you will take some time, a week at least, to do the very things that have paid off for you thus far with your present comfort zone. If you are afraid of losing the property, then go ahead and tie it up with an extra 30 days on top of your regular due diligence period, and devote the first 30 days to spending as much time as you can to add this area to your comfort zone. Keep in mind what I keep saying about real estate being a hands-on kind of investment. The more you personally know about the property and the area, the better your decisions will be. So, for the first several investments, stick to your comfort zone and no other. As you branch out, try to add territory to your current zone rather than jumping to another town or state.

Understand the Power of Using Other People's Money

Other people's money is available because there are other people who would rather take a lower return by lending money on real estate than they would by owning it. In a way they are also leveraging their investment, because their cost of those funds is less than what you are going to pay them. Many of the loans that are made on the local level are made by community banks. That money comes from people who have deposited money with the bank; it can also be augmented by funds that the bank borrows from other banks or from the Federal Reserve. Banks borrow from each other at rates well below what you and I are likely to be quoted, so they can afford to make us decent loans. As long as a lender doesn't get caught with a lot of capital tied up in long-term loans at rates well below what they now have to pay for the funds, they will make money as long as the loans remain in good standing.

Get to Know the Money Market in Your Area

There are many sources to tap into the OPM market. Your local commercial banks and the savings and loan associations in your area are all good sources for many kinds of loans, especially real estate mortgages. It is a good idea to have a couple of good mortgage brokers in your sphere of reference as well. They deal with lenders on a broader scene than you might have access to.

Follow the Lender's Dream

All lenders have a preferred or ideal kind of loan, based on two major factors: the borrower and the property. As many commercial loans are nonrecourse (there is no personal liability tied to the loan in the event of a default), the borrower's track record and experience are important factors. We all read about people who just seem to be able to buy anything, no matter what the price. This is because lenders love them and throw money at their feet. You may never get to that level, but why not try?

You need to know what sorts of property the lenders love. You aren't their ideal person just yet, but you can invest in the kind of real estate that they like. This is the right way to ride the roller coaster of real estate. When hotels are the prime choice of security that lenders currently love, then consider getting into the hotel business; if big box tenants are the ticket, then consider that kind of real estate. Note that I said "consider." Never make a move into something solely because this or that lender loves it. Remember, there are more lenders out there, and you bend to their preferences only when you can't find one who loves the kind of property you like.

Fill a Void

To maximize any aspect of real estate investing, you want to invest in a property that has the best opportunity to go up in value. Your selection of property will rely on how well you have developed your comfort zone, and whether you have worked hard at becoming a real estate insider. But there are also other factors critical to getting the most out of your investment capital. I have mentioned some of them already, such as following the lender's dream and picking real estate where your talents aid you in creating *"added value"* to the property. But when it comes to leverage, the single most important factor is that the property should fill a void in the marketplace. Not just any void—it should be a void that is in demand.

This kind of void is often very easy to see. It is the hot property, the "in" neighborhoods, and so on. But if you keep your eyes open you will begin to see that real voids are not always so obvious. Take, for example, a neighborhood that has a lot of small rental properties scattered about. That evolved because there were investors who wanted to own that kind of property and there were builders who supplied that demand. Okay, that was the easy-to-see void. But what about now? It is hard to find good rental properties to purchase. In neighborhoods where older rental properties exist, they sell the instant they go on the market. The only problem is that very few go on the market. See a void? It might be time to build new small rental properties for the purpose of selling them at a profit. This concept can be applied to any kind of real estate. Check it out in your neighborhood.

Get the Facts Right

You know what they say about the reliability of a computer: Garbage in, garbage out. The same is true with real estate and, because of the Rule of Small, even the smallest error in the data you collect will turn a property that looks like it will be a winner into a quick loser. Because you cannot rely on what you are told, you have to pay close attention to the actual documentation of the income and expenses of a prospective property. This means looking at the bills, and questioning the absence of expenses that should be there and aren't, or the amounts that appear to be much less than they are in other similar properties.

How do you do this? Start looking at the financial numbers of as many properties as you can. Every property listed for sale through the local realtors' listing services is fair game for you. Narrow down the listings to the kind of property you most want to learn about. Ask the listing agents for the details on properties. Make a comparison between different properties. Does each similar property have the same list of expenses? How do they compare as an overall percentage of the gross income collected? For example, if the property has $100,000 of gross rents, what percent of that is made up of utilities (all lumped into one), real estate taxes, property insurance, general reoccurring maintenance, management, pest control, and nonreoccurring repairs and replacements? "Reoccurring" and "nonreoccurring" expenses are accounting terms that you must pay close attention to. If you don't see any nonreoccurring expenses such as roof repair, heating and cooling systems, or exterior painting, ask when repairs or replacements were done. If it was a long time ago, be extra cautious. If you see a large disparity between the percentage of revenue to these expenses in different properties, you need to question the agent about them. There will be other expenses too, like legal expense, bad debt, accounting, yard maintenance, pool service, elevator service, and so on. One thing you can count on is that similar properties in the same city should have similar expenses.

Question expenses that will change when you purchase the property. Taxes are likely to go up the minute the tax assessor sees the recorded deed at a double value to the previous year's assessed value. This is something that comes as a big surprise to many buyers. Be aware of this, and count on the new tax level and not the old one. Insurance may go up, too—as the seller gives you last year's bill to review and it is already out of date.

Pitfalls in Highly Leveraged Mortgages

Any highly leveraged loan can create problems in the event of sudden vacancies reducing the income of the property to levels that cause the property owner to struggle to meet debt service and operational expenses. When there is a shortage of revenue, most property owners will begin to cut back on maintenance. If that doesn't reduce the shortfall to the level where debt and essential operations can continue, then the owner will have to dig into his own pocket to meet expenses, including the mortgage payments.

When there is a severe shortage of revenue and a property owner is faced with the loss of a property, the options may become limited. If refinancing is not possible, then disposition of the real estate may be the only remedy.

At that point, hindsight is no consolation, but remember that every debt against a property can one day become the mortgage that forces the property into foreclosure. Of all such mortgages, those that have early repayment dates are more responsible for this situation than any others. A 30-year term with a balloon in five years is really a five-year term with payments based on a 30-year amortization. No matter what the loan looks like, it will be due to be paid off in five years. This can cause a lot of pressure in any real estate transaction, and will necessitate finding a creative approach to dispose of a property in this situation. The key is to stay ahead of a pending disaster. If you have a loan that is coming due, or a major debt payment that must be met, and you think you are going to have economic difficulties meeting those obligations, then do not wait until the due date is upon you to start to seek a remedy or other solution to the pending problem.

CHAPTER 7

How to Maximize Your Financing

The goal of this chapter is:

To Help You Get the Best Loan Terms Possible

Unless you are an institutional buyer, such as a real estate investment trust (REIT), home buyers have the best opportunity to borrow at low rates, unless their credit is shot full of holes. Even then, many poor-credit buyers manage to make decent investments in single family homes. VA and FHA loans help those who qualify for them, and seller-held financing can give any buyer a boost to get over the financing hurdle.

The sellers of commercial property are often motivated by profit. When this is the situation, you have many options in dealing with those sellers. Generally the first place to look for a commercial loan will depend on the size of the loan. Small commercial loans, up to $7 or $8 million, might be obtained locally from a commercial bank or savings and loan association. A commercial lender takes the property into consideration, and in some cases give the property greater weight than they do the borrower. But one factor is universal: If the intended use is risky, then the whole deal may not be easily financed. In the end, the best commercial loan will boil down to the lender liking the project, then liking the borrower, then making the loan.

The key to getting the lender to like the project is to make sure you are bringing the lender a development or loan package that is backed up with a sound business plan. The economics of the deal are what it will take to convince the lender. Once that is accomplished, then you can emphasize the fact that the combination of you and the project is worth their taking a chance on the loan.

On the positive side of commercial loans, lenders love to advance money on commercial real estate more than on residential lending. The reason is that commercial real estate produces revenue that will pay off the loan.

Key Words and Concepts to Build Your "Insider" Knowledge

Seller-Held Financing
Loan Officer
Wall Street Financing
Acquisition and Development Loans
Income and Expense Projections
Loan Draw Schedule

Seller-Held Financing

If there is any truth about financing, take this as an absolute: When available, a motivated seller is potentially the best source for creative financing of the property you are about to purchase from him. There are many reasons for this, and I touch on all of them in this book. The key, however, is for you to recognize several factors about seller-held financing and what motivates the seller. Let's look at the seller's motivation. Generally there are nine primary reasons a seller may want to sell. Here is the "why sellers exist" list.

1. The seller cannot afford the debt. There are many reasons for this, and it may have nothing to do with the property offered for sale. It could be that this is the seller's only saleable property. In the case of income-producing property, a prudent investment will cover its own debt, so if the problem is poor management, you would approach that seller differently than one who simply has a bad and costly habit (drugs, gambling, or other vices) that has put him or her into big-time debt. It can be a difficult sale if the property in question is the problem and is already so soaked with debt that the seller doesn't have any real equity in the first place.

2. The seller no longer needs the property. Of course it could be that he never needed it in the first place but ended up with it. Perhaps he inherited it, took it in lieu of foreclosing on a loan, or got it as a part of an exchange or payment owed. Or perhaps the seller simply outgrew it. These are generally motivated sellers that are easier to deal with than those deeply in debt.

3. The seller needs to raise capital for another project (to save or to buy). Cash is the motivation here, so unless you can meet the cash requirements this seller will be difficult to deal with. However, if the need for capital is such that he can let the property go for a real bargain, then the buyer with just enough cash to save the other project might get a really good buy.

4. The seller is sick and tired of property management and wants out. Most property owners have their moments when they are tired of dealing with the headaches that go along with property ownership. For most of us, those days are offset by looking at our growing bank account and the yield we get on our investments, way ahead of our friends who are locked into the stock market. However, this is a genuine reason to sell and is often coupled with one or more of these nine reasons, like, the desire to travel. This is a truly motivated seller and is often the best one to work with when you need seller-held financing.

5. The seller's spouse is sick and tired of dealing with the property and its headaches. This is a logical and a primary reason many mom-and-pop types of real estate holdings are offered for sale. Take the motel the couple retired to, thinking it would be like a 365-day vacation each year and they could live free (in the manager's apartment) and rake in a ton of money. But that's not generally the way it turns out. If the seller who does the talking confides to you that his or her spouse is the driving force, then find out what's up and work to help the spouse reach his or her goal.

6. The couple has a divorce in progress or is facing a court order that says they must sell and divide the proceeds. This can be a motivated seller, but there are often a lot of complications in closing the deal. Cash is usually the key factor. When the right situation comes along and you have the cash or financing available, then go for it.

7. The owners are looking to form a new investment format to improve their estate for future generations. These owners may or may not know what kind of investment will improve the estate, so they might be a likely candidate for an exchange into a property that you own that will make an ideal down payment for you. Creative financing is also a potential here. A long-term land lease they hold on the shopping center you want to buy can save them taxes and create a management-free income for now and future generations.

8. The owners want to travel. This is usually a side effect of one of the other reasons, or it might just be that their pet dog has died and they are now free to travel. This can also be an excuse and not a reason at all. When you hear this given as the reason for selling, then ask some more questions. If this is indeed the motivation for a sale, a creative approach, such as a joint venture, land lease, or exchange, might work wonders.

9. The old owners just died, so move to the top of the list. When a property is a part of an estate, there can be opportunities to be had. This is especially the case when none of the heirs are interested in taking over the property. However, probate and other after-death problems can put roadblocks in the way of a final deal, so be patient.

If you can learn whether your seller is motivated for any of these nine reasons, then you will be able to negotiate a deal that can better serve his goal as well as yours. The kind of financing a seller may hold will generally fall into one of these categories: a first mortgage or a loan that is in a secondary position (second, third, and so on); a land lease (subordinated to existing or future debt, or unsubordinated and in a secondary position); an option; a joint venture position; a partial exchange; or a full exchange. As you can see, not all of these categories are actually mortgages.

A land lease, for example, allows the seller to retain a part of the property while at the same time giving up the use of it. In turn the buyer pays rent on the leased portion of the deal. A prospective buyer can obtain an option to buy at the end of a specific term. In the meantime the buyer may gain use of the property and can increase the value of the property to the point that outside financing can be obtained and the seller eventually paid off. This option technique can be combined with the lease situation, and a *lease option* form of acquisition may result.

A joint venture may result when a reluctant seller is enticed to accept a proposal from a developer that keeps the present owner in the deal for a piece of the action. This type of transaction can also be combined with a second mortgage the seller holds to secure his position. Other development type contract provisions may give the seller a *preferred* return, which is paid to the seller before the other joint venture members are entitled to their share of the profits.

Real estate exchanges can also play a role in financing. If you consider anything a seller will take, other than money, as financing, then a buyer can exchange labor (often called *sweat equity*) in a deal as a down payment, or an option payment to seal the deal.

A motivated seller may be at the end of his or her rope, or just in need of getting capital out of one deal to put it into another. Whatever the situation, the buyer who makes the deal will be the investor who knows that helping the seller satisfy at least one of his or her major goals can assist in making a deal possible.

Loan Officer

The loan officer is the person you deal with when you go to a lender to discuss a loan. Knowing some important things about this person will help you to understand how they function, what their hot buttons are, and where their limitations lie.

Let's start with how they function. A loan officer's job is to deal with the paperwork of mortgage applications, make initial assessment of the borrower, review the loan presentation, and formulate a report to the loan committee. The larger the loan amount, the more hands-on the relationship between the loan officer and the borrower might become. The loan officer also deals with the other players who come together to make the loan work. These include the appraisers that are hired sometimes by the lender and sometimes by the borrower (but always paid for by the borrower, one way or the other). These appraisers assess the value of the security being offered. The ones that work directly for the lender tend to be a bit conservative in their appraisals. They need to protect their clients, and conservative appraisals help protect the bank against making loans on over valued properties. This should be a red light for borrowers to make every effort to hire their own appraisers that are approved by the lender. As the borrower will end up paying for the appraisal anyway, this separation of control over who actually does the appraisal, no matter how slight, will be to the borrower's benefit.

The loan officer also interacts with the legal staff and the lawyers who are processing the technical aspects of the proposed deal, and of course the loan officer is either a member of the loan committee or is at their beck and call.

Formal education does not prepare a person for this job, no matter how many accounting courses one has or what vocational school one might have attended. A master's degree in economics is no real help either. Many loan officers are people who gravitate to this line of work from other banking positions, either up or down the ladder, and when they are good at the task, they tend to stick with it. In most instances it is a comfortable but not highly paid job. Yet, depending on the lender and the level of loans we are talking about, a loan officer can do well, raise a family, and retire with a nice pension. Very lucky ones might also make a few investments along the way and be able to have a second home by the sea or in the mountains.

The loan officer's hot button is any loan that has the absolutely 100 percent guarantee that not one payment will ever be late, and that the borrower will keep coming back to that same loan officer year after year, borrowing millions of dollars and paying it all back early. The reason for this is simply that no loan officer—no one who works in the lending institution, for that matter—ever wants their name associated with a bad loan that ends up in foreclosure. There is a standing rule in the lending business: When a loan officer's loans go sour, a nice, shiny red star, either real or imaginary, will be stuck in the book next to that officer's name. Get too many red stars and you are history.

Loan officers have their limitations, and unfortunately you discover them at the worst possible moment. When is that? When the loan committee has turned down the loan request or has sent the loan officer back to renegotiate the terms. Remember the hot buttons? Well, when the going gets tough, many loan officers take the avenue of least resistance. They don't step up to the bat and fight for you. And why should they? This is where your relationship needs to be directed. The whole essence of dealing with loan officers starts with you knowing these factors about them, and doing all you can to light up their hot buttons. As a commercial real estate investor, you are not a once-every-eleven-years-or-so home buyer. You are headed for the big time, and you appreciate every moment of their time helping you along the way.

How do you keep that fire burning? I have a simple rule: Be an appreciative person. What this means to me is to let people know that you appreciate the service you got from someone who works for them as well as the person's peers. How do you let them know how great you think this person is? Well, this reminds me of the 85-year-old guy who shows up in the confessional. When asked by the priest, "What can I do for you, my son?" the man starts telling the priest about the 30-year-old girl he is living with. He tells the priest how great their sex life is and how wonderful she thinks he is.

The priest asks, "Are you Catholic?"

"Why no, father," the man says.

"Then why are you in a confessional telling me this?" the priest asks.

"Father," the 85-year-old man replies, "I'm telling everybody."

I think you will remember this analogy, and that is good, because when you find any service above mediocre, it needs to be encouraged. Only through encouragement and appreciation will "above mediocre" improve to "great." As for loan officers, I do not single them out for this treatment. All hardworking people should be treated as though they are someone special when they give above-average service. If they give outstanding service then so much more accolades should come from you. And to whom do you give these accolades? To their employers, of course—but not just their immediate superior. Praise at more than one level or the praise will stop at the first level.

I'll pat your back and hope you'll pat mine in return. This works wonders in business, and in just about everything else, so be sure to tell everyone the good news.

Wall Street Financing

All the major stock brokerage houses get into real estate. They do so by raising funds for big projects and in the end often become a partner in the venture. This is big-time real estate financing and is a great source of funds for the big-time investor. Guess what? You don't have to wait until you are already a big-time investor to take advantage of this source, because that will take longer than you might want to wait. Get in on the inside of this source early. How do you do this? Sit down with one of the vice presidents at a local office of one of the big Wall Street brokerage houses. If you don't know which firms are big Wall Street firms, then pick up a copy of the *Wall Street Jour-*

nal and read it from cover to cover one afternoon. You will know who most of the big houses are by the end of the day.

Explain to the vice president of the firm you have selected that you and several of your partners (who knows, one might be Mr. Trump himself) are looking at a couple of real estate projects and would like to discover if his firm is interested in becoming a joint venture partner in the deal. Would he or she (the vice president) kindly explain how the firm can be of help to you?

But remember, the vice president of a stock brokerage firm functions a lot differently than a loan officer at the local savings and loan association. All stock brokers, no matter their rank, work in a commission-based environment. They get commissions on stock sales and on joint venture deals that are brought to their Wall Street firm. Learn all you can from more than one of these vice president types. Then pick the one that you best relate with, and try very hard to help each other become wealthy.

Acquisition and Development Loans

This term relates to a package loan that is used to fund two things: the acquisition of a property and its ultimate development. These loans are generally made by a local commercial bank, a savings and loan, or a combination of several banks or other lenders that unite to make such a loan. In large, multimillion-dollar projects, insurance companies, credit unions, or Wall Street itself may be a part of this kind of financing. This type of loan is also called an A & D loan, and they often carry the project through to its final development. When the development is completed, the A & D loan is then paid off from proceeds of new financing, or from a combination of financing and sales.

Examples of A & D Loans are found in many different types of development. A condominium project, for example, may have this kind of financing. The developer goes to a lender, let's say an insurance company, and obtains an A & D loan to fund the acquisition of a site and the development of 150 deluxe condominiums in Naples, Florida. The lender has a restriction to the loan that the developer must obtain pre-sales of the condo units of, say, 50 percent of the project. The developer has to tie up the property, pay for all the pre-development costs, and begin the sales campaign, all without getting any money from the lender. Once the presales criteria are met, then the loan is funded and the project moves into the actual acquisition and development stage. The lender will have negotiated terms that are highly favorable to the lender, which might include a nominal interest rate and a hefty piece of the action from the overall sales of the condo units. The lender would likely have a preference on return of profit so that the developer will not receive its full percentage of profits until the final wrap up of the deal, the payoff of the loan, and the sale of the last condo units. The buyers of the condo units would either pay cash for the condos or finance them through local lenders that are conventional savings and loans, or other similar sources for residential loans.

Income and Expense Projections

In accounting terms, income and expense statements are a record of a past period of income and the expenses that occurred during that same period. Add the term *pro forma* to the equation and we are now talking about a future projection as to how the finished development will perform. This is an estimate of what the future will bring for any new venture, building, or development. These projections are important for new projects and redevelopment of old projects. If you are buying an existing commercial strip center, and it needs of a lot of tender loving care, then you will want to borrow based on what the income and expense picture will look like when the work is finished. You will project the end results, showing in great detail how you plan to achieve that increased level of income. For brand-new development, there is no existing history of income or expenses to look at, so you will need to provide the lender with a realistic projection of the project's future income and expenses.

The borrower must clearly articulate several factors, including costs to arrive at the end product; time it will take; estimates of cost, time, and absorption of new tenants or sales; current market conditions for similar projects; and the developer's background and success record. Unfortunately, many pro formas turn out to be crystal-ball guesses, full of shoddy information. Clearly, many such projects are turned down at loan committee or never make it that far.

As you go through the loan process, do not skimp on getting professional advice on how to make a good loan presentation sparkle. A good source for this knowledge is an accounting firm that has experience working up such projections for real estate development companies. If you have trouble finding one, then get to know some executives in development companies and ask them who they might recommend. If they are reluctant to give you such information, then try several top commercial loan officers at one or more of your local lending sources. You will eventually find a good place to outsource this work. A professionally made pro forma can mean the difference between moving forward or sitting that dance out.

Loan Draw Schedule

When the development part of the loan kicks into high gear, construction starts. The construction loan is tied to a series of *loan draws*. What this means is that, as the construction progresses, the borrower is allowed to submit requests for a draw against the total loan committed to the project at certain stages of the development. These stages will vary depending on the type of project and the lender's experiences with that kind of development. The overall loan will never pay out fully during the construction period, as the lender will retain a certain amount until the conclusive draw, which is generally after the certificate of occupancy has been given by the local building department. It is important to work with the loan officer and your construction supervisor or general contractor in advance of making a presentation as to what your needs will be. Generally there is some flexibility in the draw process, but if this is your first loan in process, make every effort to hit every construction plateau on time and on budget.

Seven Important Factors to Maximize Your Financing

1. Provide an economically sound reason for the loan.

2. Select the right lender for your project.

3. Establish rapport prior to making a submission.

4. Use their forms and follow their procedures,

5. Know how much you need to borrow.

6. Introduce your investment team.

7. Have a positive and honest personal resume.

Provide an Economically Sound Reason for the Loan

The loan you are seeking might be an acquisition loan on an existing project, or it might be for the purpose of buying a project that needs a new spark of life that only you can bring. The reason for the loan is important. Commercial lenders want to believe that the security for their loan will be economically sound, and that the income projected or reported is real and realistic. They want, more than anything, to know that the loan they recommend to their loan committee will be repaid.

The believability of your projections is dependent on the quality of your investment team and the local conditions of the real estate market. Never assume that the lender is unknowledgeable about local conditions. You must reinforce and/or supplement their knowledge by providing clear and accurate documentation to support the revenue you expect to receive. One of the best ways is to have a triple-net lease executed by a triple A-rated tenant. (A triple-net lease is one where the tenant pays rent, plus all costs related to maintenance and upkeep of the property, including insurance, taxes, and local assessments against the property).

Each type of loan will have its own criteria that the lenders will insist you clearly document. A project appraisal may be needed, which will show all the competitive properties in the same market area, as well as a history of other existing and future planned development that may impact your project. Any local infrastructure changes that could have an impact, either positive or negative, should also be shown.

The distance the lender is from the project is important for you to consider. The greater their distance from the project, the more background data you will need to provide. Clearly, if the lender's office is across the street from the project, there are many details that your pro forma may not have to contain. However, if you are dealing with an insurance company located a thousand miles away, then you have to assume that the loan committee will know little or nothing about the area.

Select the Right Lender for Your Project

This is a slightly different point of view from my earlier advice, which was to pick projects that your lender likes. Let's assume that you have been working on a project that you know will be a winner—say, a fresh approach to a private student apartment house that is convenient to two different colleges. You have done your homework with the student housing officials at each of the two colleges and know that there is a shortage in close-in housing for students. You have run the numbers and, based on a 90 percent occupancy, the project will give you a solid return of 17 percent on your anticipated capital investment. All you need now is a lender who agrees that student housing is a good enough project for them to give you the needed financing at their best loan terms possible. As you are starting without the lender's advance blessing on what kind of projects they like to loan on, you now need to look around for a lender that loves anything that has to do with the college environment.

The answer is pretty straightforward. Go back to the student housing officials and ask them who they would recommend you approach for the financing of this project.

Somewhere, between the two colleges and their respective housing departments, someone will come up with a suggested lender. It might be a bank whose president is a graduate of one of the colleges, or who is on the board of directors of both of the colleges. Dig down deep and find some connection between the colleges and a lender to approach.

All good projects, unfortunately, do not have ready, willing, and hot-to-lend lenders waiting for you to knock at their door. Not so many years ago, most lenders in Florida wouldn't touch a hotel refinancing loan unless the loan-to-value ratio (percentage of the loan to the total value of the property) was so low that even if they had to take the hotel through foreclosure they could not lose. Naturally, there is a point in any financing deal where the loan-to-value ratio is so clearly in the lender's favor that the amount of the loan may not be enough to satisfy the reason for the loan request. If you get caught in one of these financing binds, and the lenders are hanging tough on a specific category of real estate, you will either have to change categories or find another source for financing. When one way is no longer a viable option, find another. Needed capital can come from sources other than banks and savings and loans; sometimes a private lender can save the day.

You find private lenders wherever there are wealthy people. By the way, you discover if a wealthy person would be interested in lending money on a specific project by asking them. Or you ask someone who knows wealthy people and is in a position to know if they would lend money. Who would that be? I would suggest you start with your own accountant, lawyer, stock broker, banker, or student housing official.

When you are given a tip as to who makes private loans, make an effort to find out as much about the person as you can. If the person has been around the community for a while, look them up in the local society register. Many of the prominent and wealthy people in town are found in these social directories, which are sometimes sold in the better book stores in town or found in local libraries. If you strike out with those two sources, check with an officer of one of the local society organizations to see if they know of a source for such a registry. Start with something like the Opera Society or the local chapter of the Daughters of the American Revolution.

Even the slightest bit of information about someone can be helpful when you make your first appointment. If you have discovered that the individual graduated from a specific university, know something about that university that can be a conversation point. Then make your appointment with a goal you absolutely know you can attain. Here is a good one that won't let you down: "My goal in meeting Mr. Goldfinger is to make a good impression and demonstrate that I am sincere in my quest to become a successful real estate investor." You attain that goal by explaining to Mr. Goldfinger that you wanted to meet him because he has been recommended to you as a good person to know within the real estate insiders club. You might mention the name of one or two people who had nice things to say about him.

Oh, yes, one thing more: Do not ask to borrow money on this first visit. You will do that only after you have successfully attained that initial goal.

Establish Rapport Prior to Making a Submission

This is the logical process of almost anything you do in business. You either demonstrate that you are the kind of person that would be a good loan risk, or you enlist the help of friends or business acquaintances to pave the way before you. Usually it is a good idea to have some of both elements working on your behalf. But remember to avoid tooting your own horn. Do not deliver a canned speech that begins just after you shake Mr. Goldfinger's hand for the first time, spelling out how wonderful you are and how many fantastic things you have done in your life. If there is no one available to toot your horn for you, work on that problem first. Chapter 9 has some tips on this subject.

It pays to look and act the role of a successful real estate investor, too. If you are a general contractor who is making the move from working on other people's projects to building your own office buildings, then it might be okay to look like a really hands-on and just-in-from-the-construction-site person. Otherwise, any smart business attire should be the uniform of the day.

Sometimes getting to first base in this rapport stage is difficult. The key is to start as high as you can with the decision makers, and those people are often hidden behind walls that are difficult to penetrate. The toughest of these walls might be a secretary or assistant.

I have learned that one of the best ways to insure you get better than average treatment during the appointment stage, and at later meetings with the potential lender, is to establish a good rapport with their secretary or personal attendant. One good way to do that is to stop in unannounced at the office and ask to speak to Mr. Goldfinger's secretary or personal attendant. If a receptionist challenges you with, "What is the nature of this visit?" or something like that, smile and say, "It is about the appointment next week with Mr. Goldfinger."

When you are face-to-face with the secretary or assistant, you thank them for seeing you, and because you value their time you will be very brief. You introduce yourself as a real estate investor in town, and then drop one of the names of someone who came up with Mr. Goldfinger's name for you, like, "The mayor suggested that I might find it beneficial to meet Mr. Goldfinger, and as I was nearby I thought I would drop in and find out when it would be possible to set up a short appointment with him. Does he have 15 minutes open any day this week?"

One word of warning: When you make this approach, you must be prepared for a meeting with Mr. Goldfinger right then and there. That has happened to me on more than one occasion, especially when I am not in my own hometown, such as on business in New York City or Los Angeles. I've said to a secretary, "I am in New York generally once a month, and I have some flexibility in my schedule, so if you can give me a date when he is available early next month, I will make sure I am also available." Her reply: "Just a moment, Mr. Cummings. Mr. Goldfinger just had a prior appointment cancel. If I can get you in right now, do you have time to meet with him?"

Use Their Forms and Follow Their Procedures

Every lender, even private lenders, will usually have their own forms to be filled out. They may all look similar but generally are not exactly the same. Lenders know where to look on their forms to find pertinent information that you have filled in, so do not aggravate them by filling out your own forms that you might have copied from another lender. This will aggravate them to one end: You don't get the loan.

When you fill out forms, it is a good idea to be both as accurate as possible and as brief and concise as you can. Give the reader the right information without being wordy.

Know How Much You Need to Borrow

A loan application should clearly state the amount you require. It is a good idea to ask the loan officer you are working with if you should state an amount that is net of loan costs or include the loan costs in the total loan. Some loan committees have a preference to how this is done, whereas others have none.

If you are requesting an acquisition loan, the loan committee will lean very heavily on the property appraisal. This establishes that important loan-to-value ratio. This ratio is more critical in single family or small apartment buildings, because some lending regulations may establish different payback terms and interest rates, the closer the loan gets to the value of the property. Commercial loans may also have different payback terms and interest rates, but this is usually because of the nature of the transaction and not due to lending regulations.

Introduce Your Investment Team

If you don't have an investment team, then put one together. Remember, this is a team you choose, so keep in mind that to a certain degree, you may be judged by a lender and others as to how well you have built your investment team. Who are these team members? They will vary depending on the nature of the transaction, of course, but will include the four most important areas, from the lender's point of view: legal, accounting, development, and management.

1. Your lawyer. Is he or she well known as a real estate lawyer? If not, you have chosen poorly, no matter how great a probate lawyer you've found. Your team lawyer is the most important name on the list. Your choice of legal counsel demonstrates your willingness to get quality in the areas where it is important. This does not mean you have to get the most expensive lawyer in town. Just get the one that best rounds out your team for the project or acquisition at hand.

2. Your accountant. I recommend you retain an accounting firm with a sound national reputation. This firm should specialize in the kind of real estate accounting that matches the property.

3. Your development team. If you are not a general contractor or architect, then make sure you have details on the background of those you hire. Certain specific data that fits the lender's requirements about these team members may be needed here. This would include a history of similar projects these team members have been involved with in the past. The general contractor's bonding ability would be of obvious interest if the lender requires a construction bond on the project.

4. Your management team. Do you hire out management or do you have an in-house management department? Either way, show who is the head and who else works in that department. A brief resume of their experience should show that you, through your choices in the management of your real estate investments, are capable and qualified to give the property more than adequate management.

Have a Positive and Honest Personal Resume

When you have a positive attitude, everything you do shines through to everyone you do business with. There are some steps you can take to improve that, and I go over them in Chapter 9. The key to having a positive attitude is that you eliminate all the negative aspects of your life—including those negative people you used to hang out with or who were included in your business circle of friends. This same positive attitude should be reflected in your personal resume.

CHAPTER 8

How to Become a Commercial Real Estate Insider

> The goal of this chapter is:
>
> **To Show You How to Become a Real Estate Insider**

This chapter is designed to help you build a foundation that will ease you into that important club: the real estate insiders club. This chapter will help you jump-start your entry into this special club by pointing out where mistakes are usually made. By witnessing insiders in action, you will discover how to avoid these errors before you run into a brick wall.

A Real Estate Insider Defined

A real estate insider is what you will become if you follow the steps outlined in this book. The term describes a person who understands what makes real estate tick and has made the commitment to build comprehensive knowledge of their chosen comfort zone and category of investments like the back of his hand.

Nothing happens to a real estate market that does not have some advance warning. Real estate values rarely react suddenly up or down. However, they often appear to because most people are unaware of how to recognize the advance warning signals that the real estate insider has been following for months or longer. Even a chaotic event, like a tornado or a terrorist attack, has a predictable outcome that can be followed, despite the fact that the event itself could not have been predicted. The insider already knows what is going to occur in the aftermath of such an event and is prepared to act quickly to protect his or her existing wealth, and to take the proper moves to investment potential following the event.

Because most upward or downward movement of value comes from new infrastructure or governmental action, the insider spends a substantial part of his time studying the governmental approval process. Once an insider has gotten to the heart of the decision-making process of all such infrastructure change or governmental action, the future trend for that insider's area is no longer a secret or a surprise. The simple secret to your success will be to do exactly what other insiders have done before you. The process they followed is the path ahead of you.

I would offer a caveat here. A lot of people have the knowledge of all the events I have mentioned but have never become real estate insiders. Just having the knowledge is not enough to allow one to benefit from that knowledge. You have to understand the event's consequences and what will follow, and then *act* on that knowledge. Real estate insiders act, and so should you.

Local Governmental Control over Real Estate

Local governments are made up of elected officials who take the lead roles in the way the city functions. Their jobs are augmented by salaried people and by volunteers who are appointed to different boards that deal with a multitude of decision-making processes within the city. These board members are usually not paid, and are given a mandate of their objectives and responsibilities by the city or county commission under which they serve. From a real estate point of view, there are several such boards that are important to any real estate investor and, for that matter, to anyone who owns real estate within that city or county.

These boards meet on a regular basis and make decisions that are often judgmental in nature. That is to say, issues that the board discusses or hears ultimately require the board to make a decision that will affect the outcome of that issue. Because these boards often act as would a court of law, this kind of authority is called *quasi-judicial* (which literally means "seems-to-be-judicial"). That is a word you will hear frequently when attending any city or county board or commission meeting. All of these meetings are quasi-judicial and, as such, must follow certain rules of protocol. Each board or commission has a leader, which may be a chairman, in the case of a board, or a mayor or commissioner in the case of city or county commissions. Other titles may be used. but the result is the same: There is one leader, and the rest of the members follow the directions of that single authority.

There are ancillary players, who may be salaried people. They could include a lawyer or lawyers who would advise the group on the proper legal protocol to follow or answer legal questions that may come up; a secretary; city staff members from the planning and zoning department; as well as staff from other departments, such as the building department, the fire department, the department of transportation, the health department, and any other division or department of the city or county which may be required to give testimony or advice on any issue that is before the board or commission.

The issues that come before the board or commission can be decided at the meeting or else postponed for later decision. If ultimately decided by a board, the higher authority (either the city commission or the county commission, depending on which authority the board serves) has the ability to make the final decision on the matter. Sometimes the higher authority must call the issue up for review. Unless one or more of the commissioners wants the commission to consider the matter, the issue can remain as the lower board or authorities has decided. You will see several examples of how this happens in the following discussion of the two most important of these boards: the board of adjustment and the planning and zoning board.

The Board of Adjustment

This board hears a variety of issues, most of which deal with matters where a person or entity is requesting a modification or relief from a city ordinance. One such request is called a *zoning variance*. This is where the property owner claims that the zoning rule for a specific property is causing undue hardship on that property owner.

The kinds of issues the board of adjustment will hear and rule on usually deal with a building modification request or setback modifications. Each of these kinds of modifications can have an impact on what new development occurs. Sometimes the issue arises because a change in the building or zoning ordinance creates a conflict for an existing building that does not conform to that new rule.

Generally, when a conflict occurs because of a change in the ordinance, the building becomes *grandfathered* to that use. But what if another rule that forces the property owner to comply to something gets in the way? For example, fire code provisions are rarely grandfathered. When a new fire code rule is made, owners of properties that are affected may be granted a deadline to comply to the new code. They must either comply, show good reason why they are not obliged to comply, or face actions to make them do so. To comply might mean the construction of a new exit or enclosing a fire escape route. If that route needs to be constructed in an area that is within the new setback, there is a conflict that, unless there is another administrative remedy, must be presented before the board of adjustment.

The so-called hardship imposed by any rule or ordinance cannot be financial in nature. This is often a difficult area where compromises are made. Yet many real financial hardships are imposed because of changes in building rules. Owners are forced to comply no matter what the cost.

The Planning and Zoning Board

This is the window to the future of any community. The planning and zoning board hears issues that shape the development of new neighborhoods, redesign old neighborhoods, and can affect the lives of all its citizens. The decisions made in planning and zoning boards can also govern the future value of your property.

Let's look at an example of this process. A real estate investor purchases a site that is zoned for medium-density, multifamily apartments. One such example was a tract I assembled for such an investor. The zoning rules indicated that if all the rules were met, the investor could build 25 apartment units per acre. In this example, that would amount to 21 apartments. As the investor intended to build condominium units that would be for sale, the actual number of units was less important than the actual saleable square footage that the building would contain. In essence, if the maximum size of the building, established by setbacks and height limitations, was 60,000 square feet of saleable space (total volume of the building less parking, halls, stairs and elevators, and other common areas), it would make little difference if this was divided between 15 or

21 apartments. The per-square-foot price would generally determine the same gross sales potential in either event. This is important to understand, because within some zoning, as was the case here, there are restrictions that will govern the maximum square footage you can construct, and those restrictions can be more restrictive than the number of units one can build.

This kind of restriction occurs because there are maximum height limitations and minimum setbacks from all property lines, as I mentioned earlier, but there can also be other limitations such as dry area for water retention, greater parking requirements as the number of bedrooms increase, and guest parking, as well as fire codes to deal with. All these things take their toll on the maximum square footage that can be constructed, even if the zoning code doesn't specify a maximum square footage.

Because a condo (either residential or commercial space) is sold by the square foot, it is possible and often desirable to build fewer units than the maximum allowable, in exchange for more square footage within those units. Fewer residential units means fewer parking spaces required, along with other elements such as fewer elevators, fire escape wells, and so on. All these factors give that space back to the developer to add to the units that will be constructed, thereby increasing the developer's overall gross sales volume at an increased bottom-line profit.

A developer ready to follow the zoning rules hires a design team that consists of an architect, a civil engineer, a traffic consultant, and a good lawyer versed in dealing with planning and zoning issues. The first step in obtaining overall approval to build is a meeting with a development review committee (DRC).

This group will include the city or county building department heads, as well as the fire marshal and other city staff as might be applicable to the project. The first meeting is an informal one, sometimes called a pre-DRC meeting. Here the design team discusses what they want to do, and some of the issues are discussed with the DRC personnel. If there are obvious problems that the staff feels will prevent approval, those are first aired in the preliminary meeting. The preliminary DRC is almost never advertised as being available to the public, although, in most communities, if you showed up it is likely you would be allowed to sit in, especially if you might be affected by the development.

Following the preliminary DRC, a formal DRC is scheduled. The design team makes whatever changes they must to adjust to the recommendations made in the preliminary meeting, and then the formal DRC is held. Again, the public is not invited, but these meetings are usually not closed to the public.

The design team makes its presentation at the formal DRC. The members discuss the issues, and the committee members will each submit a report on their areas of authority—the fire marshal, the traffic department, the different building inspection departments such as structural, electrical, plumbing, landscaping, and so on. The design team ends up with a full set of reports from all the members sitting on the DRC, spelling out what it is going to take to get these departments to sign off on the final building plans.

In the formal presentation at a planning and zoning board meeting, there are a number of players. Many of them are the local real estate insiders, and these meetings give you the opportunity to rub elbows with them all. Here are a few of those players. There is the design team and the investor on one side of the fence. The city planning and zoning staff will discuss the issues with the board in an open forum meeting before the public. The city staff will then make its recommendations, which could be to approve the plan as presented; approve but insist on further changes; request the petitioner to make changes; insist that the developer meet with the neighborhood homeowner associations to try to iron out matters of contention between the parties; or deny the request to develop as presented. The design team and its lawyers make their case, and then the public gets to speak. As this is a quasi-judicial meeting, everyone who speaks must take the oath to tell the truth, and should be sworn in by a city official (usually one of the city's or county's lawyers); however, in some small towns the protocol may be much more relaxed and a formal agenda may not be followed.

In a development proposal where there is neighborhood opposition, these meetings can run for hours. This occurs because each side of the proposition takes every effort to document their case, should there be legal repercussions later on.

If the investor receives approval to proceed, that might be the end of the matter, and it would go back to the architect for the plans to be completed. The project's final building plans will go to the building department for issuance of the building permit.

However, if one of the city commissioners (or county, if that is the higher authority) were to call the matter up for a presentation before the full commission meeting, the process could go back to start with the same or similar process that went before the planning and zoning board. This means more presentations, more time and expense, and even though the project was earlier approved by the planning and zoning board, it could get voted down by the commission.

The entire process is very expensive and time consuming. The whole exercise is to protect the public, administer the rules and ordinances of the city, and insure that the development of a community is orderly and aesthetic, as well as safe.

The Nine Stages of Becoming a Real Estate Insider

1. Identify existing real estate insiders in your area.
2. Meet the people who can change real estate values.
3. Build insider contacts.
4. Ask pertinent questions.
5. Learn the key elements of the local zoning codes.
6. Inspect "for sale" properties.
7. Follow the rental market in your investment area.
8. Learn the basics of income and expense statements.
9. Study what you are weak at.

Identify Existing Real Estate Insiders in Your Area

Distinguishing a real estate insider from someone else (say, someone who rents where they live) is not all that difficult, once you discover what insiders are and what makes them different from the renter. To do this you need to be observant of what is going on in your community. If you think you already do this, then you should be able to name at least two members of your city commission, the head of the building and zoning department, and the mayor's secretary or assistant. Did you pass that test?

You will begin this learning process by reading the following four sections of the local newspaper: society, business, legal, and real estate. These sections will have a certain overlap of important information. Many of the local real estate insiders will show up in all four of these sections. This overlap provides a major shortcut for you if you plan to eventually meet some of these important people. It gives you insight as to what they do and how they give time and money back to the local community through their social and community organizations. It also gives you a starting point of what to talk about when you do meet them.

As this book sticks to the concept that everything you accomplish is through setting goals, then following through with the steps to attain them, a worthwhile goal you should set is to *attend the next three planning and zoning (P&Z) board meetings and then the following three commission meetings.* It is critical that you tie this commitment to three meetings of each body. It will take that long, but only that long, to get a good grasp on what is going on within the most important steering body of your local real estate values. Remember that the task is simply to be an observer at these meetings, but you must be prepared to hand out your business cards that introduce you as a real estate investor. Some people have these cards made up with their photograph on them. This is generally a good idea, as people will not only be able to remember your name but they can tie it to a face, too.

Don't skimp on your business cards. Have one designed that is unique and of high quality. Other than your photograph, be sure it has color in a logo or heading. The goal you will strive for is to get to know the members of the board and the commission and the supporting players that advise them. But at the same time, you want them to get to know you. It is this two-way street that is essential to breaking into any insider club.

Start with the planning and zoning board. You have three of their meetings in which to attain the following goal: "By the time I have attended three of the P & Z board meetings, I will have introduced myself to each board member present, and they and their advisory staff will have gotten to know me as a local real estate investor."

The best ways to insure that not only do you know them, but they know you, will be through a carefully planned introduction, a good first impression, and your follow-up to that meeting. Chapter 9, "How to Build Effective Contacts," will give you additional tips and suggestions on how to make these encounters profitable ones.

While at these meetings, it is important that you be an observer and not a participant. Sit back and watch how the real estate insiders conduct themselves as they present their cases before the board or the commission. Pay close attention to the lawyers and other experts who testify for and against the investor or his team. You will see mistakes made, though you may not recognize them as mistakes right then. If you think about the meeting the next day, you will come up with a lot of "Why did they say that?" questions. When that happens, you are beginning to see that there might be better ways to get things done. You are also starting to recognize a mistake when you see it, and that is the very best kind of a mistake to experience. It belongs to someone else, and you get to learn from it.

Meet the People Who Can Change Real Estate Values

By the time you have attended three P & Z board meetings and three city commission meetings, you should be well on your way to being recognized by sight. Commission members will nod their head toward you in recognition; they might even smile or say "Thanks for the photo of my wife and me at the Boy Scout benefit," or whatever shows appreciation for your being attentive to their commitment to the community.

As you go down the list of people you should meet, always start at the top. For the P & Z Board, that would be the chairperson. At the city commission meetings you would start with the mayor and the commissioner from your district. Branch out to the county level of government, too, as they deal with a broader scope of issues that can have an impact on your future as an investor in the community.

After those initial three meetings you committed to attend, you will begin to know many of the building and zoning staff members. These are the people who may speak at the meetings or be asked by the board members for advice. Meet with them in their offices. You have a perfect reason to be there—you want to discuss with them one or more of the issues that came up at the last P & Z board meeting or the commission meeting. Review their opinion and ask them why the other side took the position they did. Remember to play this game carefully. You are a neutral observer and not there to challenge the people you want to meet.

Think of this process as the rule of three: three meetings of three different boards or commissioners (planning and zoning board, city commission, and either the board of adjustment or the county commission). At each meeting all you have to do is concentrate on three of its members and three staff members. By the time you finish the third meeting, you pretty much have the major players in the bureaucratic side of real estate covered. From then on out, expand your rule of three into the private sector—where the investor insiders live.

Build Insider Contacts

Once you have established a rapport with one of your new acquaintances, you should pyramid that into introductions to other insiders. Here is how this works.

You have been to a city council meeting and have introduced yourself to the head of the P & Z department, who was at that meeting as an adviser to the commission. You follow up with a short note, thanking him for the opportunity to meet him, and you go on to say that you found his explanation of the new zoning code, which he gave to the commission, very informative. You end the note saying that you would like to meet with him at a future date and that you will call his office for an appointment.

You get the appointment for what you promise will be a 15-minute meeting to discuss the zoning uses of a property you are interested in acquiring. You arrive at his office at least 10 minutes early and have your questions neatly typed out, with an extra copy for the person you are meeting. The meeting goes as you have indicated it would, except that you have stressed the fact that you are a real estate investor new to this area and you hope he will not mind giving you some pointers on the direction of real estate in the area. Be ready for some questions you will be asked, such as what kind of real estate, where, and some background questions about yourself. Be honest in every way, and stress the fact that you hope to make this community your home (even if you have already lived there for 50 years). One of the last of a very few questions you ask is, "Who should I meet next to best expand my knowledge of the area?"

I have never had less than two names recommended to me when I asked this question. I suggest you limit the list to no more than three, no matter how many names might be given to you. You can do this by asking which of those names (if more than three were suggested) they would say are the top three you should get to know first.

Once the list is narrowed down to three, then ask the person you are meeting with if he would mind giving you three of his cards (in addition to the one he gave you earlier), and write the name of each person on the back of one of those cards. Later, when you call on those people, you will hand them the card and say, "Jim Naugle, our mayor, suggested I meet with you."

Ask Pertinent Questions

You build rapport with people by letting them know that you respect their position and their knowledge. You should be sincere in this as you are there to learn from this person, as well as add them to your sphere of reference. They are, after all, little gold stars that go onto your report card and help earn you the right to be called a real estate insider. So do your homework and do not ask stupid-sounding questions. If you are meeting with the fire marshal, don't ask how many fire trucks are under his control, or what is the name of those spotted dogs that ride with the firemen. Both of these are questions I have heard asked of a fire marshal in the past, and thank goodness no one remembers I was the person who asked them.

Here are examples of some good questions to ask the fire marshal: What is the code as it relates to when a building must have fire sprinklers installed? How long do I have to install them, after I have been notified by the authorities that they are needed? What is the greatest distance a person in a building can possibly be from a fire escape? Is that distance a direct line, or is it a distance that can be traveled? These are questions that show you have thought about an issue and give the fire marshal a chance to expound on his knowledge of the job that he's the authority on. Be sure to have a plan B that will cover the situation if you ask a question that the person cannot answer. A good plan B for me has always been a backup question: "I'm sure the answer is more complicated than the question. Would you mind if I stopped by your office one day next week to discuss the matter? Is Wednesday at 2:30 okay?"

Make sure the questions you ask have a connection to the meeting or to the subject matter that the person has dealt with in the past. This ties things together and helps set up the next meeting when your rapport begins to deepen.

When you are meeting with one of the future project decision makers, always ask what new projects are coming up that you should know about. The mayor will generally know of things that are soon to be discussed at an upcoming city council meeting weeks, if not months, prior to the actual council meeting. He knows what's going on, so why not try to get some advance information yourself.

Virtually all city employees or committee members want to give the impression that they are not antidevelopment in the city. Give them a chance and they will tell you the positive reasons why you should invest in this city instead of a neighboring city.

Guess what is next. Drop them a note, thanking them for the information and good advice as well as for the three introductions they gave you. Remind them who they recommended you visit with next, and end by saying you will keep them informed on how your meetings with those people go.

When you do this, people will respond to you in a very positive way. They will appreciate that you respect their advice and think highly of their time.

Learn the Key Elements of the Local Zoning Codes

By now you understand how important it is to know what use a property can be put to. Use is everything, in the long run, and as I have mentioned before, use is a factor that is governed mostly by zoning and city ordinances. Getting a solid grasp on this issue is the dust that grows into solid gold bars. How do you win? You win by paying close attention to the zoning codes and issues in city meetings when possible changes to those codes are discussed. Every time a zoning code is changed, even to the slightest degree, some people's property may lose value, and some real estate investor will profit.

Unless you know what the zoning is today, a change may mean nothing to you. As with real estate, zoning is a very local matter. It is common for adjoining cities to have different city codes and zoning categories. When you learn the codes, you will want to apply them to the property in your investment area. If the zoning says RMM-30, what does that mean? If it indicates that you can build 30 units per acre, what other uses are allowed besides units? What kind of units? Hotel rooms or apartments or both? Can you build seven single family homes on a one acre site with this zoning? Is there the potential of building a 100-room hotel with restaurant and lounge on a three-and-a-half-acre tract of land with this kind of zoning? The answers to each of those questions might mean a windfall profit to the owner of such a tract, or to a developer who buys the land from an owner who doesn't understand what the zoning means.

Once you have a list of possible uses down pat for every zoning that is in your investment zone, and the possible uses that each can be put to, do your homework on the restrictions or regulations that will apply to those properties that require a modification of the codes that regulate those uses. There are major rules. There is no real order of importance of these, as the one that is most important to the use you want to apply may be different from the ones pertaining to my use. The following key factors in zoning codes can also be used as pertinent questions to ask of the appropriate city officials or board members. Each of the following factors can make adjoining properties unique, because one property may incorporate more of these factors than the other, even though they both may be the same category of zoning.

Building Grade Requirements: Building grade is the height of the ground at the site of the foundation. This height is established from a set benchmark (a previously established height) and will determine how much fill you have to bring in to raise the building to its proper grade level, or how much you might have to remove to have proper slopes for drainage and water retention. This level or height is important because it sets the minimum level of the first floor. What about the slope of the property to adjoining properties? What is the benchmark from which building grade is measured, and exactly how is the code worded? These are questions that only the local code can answer for you. Some areas may set the grade at 18 inches above the crown (highest point) of the road the property adjoins. Other benchmarks (even in the same town) may set the grade at a height above a marker that governs the area, or so many feet above sea level, or other such criteria.

Building Height Maximums: How high can you build? This can be given as a number of floors but is generally shown as a certain number of feet. But how is this code applied? Say the building height is stated as 45 feet. Does that city start the measurement at the first floor where people can live (in an apartment or home) and not in the parking garage under that floor? Some codes vary on that point. And what is meant by *top*? The 45th foot, according to the code, might be the top of the highest floor where people can live, and with nothing allowed above that under any circumstances. Or the definition of *top* may not take into consideration utility and decorative structures above the roof of the top floor. If the latter case applies, the elevator equipment, air-conditioning towers, decorative structures, and so on can extend above that maximum height. Alternatively, the 45-foot limit might simply mean from the bottom of the lowest level to the top of the highest part of the building. Learn which it is, because it can make a big difference in the maximum volume that can be built.

Easements Within the Property: Most properties areas have one or more easements that run through the property. Traffic and utility easements are the most important of these, because without them you may not have access to any city utilities. But there are other easements that can run through the middle of your property that were there long before the land was subdivided. A gas line, water or sewer service, and storm drainage systems, for example, all may have rights to cross a part of any property. Other easements, such as power or phone cable easements and so on, can all mess up your plans, because you may not be able to build over an easement area—or under it, if the easement is above the ground. (Some of these exist but are not in use or even currently intended for use).

Easements that are not presently in use can sometimes be vacated by the party or parties to which the easement was given. Others may not be easily dealt with. These easements can be very important to the development of a property. They can be a critical issue in urban development, where entire blocks of older buildings are razed to make way for new development. Removing old easements can be expensive and time consuming, and sometimes impossible.

Federal Requirements: A few years back, a national law called the Americans with Disabilities Act (ADA) went into effect to protect the rights of physically challenged people to access buildings and services. This was a far-reaching law designed to insure that people in wheelchairs can enter buildings (via walkway ramps, large doors and corridors, and so on), that there are special parking spaces for their vehicles, that they can have access to toilet facilities, and that there are special criteria to meet the needs of blind people who may need the assistance of dogs, raised brail markings for elevators and marquees, and so on. There are special exceptions for building owners when the cost to comply is unreasonable, but that is decided case by case, so these are requirements you should be especially careful with.

Fire Code Requirements: I have mentioned the importance of fire codes before because they rarely are grandfathered in. If a fire code changes, you must comply within a certain time period. These codes account for most of the potential code violations in older properties. When buying an older building, be sure you double-check existing code violations that have not been corrected, as well as have a new check done for current code violations that have not been discovered by the authorities.

Green Area Minimums: Green area does not have to be green. The term refers to landscaping area. Most zoning categories, and especially commercial zoning areas, have enacted strict green area minimums to insure that no more vast, paved parking areas are created to surround shopping centers without breaks for plants, trees, and decorative landscaping areas.

Landscaping Requirements: A building code that has a comprehensive landscaping code will list all the types of plants that can be included. Other plants may be supplemented, on a case-by-case basis, especially if they are already on the site, but in general, to vary from the approved list may mean a denial of a permit. These codes not only list the type and name of the plant, but usually indicate the size as well.

Parking Requirements and Space Needed for Them: These codes will vary between adjoining cities, so learning how one city structures its parking code does not insure that you know how other cities do it. Most commercial parking codes assign one parking place to a certain amount of square footage of building or of use area within the building. The amount will depend on the kind of use. For example, is it a day care center, a shopping center, or a restaurant? If a food service, is it fast-food, take-out only, or a full service restaurant? If you are building a strip store or shopping center, you have to plan for a use that might require more parking than just what your tenants need. Each use may create different parking requirements, which will, in turn, have an impact on some or all of the other restrictions. For example, greater parking will impact the area needed for green space. This might require that the *footprint* (the area the building takes up on the land) be reduced. There are only two ways to do this: Reduce the size of the building, or reshape it as a taller building with more floors, thereby cutting down on the footprint. This may not be permissible, or viable for the intended use.

Restricted Use Due to Other Uses in the Area: Some cities restrict certain uses within a certain distance (which also may vary) from bars, gas stations, and paint and body shops, as well as many other types of businesses. If some of these elements are near a property you are considering buying, you need to know what uses are prohibited for that location because of something else being nearby. This restriction may limit the kind of tenants you can have, or some of the services those tenants could offer.

This restriction can create opportunities for properties that are far enough away from the use that causes the restriction—for example, a school or church. If there is a shortage of good commercial sites for auto body shops, as an example, then a site that can be approved for such a use may bring a premium price.

Special Exceptions to Allow a Use: A day care center is a good example of a special exception. I know a lot about this use, as I am in the process of building a day care center for a tenant on a property I own. This use, as well as many other uses, may be allowed in a specific zoning, but only with the city commission or county commission (whichever has the control) approving the use. This is accomplished by going before the P & Z board to get their approval, then to the commission to get their approval. If you get denied then you are out of luck and have to wait a period of time before you can apply a second time. Why would you do this? Commission members change, and a new vote might go your way.

Water Retention Requirements: What do you do with rain that falls on your property? Many buildings do nothing about it. They let it run into the city storm drainage. But what if there is no such system to dump the water into? This is a problem that is becoming an expensive item for many developers to face. For large projects the solution may fit nicely into the layout of the property and the development in the way of a pond. For others, however, it can be an expensive nightmare.

Yard Setbacks for Buildings from the Lot Borders: Setbacks are very important because they are one of the elements that define the building envelope you have on a lot. A *building envelope* is the box created by application of all the developmental restrictions that will affect any development on a vacant tract of land. If we were to consider only yard setbacks and building height, on a lot 200 feet wide and 200 feet deep with a 50-foot minimum setback from every lot line, the maximum building footprint allowed would be 100 feet x 100 feet. If the building height was four floors maximum, then the envelope would be a box that is four floors high (say 45 feet high) by 100 feet square at its base.

But keep in mind that other elements might cut that footprint down—the green area codes, parking codes, water retention provisions, added setbacks to move away from underground utilities, and so on.

Inspect "For Sale" Properties

You will only learn about the real estate market in your investment area by inspecting firsthand all property that is for sale. Even though a particular property offered is not of interest to you, it is essential that you understand values of all the real estate in your area, not just the kind you want to own. There are two very important reasons for this.

1. A rise or drop in the value of one category of real estate may be a signal of a trend for the area. When industrial properties suddenly drop in value, or modestly priced single family homes jump through the roof, your small apartment houses might be

the next thing to become really hot. Think of these two situations. Industrial properties going down in value might signal a near-future rise in unemployment as the job sector is suffering. This could cause some of the more modest single family homes to go up in price as working people begin to downsize their lifestyle. But, as the modest single family homes rise in value, then downsizing might mean more people will be renting. If other real estate sectors start to drop in value, such as shopping centers, restaurants, and other services that are not essential, this might be a prelude to greater unemployment, and a downturn for expensive single family homes may shortly follow.

2. A sudden rise in real estate in one part of town may suggest that good news is closely held. Not everyone knows what is going on everywhere. This is a simple fact of life. But it's dangerous when you don't know what is happening in your own comfort zone and investment area. Did you miss that planning and zoning meeting when the investor/developer submitted plans for a new entertainment complex? Were you out of town when the city announced that a blighted area of town was going to be torn down and in its place a new office park and affordable housing would be going up? These things tend to happen this way. The real insider does not run around telling everyone, "Did you know about the new cruise port, or exit off the turnpike, or . . . ?" I hope you get the point. Nothing happens in the development arena of real estate without someone knowing about the impending development for a very long time. Many other people may have known about it for almost as long, but few people act on that knowledge. Most never even know about the plan for a project until they return from a vacation and see it already built.

Follow the Rental Market in Your Investment Area

No matter what category of real estate exists in your comfort zone and its adjoining area, you should pay close attention to the rental market for each kind of real estate that exists there. The details of the rental market can give you advance information about the health status of the both the business and residential communities.

When things are going well, commercial activity is brisk. There are very few, if any, "For Rent" signs in good commercial areas, and only poor locations show any sign of vacancies. The few "For Rent" signs that you find will likely be recent vacancies, and the new rents quoted will be higher than they were a year ago when you checked similar types of rental space. A healthy rental market means that shops, offices, and the support facilities for these businesses are all doing well. This means that as new vacancies occur, new rents will be higher than before. When this happens you should take note that it is an advance signal of a strong rental demand (in the categories of real estate that fit this trend) and that there is a greater demand than supply. This information provides you with advance notice of new sectors of your investment area to consider.

If, for example, rents for buildings that can be used for showrooms or distribution facilities are in great demand, the next thing you will see is property with unprofitable buildings on them, but with the proper zoning, converted into showrooms or razed to make room for new showrooms.

When any category of real estate starts to get tight and prices or rents start to go up, ask yourself why. What is occurring that has caused this new demand? Start checking around and find out why.

Who do you ask? Start with some of your newly found real estate insiders within the building and zoning departments in the various cities that might be involved. Someone will have the information that will lead you to the right answer.

Learn the Basics of Income and Expense Statements

Think of this activity as a shortcut lesson on the economics of the area. To get started, pick any for-sale income-producing property. Ask the broker or the owner for an annual income and expense report. This might be called a P&L (profit and loss) report, or just a year-end statement. These statements, if made by an accountant, will all look about the same for the same category of real estate, but when you see something that you have not seen before, ask the owner/broker or the accountant what it is. What might you see? A different format, a type of expense you have not heard of before, a term that you do not understand—anything like that.

The most important key to understanding income and expense data is not to be intimidated by it. All such statements follow the same format which is

Gross Rents–Expenses = Net Operating Income (NOI)

Let's review the relationship of this simple formula to the other elements you will encounter when examining income and expense statements.

Income: The income of any property is the rent and other income paid to the owner in the course of the reporting period (week, month, quarter, year-to-date, or full 12 months). Income may be shown by department if there is more than one source of revenue from the same business operation. A hotel, for example, might list rooms, telephone, safes, food and beverage, game room, tours, and more as separate departments. An apartment complex might also have several departments, such as unit rents, pet supplements, vending machines, covered parking, and so on. These separations give the operator and/or owner additional ways to keep track of the overall revenue by seeing which departments are doing well or poorly.

Operating Expenses: When income is separated by department, it is common to separate operating expenses by department as well. This can be very cumbersome, however, as many businesses or income property operations do not have separate management for each department. So, with the exception of a hotel operation that may have, say, a food and beverage department for which the operational expenses could be separated, most real estate will show all expenses under one section.

Accountants divide expenses into two categories: operating expenses and fixed expenses. When you subtract the operating expenses from income you get the NOI.

Fixed expenses, when properly reported, include income tax paid and debt service paid (principal and interest on property debt). A note of caution: There are some expenses that get reported as fixed expenses when in reality they are not. Two that are most often listed as fixed when they should be in the operational expenses category are land lease payments and outside management expenses. When you see that mistake, make the adjustment by moving those costs into the proper place and deduct them from income.

One item that may show up in the operational expenses is titled "depreciation." This is a paper deduction allowed by the Internal Revenue Service but is not an actual cash payment made by the business. Some investors will remove this number from the expenses because it looks as if it will distort the actual return made from the property. Their argument is, if it was not spent, yet it has been taken as a deduction from income, I should add it back to get my true cash flow after deducting the fixed expenses. This is a good approach, and should be done, but only when the property has been well maintained and there is evidence that capital expenditures have been made during the past few years to keep the property in good operating condition. Depreciation is, after all, a reflection of the deteriorating condition and value of a property. You will have to make a decision on whether or not to add back the amount of the depreciation to reflect a more realistic NOI.

Once you have made those corrections, the resulting NOI will be correct. Failure to make these adjustments will distort the NOI by the amount of those incorrectly listed expenses. The NOI is the most important number when comparing one investment property against another, so it's crucial to have accurate figures.

Net Operating Income (NOI): Once all the expenses have been deducted from all the income, the balance is the net operating income. This is either a positive number or a negative one. Losses are shown with parentheses around them, such as "($50,000)," which, at the NOI line of the report, would suggest that the operation has spent $50,000 more than it took in for that reporting period.

The NOI is the unleveraged return you or any other investor will get if you operate the property exactly as has the current owner. The kind of debt you structure will give you either a positive or negative leveraged situation once you have acquired the property.

Fixed Expenses: Once you see what the NOI is, you will deduct all the fixed expenses that have nothing to do with the income or the operation of the business. These are expenses that are outside of the operation, such as any cost or payment made on a mortgage or other debt. Fixed expenses should be mortgage service and income taxes only, and they should be expenses that are paid during the period.

Sometimes an owner gets behind on payments and will suddenly catch up on a tax payment due or a finance charge or penalty assessed from a previous year. These are non-reoccurring expenses and should be adjusted by removing them from the period in question. Look back on the previous year, and adjust that year's income to reflect the actual expenses that should have been paid that term but were passed on to the current year. Be sure you apply this same cross-check with the operational expenses too. I have seen very large payments made at the end of the taxable year that were advance payments of an expense that was going to occur the following year. That would then distort both the current year's NOI, and next year's, too.

The key is to question any expense you see listed as a fixed expense.

To make sure you are comparing apples to apples, I suggest you first locate "depreciation" and then review the "fixed expenses" shown. If a fixed expense listed should be an operational expense, then move it to its proper place and adjust the numbers accordingly. If the fixed expense is really a debt charge, or an income tax payment, then label them so you will not get confused when making comparisons to income and expense statements of other properties.

Cash at End of Year: Identify the actual cash left over at the end of the year. To do this you must be sure that depreciation has not been taken, or, if it has, add it back into the net operating income. Also adjust for any fixed expenses that are really operational expenses, which would require you to deduct them from the reported NOI to end up with the real NOI.

Repair and Maintenance Expenses: Compare the condition of the property to the amount of repair and maintenance expenses reported. This is where you can get an idea of how well a property has been taken care of. To get a full picture, however, you need to look back on the past several years' reports. There is no standard that says repair and maintenance should be a certain percent of the revenue, because each property is different. But with appropriate maintenance of a property, the cost will not vary much from year to year. When a property is poorly maintained, there can be big jumps in these expenses one year and then only half the amount for another three years. You will start to see a pattern when you make comparisons between properties. If a property looks well cared for, then the repair and maintenance expenses should be within a small percentage each year for the past three years at least.

Seller's Personal Expenses: Beware the seller who says that the expenses listed include a lot of his or her personal expenses. This is likely true, but how much and which expenses are not shown. Some sellers will actually tell you that a lot of their business is cash and they don't always put that down. This is often a seller's excuse when the income shown in the year-end report doesn't support the asking price.

Management Expense: Income and expense reports that show very little in the way of management expense should be questioned. Again, this is often a seller's way to hide just how bad the business is doing. All real estate requires management, and if the seller is managing the property or if you plan to manage it when you own it, calculate what you should pay yourself for that job. You can discount it a bit, because after all, being your own boss is worth something, too. But don't simply overlook it. You will wish you had been more cautious later on.

Study What You Are Weak At

It is a wise person who knows what knowledge he or she lacks. Remember when I said there are always a few people who know what is coming (as in the future planning of a city), but few of them ever take action to their advantage. So it can be with areas of real estate that you may find complicated. If the whole idea of understanding income and expense statements blows your mind, then consider taking an adult course in Accounting 101. I promise you will find such a course (although it might have a different name) in your local adult education courses, or a local community college. Often you can audit or take a course at a university or college without having to be accepted as a full-time student. Get the best education you can, within your timetable and at a price you can afford.

A graduate from Yale will be no better at real estate than you. You are the local expert on what is going on in your area, and the Yale graduate is a graduate of theory. Theory is old-time thinking. It is the mathematician's or the scientist's approach to any problem, and for them it works. Speaking of real estate theory reminds me of a friend who used to lecture about real estate investing. He and I appeared in the same investment programs once or twice, and I found his approach to real estate investing absolutely fantastic, in theory. It was simply this: Buy cheap, sell expensive. Of course this makes things sound simple, and in reality that is the fundamental element of success. But *how* do you buy cheap and sell expensive? By knowing your comfort zone and your investment area like the back of your hand.

CHAPTER 9

How to Build Effective Contacts

The goals of this chapter are:

To Understand How Interim Goals Work

To Fine-Tune Your Positive Attitude

To Sharpen Your People Skills

To Shorten Your Path to Becoming a Real Estate Insider

This is a great chapter to read no matter what you do with this book. Because these goals apply to any endeavor in life, let's begin by taking a closer look at each of them.

Interim Goals

You have seen interim goals at work in earlier chapters. Your long-range goal might be "I want to retire by the age of 58 and be independently wealthy," or "When my wife and I reach 65 we want to be financially independent, move to California, and live in Napa Valley," or some other worthy goal. If you have chosen real estate as one of the steps that will take you toward that goal, then one of your long-range *interim* goals would also be something like, "I will design a plan of action that will make me an expert in commercial real estate investment in my comfort zone within 18 months.

Remember, everything in this book is goal oriented, so each individual goal has stages that guide you toward the completion of that stage and the attainment of that goal. The successful attainment of a goal, in turn, moves you toward other, longer-range goals. One goal is just a stepping stone to another. These are your interim goals.

Interim goals come in many different forms. There is the long-range interim goal, which, at the time you make it, might appear to be your final goal. All long-range goals are really just long-range interim goals. The reason is that prior to your reaching that goal, you will already be reaching beyond that goal. As you get close to any goal you should have added another step in your life.

Take the one of the goals stated above as an example: "When my wife and I reach 65 we want to be financially independent, move to California, and live in Napa Valley." By the time you have sold your home in Chicago and purchased a nice place in Napa, your new goal might be "We want to be successful with a new vineyard on the 120 acres we own in Napa." One long-range interim goal gets replaced with another as you go along.

The shorter interim goals can take care of all the steps that take you to the end product. In this example, you would have goals designed to direct you to all that you need to know to be successful with a new vineyard. These short goals actually can be as short as "I will be accepted in a wine making course at the University of California," or whatever short-term step you need to take. That goal, by the way, would likely have several interim goals that would insure your success in being accepted.

To help you get started in this process, there are two steps you can take that will help you reach any goal you make. First, agree with the premise that a particular interim goal is one that, if obtained, will help you to attain the higher goal (which, in this chapter, is to build effective contacts). If, for example, the interim goal of fine-tuning your positive attitude will not help you build effective contacts (or if you believe it will not), then it will be impossible for you to fully attain the higher goal. Second, once you accept that the interim goal is something that should at least help you in that direction, then you must also accept that there are things that can be done to actually reach the higher and longer-term goal. As you discover things you need to fine-tune, then those items will, in turn, become subjects of new interim goals.

Your success in attaining your interim goals will reinforce your confidence in the goal system. "I will send out 10 thank you cards by this Friday" is a goal you know you can achieve. When you have finished that 10th card, you will move to another interim goal: "By Friday of next week I will have called five of the people on my list as a follow-up." Again, an achievable goal. "I will attend the P & Z meeting this coming Wednesday" is not only achievable, it will be highly rewarding.

Fine-Tune Your Positive Attitude

This goal incorporates several elements, each of which will require you to establish interim goals. They need to be *your* individual interim goals, of course, as everyone will have certain positive points that may not need fine-tuning, while others need to work on the whole gamut.

The first element is to recognize that your attitude can use some fine-tuning. It is possible, isn't it, that no matter how positive your attitude is (in your opinion), it would not hurt to fine-tune it a bit. For most people, that fine-tuning can turn out to be a major rebuilding job, so don't give up hope or get bored trying. The reality is that maintaining a positive attitude about anything takes work. It is very easy to have a down time when you are disappointed or even disgusted with a certain turn of events in your life. This can cause you to temporarily suspend whatever positive outlook you had. Jump right back into reality as quickly as you can, and use the interim goal process to retune your positive approach. This chapter takes you through steps that you need to accomplish to fine-tune your positive attitude, sharpen your people skills, and shorten the path to your becoming a real estate insider.

Sharpen Your People Skills

The other day I was watching *Good Morning America* on TV, and there was a program segment on the subject of meeting people. It was designed for single men and women, and it was all about saying and doing the right thing when you are attempting to meet someone at a social event, in a bar, at a professional meeting, or just out on the sidewalk. As the program progressed, I could not help thinking how desperately the producer of the program and the originator of the techniques shown need to read this chapter. The goal, as best I could ascertain according to the hype of the program, was: "How to meet your soul mate." Sorry, ABC, but there were no interim goals present. Just as in becoming a fighter pilot there are interim goals needed, such as, "I will get accepted into the United States Air Force flight school," so when meeting people, you do not blunder into a meeting of Young Republicans, pick out a potential soul mate from the crowd, and say, "Hi, I'm here to meet you—you might just be my new soul mate." Talk about pressure on both sides of that conversation! Instead, the first goal you need to set, for any kind of person-to-person encounter, is to say something that gets the other person to respond positively in a way that will prolong the conversation—not, "Get lost, buster, I've already got a soul mate."

What you say and how you say it are part of the people skills that are covered in this chapter. The interim goals that target the task of fine-tuning your positive attitude, sharpening your people skills, and shortening your path to become a real estate insider or anything else, are worthy of your time and effort to attain. Once you agree with and accept that fact, then you will quickly see how these three goals are tied together. As each is obtained, you get closer to becoming highly successful in commercial real estate, and in life in general.

Shorten Your Path to Becoming a Real Estate Insider

As the theme of this book is real estate, the final path of effective contacts is also oriented to real estate. If you were to write a chapter about building more effective contacts in another field, the tools you would use might differ from those in this chapter, but the results would be the same. Remember, when you establish any goal that requires something else to happen, you will be more effective at that task when you are working with interim goals. The path to becoming an airplane pilot does not start with sitting in the airplane—it begins much earlier. For me, one of the first interim goals on my way to becoming a pilot was the interim goal to overcome motion sickness. The next one was to be accepted into Air Force flight training, and so on, until I had attained each goal.

The goal of becoming a real estate insider is filled with many interim goals, all of which are sprinkled about in this book. But keep in mind that there will be specific interim goals that are personally yours. They can only be set by you, and it will be up to you to make sure that they are oriented in a way that will carry you through to the time when your goals are updated and raised to a higher rung.

Key Words and Concepts to Build Your Insider Knowledge

Recognizing Positive People
Negative Washing
Fluid Interim Goals
Building Self-Confidence
Effective Listening
Cutting out the Blah Blah Blah

Recognizing Positive People

The nicest part of being a positive person is that people will quickly label you as one. To stress this point, lets look at some of the characteristics of positive people. They smile a lot, always have something nice to say (often about you and how you have been), ask questions and then listen to what you have to say, rarely complain, never gossip, appear in control, are well organized, are both good leaders and excellent team players, can make you laugh, and seem to know when not to say anything. Now, how many people do you know who fit that bill? If you can't think of anyone, you need to pay close attention to this chapter.

Negative Washing

This is simple to understand but often very hard, at least in the beginning, to accomplish. The concept is that one of the best ways to build your positive attitude is to get rid of everything negative around you. To do this you must separate yourself from all the negative people around you. Why? Becoming a positive person is like trying to give up smoking while still hanging out with all your buddies who smoke. Hanging around a group of negative people will not only make it difficult for you to get rid of your negative habits and thoughts, but it will make your life miserable. You don't believe this? Well, try to stop smoking while hanging out with people who do smoke. They will do everything possible to keep you from reaching your goal, even if they don't consciously recognize what they are doing.

The best assistance is to find out where the positive people hang out and to begin to associate with them. Later in this chapter I offer some tips on how to find positive people.

Fluid Interim Goals

By this point, you should be getting the idea about goal making and the achievement of the goals you set. You establish a long-term goal, and then build the interim goals that will take you to that goal. Some of these interim goals are easy to establish and, like all worthy goals, they should be measurable and have a timetable.

Other interim goals are not predetermined but added as you are on the go. These are what I call *fluid goals*.

A fluid goal is one that will be easy to obtain, but only if you do something. A good example of this would be the goal to create a situation where a new contact you have just made will commit to continuing the relationship. One way to do that is to make a statement about a future recontact with that person and get a positive reply. By *recontact* I mean anything from a phone call to a meeting for dinner. Anything that reestablishes a connection between you meets the intent of the goal.

Often this will occur on the fly. For example, you have just introduced yourself to the mayor of the city. Your original goal was simply to make that introduction and then follow up with your usual procedure of sending him a card a few days later, thanking him for the opportunity to meet him. In that card you might also say you are looking forward to seeing him at the next city council meeting. However, in the initial conversation, the mayor asks your opinion on something. It might be something that was discussed in the current city council meeting, or something that was brought up by another person who is a part of the present conversation. This is your chance to throw in one of your fluid interim goals: "Get him or her to give you a positive reply to a recontact." You begin with, "Mr. Mayor, I agree with your method of handling that subject, and I've recently read an article that supports you completely, but at the same time it points out some rather unique, contrary points of view. I'll make a copy of it and if you don't mind, I'll drop it off to you tomorrow." If the mayor was listening, you will get a positive reply. Of course, if you don't have such an article, try this tactic: "I would very much like to discuss this matter with you. Whom should I call to set up an appointment with you?"

Building Self-Confidence

One of the side benefits of developing your positive attitude will be that every time you achieve a goal, no matter what stage it is, long-term or interim, you are adding another brick to your wall of self-confidence. Self-confidence is a fuel that makes everything seem easier. And best of all, the more self-confidence you get, the better and more efficient you become at everything you do.

Effective Listening

I have a friend who never seems to listen to anything other people say. Yet, when you talk with him, he *appears* absolutely glued to every word you say. This reminds me of an after-dinner speech I was asked to give to a local Lions club. I had been asked to give them an update on the status of the real estate market and local trends. The location of the dinner meeting was a restaurant/bar that was part of a bowling establishment, and the noise was horrific. Most of the people at the table had already had a couple of cocktails and were not the most attentive of audiences. Nonetheless, I found solid eye contact with one man seated at the opposite end of the long table from where I stood. So I launched into my 15-minute speech with my usual positive attitude because I could see one person who was absolutely engrossed with my every word. Every few sentences that I uttered caused him to take feverish notes.

At the end of the speech there was polite applause, and this one person, who had been my contact for the night, came rushing up to where I stood, his notes clutched in his left hand. I was sure he wanted to shake my hand and congratulate me on how the information I had provided that night was going to make him a millionaire. Instead, he addressed the person next to me, who was the president of that chapter of the Lions organization, and, handing him the stack of notes, said, "Here's the minutes of last week's meeting—sorry to be so late."

The goal here is not to be a pretend listener but to really listen to what is being said and to comprehend it. This is especially important when the conversation is with a new contact. Far too many people are not listening at all, but simply waiting until it is their turn to talk.

Cutting out the Blah Blah Blah

One of the best ways to make sure that people are listening to what you have to say is to keep the conversation interesting and to the point. There are some simple tricks to this, and here are several of the best I know. When the other person has just told you a story that sounds like pure fiction, instead of saying, "That's a lot of b___s___," say, "That's fantastic." And never, but never, follow up with a story of your own that tops the one you just heard (this is a very hard habit for most people to break). Ask the other party to your conversation something that will get them to speak about their connection to the topic at hand. For example, if they are the owners of a property you want to buy, ask them how they became the owners. Did they build on the property? How long have they owned it? Try to find something that connects them and you together, and always avoid the no-no topics—religion, politics, health, and personal relationships.

One of the great ways to fine-tune your public speaking ability, as well as improve personal conversations, is to join a local Toastmasters International club. This is not a wine drinkers' opportunity to give a toast. It is a great organization that helps people become good speakers. Some members even become great public speakers, but all members of this group learn how to organize their thoughts into good communication. Almost every community in America has one or more Toastmasters clubs. They are small groups; some of the clubs meet early in the morning, others at lunch, and some at dinner times. My suggestion is to join one that meets in the morning. Why? The morning clubs (of any nature) seem to have a high percentage of positive people as their members. Perhaps it is because the morning groups are made up of people who understand the benefit of starting their day on a positive note.

Too much blah blah blah is sometimes an affliction of someone who does not respect or understand the power of silence. Salesmen and women can fall into this trap, as if five seconds of silence is more than they can bear. If you stop talking and the other person or persons do not jump in to fill the silent gap, do not try to fill it yourself. They could be thinking, which might just be a compliment as to how salient your last point truly was.

Ten Ways to Effectively Build a
Contact into a Profitable Relationship

1. Look and act successful.

2. Join quality-building organizations.

3. Become visible at public and important occasions.

4. Speak highly of people you know.

5. Be a positive person.

6. Never make an enemy.

7. Be polite and respectful.

8. Keep in touch.

9. Be a thanking person.

10. Ask for references.

Look and Act Successful

I don't know any motivational speaker or author who does not also stress this point. Looking and acting successful is essential if you are in the process of building relationships and do not want to lose those that you have already cultivated. I am talking about the impression you give when someone meets you for the first time. You never know if the first time will be the only time you have to make a connection. Therefore, you will want to use every positive factor you can muster up.

A real estate associate who once worked for me became engaged to a local accountant I had not yet met. When I eventually met him, I was appalled at how ultra-casually he was dressed. I remarked to my associate that it was strange that she, who was the absolute opposite and always looked as if she had stepped out of *Gentlewoman's Quarterly* (if such a magazine ever existed), would be drawn to such a person. Her remark was in defense of her soon-to-be-husband: "Would you rather have a bad accountant who dressed well or a great accountant who dressed poorly?"

As it turned out, he was as sloppy a CPA as he was at picking out clothes, just as I had guessed he would be.

You should make every effort to look and act successful. When do you do this? Whenever you are in a setting that will expose you to other real estate insiders, potential buyers and/or sellers, as well as any current or potential business or social contacts. During these times you need to take extra care to leave the best impression you can on all those whom you meet, or who have met you on another occasion. It is equally important to think of those whom you have yet to meet, especially people who may see you a dozen times before they approach you to make your acquaintance. (You are becoming a true insider when this happens.)

There is a great book you should read. It is titled *How to Win Friends and Influence People*, and it was written by Dale Carnegie. You can log on to a Dale Carnegie web page at www.winnerstrategies.com, or you can find this book in any library in the United States, and most book stores will have a newly printed edition. Get a copy and read it.

Join Quality-Building Organizations

I have mentioned one already, Toastmasters International, but there are many. Here you can introduce those four no-no topics of religion, politics, health, and personal relationships, and join organizations that are oriented in those areas. Become a volunteer at your church; take a Sunday School class (the best place to meet a future spouse, I have always told my women employees, and some have actually followed up on that suggestion with great success); be active in local politics; become involved with the local hospital groups and cultural organizations in the area. Look for and join social groups that are made up of people your age and who have interests similar to yours. All these organizations will help you build social contacts and business relationships as well.

In the "social groups" category, I do not mean to become a regular at the neighborhood bar, but get active in a team sport or a ski group that travels together, or a weekend hiking group, or take cooking classes or other adult courses from the community educational programs. You will meet other people who have similar likes, and lasting friendships and good social skills can be formed. These locations are sources for meeting people overflowing with positive attitude.

One excuse I hear when I talk about joining such groups is "I don't even have enough time to do all the things I already have to do." This is interesting to me, because I used to think the same way. But a good friend got me tuned in to the attitude that to get anything out of a community, you have to participate in what it has to offer and give part of yourself back to that community. At one time in my early professional life, I was president of a local Toastmasters club, chairman of the commercial division at the board of realtors, a member of the board of directors of a local college, and a member of the board of directors of the South Florida Symphony all at the same time. All this was in addition to looking after my real estate firm of 45 salesmen and women. Not only did I never feel overwhelmed with the activities, I prospered by making more contacts in a much shorter period of time than I would have ever believed possible.

One thing is as certain as anything you will read in this book: If you want to get involved, no matter what group you join, if you become a worker and not an observer, you will quickly be the center of attention. Want to become the president of that organization? Then become a worker, then the head of a committee, then head recruiter, and then—well, they will beg you to be president. Try it, and it will work wonders for your social and community esteem, to say nothing about the grand boost it will give your self-confidence, and that special look you will get from your family and friends.

Become Visible at Public and Important Occasions

There is a fine line that you must be careful not to cross when you make an overt act to be seen. The best way for me to express this is to describe those who do cross the line. You know the people who are the last to arrive at an event, such as a performance, lecture, or similar gathering, and make their way to the front of the room where they have reserved center row seats. They make sure everyone in the auditorium or theater has seen them. Then there are the people, likely the same ones, who are the first to raise their hands to ask questions following a thought-provoking lecture—only they are not really questions at all, but statements to attempt to show how smart they are and how uninformed the lecturer really is. How about the person who overdresses for the event, or comes to a city council meeting dressed in very nice golf apparel, or looks like he's on his way to a polo match, as a player, to boot. This list can go on and on, but I am sure you have an idea what I mean.

The key to being visible is to make an effort to meet people by introducing yourself to them. Be a proactive person in this way. Have your business cards ready, but don't be too quick to spring the card on someone. It is okay to hand your card to someone at a business meeting almost at the very instant of the introduction. However, in a social meeting, you will hold back and not rush to pass around business cards. Let the conversation and your charming self do most of the work. If you are nearing the end of the conversation and there has been a hint of business because either they or you mentioned it, then ask the other person for their card. He or she will follow and ask for yours, or you can simply offer it at that point.

Speak Highly of People You Know

This is one of the most powerful things you can do to solidify a relationship. Look at the following example. One evening my family and I were having dinner at a local restaurant and I noticed someone I had not seen for some years, seated nearby with his wife and daughter. I excused myself and went over to say hello. It turned out that it was his birthday, and his wife and daughter had taken him out for the evening. I spent a few minutes with them and recounted how I had first met him, and how pleasant it had always been to do business with him. I told his daughter how highly respected her father was in the real estate profession and that I had learned a lot from him. As I spoke, everything I said was genuine admiration of him. I was glad I had the opportunity to tell him how I felt, and to be able to do so in a most appropriate situation. By the time I left their table, the attitude of the wife and daughter had become very upbeat, so much so that I believe there were some real tears of pride in their eyes.

A few days later I had a phone call from someone I had never met, but knew of by his reputation. He asked if I would stop by his office to discuss my handling the negotiations for a property he was interested in buying. A day or so later we met, and that relationship lasted for many years until he passed away. Early in our business relationship I discovered why he had called me in the first place. As it turned out, his brother-in-law was the man I had seen in the restaurant. What I never asked was if it had been because of the brother-in-law or his sister or niece that he had decided to call me.

When I am asked if I know so-and-so, I try to say something nice about that person, if I know them personally, or at least say something nice if I only know of them. But you will find that, as with the example shown above, the most mileage you will get out of this tip is to say something nice about a person in their presence or when you know your comments will get back to them. Oh, you never know when that is going to happen, do you?

It doesn't matter if you are in competition with the person, or are absolutely in opposition to their position. If you know the person at all, there should be something nice you can say. If not, then certainly don't say anything bad. You never know who you are talking to—the person you are having a conversation with might be a relative.

A word of warning: If you think that a compliment you give can get back to the person you complimented, think how lightning-fast a negative comment will make that same journey.

Be a Positive Person

I have already spoken of the importance of having a positive attitude about everything. This is the first step in becoming a positive person. But there is more to the overall makeup than just having a positive attitude. I know people who are absolutely positive they are going to die tomorrow, or salesmen who are sure they are going to fail to get a contract accepted, or team players who know for certain that they will lose the race. The key is to be positive in a nonnegative way. The whole goal thing works for you in this process. Build one positive event on another. "I will get the appointment, I will make a good impression, I will establish a good relationship, I will be successful." One step after the positive other.

I know that eight times out of ten I will find a parking place right up front where I want to go. Does my being positive about this open up a spot for me? Yes, I am sure of it.

Never Make an Enemy

It is hard enough to keep a friend, so why go out of your way to make an enemy? It is easy to do, too, and often comes from some of the smallest things you do. Here is a list of some of those ways you can make an enemy: Start an argument, be uncomplimentary about someone or something, be impolite, be inconsiderate, be disrespectful, be a showoff, be LOUD, always be right, never acknowledge you are wrong, be late at everything, don't do what you said you would when you said you would do it. Are there things you can do to avoid developing any of these habits? You bet! Read the following section, "Be Polite and Respectful."

People who do one of the above things generally do more than one. Little by little this will cause other people to form an opinion as to what kind of person this man or woman really is. This then becomes their reputation.

When your reputation precedes you, it can become exaggerated until you are seen as a monster. Usually this is the result of a rumor, and it's usually spread by people who hardly know you. These may be people who love to gossip and don't care to check the validity of rumors before they pass them on to others, or it can be a negative friend, someone who is envious of your good fortune and would like to see you fall flat on your face for a change. The "negative washing" mentioned earlier will help stop this potential situation from happening.

You can repair a faulty reputation, but it takes patience and a lot of effort spent doing the right things. This chapter is filled with the right things you need to be doing. Walking away from a situation that is headed for an argument or worse is always the best tactic to take. A phone call to the person later, after tempers have settled down, to smooth over the problem might nip the build-an-enemy-today routine in the bud.

Now, having said all this, there are times when you encounter a person or two who immediately rub you the wrong way. These people, for whatever reason, should be crossed off your social list and avoided when you accidentally both show up at the same wedding or other social event. However, be polite about it.

Be Polite and Respectful

This single tip will keep you on the straight and narrow path to setting a good example and to cementing good friendships and solid acquaintances. This book is not meant to be a book of good etiquette, nor to set the standards for how to act on every occasion. But I have noticed things that some people do that set them above people who do not do those things. Here is my list of how to win friends and influence people by being polite and respectful.

Respect People's Time: This covers a multitude of sins that people commit. Let's start with appointments. If you make an appointment, then show up a few minutes early. If you know you are running late, then let the other party know of this as much in advance as possible, and give them the option of rescheduling or allowing you to be late. This is especially important if the location of the appointment is your own office. If you are late, then accept the consequences that you have upset their schedule and do every-thing possible to reschedule at *their* most convenient time. By the way, when you are on the other side of this event and are inconvenienced by someone who had to cancel an appointment, think positively. I find this can be a great opportunity for you. That person now owes you something. Just be careful not to let on that you know they do.

Be Attentive: This means showing the person you are talking to, or meeting with, that you are interested in what they have to say. Don't be looking around the room, or ac-cepting phone calls, or otherwise demonstrating that they are secondary, for that mo-ment in time.

I always reflect on this from an early experience I had as a fledgling realtor in Fort Lauderdale. One of my early clients was Ken Behring, a person who had retired to Florida as a young man and who built a fortune building retirement home communities. He sold out, lock, stock, and barrel, and moved to California, where he did even bigger things and made even more money.

As busy a person as he was, Ken was also the most attentive person I have ever known. He would meet me at the exact time of the appointment, and, if at his office, he would be seated across from me at a clean desk, on which was nothing but a yellow pad and a pen, which he used to make notes as we talked. Ken would listen to my presentations, ask ar-ticulate questions about important aspects of the topic, and pause to think about the situ-ation. After a moment or two he would render either his decision or opinion, or set another appointment, at which time the decision would be given. Not all his decisions were beneficial to me, but getting a no that was respectfully given after attentive consid-eration was an easy pill to take. Besides, there were sufficient yesses along the way.

He did not waste his time, nor mine. I have always tried to follow that example, and you should too.

Remember People's Names: I have a hard time with this, so I work hard at it. If the per-son gives me a card and it has their photograph on it, that helps me remember the name, together with the face. If there is no photograph, I write down the date and circumstance where we met, and if there is something particular about the person that will help me remember them, I make note of that too. One of the best ways, according to most memory books I have read, and it does help me, is to use the name as quickly as you can in the conversation. One way to do this is to introduce the new acquaintance to someone else who joins you. But be sure you have gotten the name right from the get-go.

I have watched people in such gatherings where business cards are exchanged and immediately pocketed. Neither person has looked at the other's card, so there is no visual association to the written name. Instead of putting the card away, study it for a moment. Does it say, "Johnathon Smyth, President, American Nuclear Warfare"? If so, then this can prompt several dozen questions you can ask that will get Mr. Smyth to begin talking. Like, "Mr. Smyth, do you make atomic bombs?"

Does your card say, "Bill H. McDonnell, Investor in Special Projects"? Something like this will make the recipient of this card think of something to ask of you.

Use Formal Conversation Until Told Not To: Use the titles Mr. Smyth, Mr. McDonnell, Mrs. Smyth, and so on. Even if Mr. Smyth says "Call me Johnny," don't do it until you are told to do so more than once. Never call Mrs. Smyth by her first name until she starts calling you by your first name, and even then, not during the first meeting.

Stand When Someone You Know Approaches a Table Where You Are Seated: This should be a natural event for men, and especially so if the person approaching is a woman. Introduce those at the table to your friend or acquaintance who has approached. Women can stay seated, but if the person approaching is a good friend or business associate, they may want to stand to greet them warmly, and then introduce them to the table companions. This is a good opportunity for the person now standing to say something nice about each person at the table.

Learn Good Table Manners: A quick read through a good etiquette book will help you brush up on things that you might need to remember. In absence of reading such a book, take a look at several no-nos. At a sit-down meal, don't eat anything with your fingers except bread, raw carrots, or celery sticks, no matter whether it is accepted to eat fried chicken and lamb chops with one's fingers. If you don't know which fork, spoon, glass of water, or bread dish to use, use the same as the host or your guest. Don't eat with your mouth open, avoid talking with food in your mouth, and never pick the most expensive item on the menu, or a difficult to eat food.

Avoid Having Your Photograph Taken While You Are Holding a Beverage (of any kind) in Your Hand: I know, there are lots of important people who have their photos taken this way, so let them be the ones who are remembered as heavy drinkers. Avoid it when you can.

When Someone Offers You a Breath Mint or Stick of Gum, Take It: You never know if they are just being polite or trying to give you a message that the shrimp scampi or liverwurst you had for lunch has made a reappearance.

Keep in Touch

This is a simple thing to do, yet you would be surprised at how few people do it effectively. There are four key characteristics of effectively keeping in touch: short and sweet, personal, complimentary, and an occasional surprise. Let's look at each of these.

Short and Sweet: Communications between people need not be long and complicated. In building effective contacts, it is important that you not overstay your welcome by sending reams of material. The first note or follow-up to a meeting would be a thank you card.

> Dear Mayor,
>
> It was a pleasure to meet you at the commission meeting last week. Your thoughts on the new sewer system proposal by city staff were refreshing, to say the least. I look forward to seeing you again soon.
>
> Sincerely,
>
> Jack Cummings.

Something like that is a good start. A second follow-up might say, "Dear Mayor, I have enclosed a clipping from *Time* which shows how one city in Texas deals with sewer smell. This shows you were right on target. Sincerely, Jack Cummings."

E-mail is the modern way to stay in touch with people, and it is a good way of establishing nearly instant communications. Many people live by their computers and cell phones that also support e-mail messages, and I recommend the use of e-mail. However, just as the telex butchered the written language, e-mail is threatening to do even worse. When telex machines were first put into use, everyone became aware that the cost to send messages was measured in how many letters and/or words made up the message. Short, cryptic, and sometimes misleading messages could be created simply by the misplacement of a comma or a period.

E-mail doesn't cost much, if anything at all, except the time to write and read it. It is a great opportunity for people to write letters that conform to standards of general letter writing, but instead most people send messages that lack any formal appearance. Often there is little or no punctuation, and rules of capitalization are thrown out the window. Instead of articulate sentences, text is choppy, words are shortened, and sometimes characters are combined to create sad or happy faces. This may be cute, but it is not, in my opinion, good communication. So when sending e-mail to any social or business contact, adopt the simple habit of thinking of the e-mail as a letter, and follow the rules of good letter composition. You might be the only one doing it— now isn't that worth remembering?

Your goal in any communication is twofold: You want to make a good impression and a meaningful contact. To do that, it is important for the person you communicate with to remember you and to ultimately become one of your inner circle of contacts. In essence, everything you do is designed to reinforce who you are.

Personal: By *personal*, I do not mean you will delve into private personal matters of yours or of theirs. Those are communications between lifelong friends, if even then. I am talking about business and social contacts here, and you do not want to get personal except in wedding announcements and bereavement notes.

But personalize your written communication. Do not send a printed copy of a letter to 50 people, describing what you did for the past 12 months, and consider that as a way to cement a business relationship. There is a place for those kinds of annual messages of "What the Cummings Family Did in 2004." My suggestion is that you follow my example in that respect and write it as a part of family history, but never send it to anyone.

By personal, I mean you are sending them something unique. No one else is getting the same text. Even if it is a printed card, or a cutout from the newspaper, you can attach a yellow sticky note with a handwritten message saying something like, "Dear Senator Graham, I thought you would get a kick out of this political cartoon. Keep up the good work. Sincerely yours, Jack Cummings."

Complimentary: You do not have to compliment the person you are writing to, but make sure that something about the communication provides a compliment somewhere in the message. It might be that clipping from *Time* that indirectly praised an idea the mayor had by pointing out how Texas used the same concept to deal with sewer odors, or it might be a direct "keep up the good work" message from you. Often a good way to include a compliment is to point out how proud we should all be that our police officers have been awarded a national recognition as the best in the state. Don't forget to enclose a clipping or newspaper photo of a local police officer being so honored. If you spend a few seconds on this point, you will be able to make this both personal and complimentary at the same time.

An Occasional Surprise: This is another twofold issue. You never want your communications to fall into the trap of being expected. It is a good idea to have frequent communication with your business and social contacts, but it can and should be a mix of written and verbal communication. The one item that should be as regular as clockwork is the thank you for any recommendation or referral that you are given. Always follow up a referral with a note on the outcome. Try something like the following:

> Dear Bob,
>
> I can't thank you enough for your suggestion that I meet with Harry Berger. Not only did he give me an excellent tip on how to finance the shopping center I told you about, he sent me data on a center that he wants to sell. It looks great, too.
>
> Sincerely yours,
>
> Jack Cummings.

Put some spice into your communications by sending an occasional surprise note or card. A birthday might be appropriate but sometimes difficult to find out. However, if you know that the person graduated from Yale and is an avid football fan, and Yale wins big over Harvard this year, then a congratulation card with a clipping from the sports page showing the score might just be remembered forever. These notes, when they strike the right cord, will set you apart from all the rest.

It is very important that in any short note you use a card designed for the note, and that you handwrite the note. Never type a personal note unless your handwriting resembles chicken scratching or is next to impossible to read. If your handwriting is of that caliber, then try slowing down, using a block print instead of script, or buy a penmanship course and practice at improving your handwriting. It won't do you any good to use the excuse that John F. Kennedy or some other famous person had impossible-to-read penmanship. Take my word for it. Those excuses haven't helped me at all.

Be a Thanking Person

How do you feel when someone thanks you for something you did? You feel good about it, don't you? But equally important is, how do you feel about the person thanking you? You feel good about them, too. This is a basic element of being polite, but it is often overlooked. I make a point of thanking people for their time, for giving me an appointment, for sending me data, for leads, and just about any other excuse I can think of to maintain contact with them. One very important thing to thank someone for is when you hear from someone else that that person has said something nice or complimentary about you. Be sure to be thankful to your friends and let them know how grateful you are for their friendship.

Ask for References

It is good business practice to ask for a reference from someone with whom you have done business for a considerable period of time. The following are three tips to getting great letters of recommendation and using your references to get maximum benefit from them.

1. Prepare a professional autobiography. A factual background history of yourself, your business, and your accomplishments is a helpful document for many reasons. One such reason is if you are feeling down in the dumps, you can get it out and read it. If you wrote a good one in the first place, it will pick you up later on.

   The main purpose of this bio is that, when you ask for a reference, you can include it along with your request. A good biography will include dates of events, number of years you were head of this, chairman of that, president of some organization, director for an event, and so on. All of this factual data can aid someone who is going to write a letter of recommendation, so they can not only be accurate but also overlook nothing that might be important. Do not be modest in this biography, but be honest and 100 percent in the positive mode. If there is something negative in your background omit it, and never try to explain it away.

2. Ask the person from whom you are requesting the letter of recommendation if they would mind if you give their name as a reference. The best way to do this is to write them a letter and enclose your bio. Acknowledge that you know they are busy, and

that it would be a special favor to you if they would take the time to write a short letter of recommendation for you. Be sure to include all the other items these tips include. Still, do not be surprised if some of your friends hedge on doing this, and don't take it personally if you get turned down. But if they do this for you, be sure to thank them immediately, and let them know later if you were successful in achieving the goal for which the letter was intended. Do not tell them if you fail in the attempt.

3. Give the reason for the requested letter of recommendation. Each letter of recommendation should be directed to a specific situation. If you are applying for a loan, acceptance to graduate school, membership in a professional society, or whatever, then explain the situation to the people from whom you seek a letter of recommendation. If it is to be directed to a specific person, explain who that person is, and what their role is in the review of the requested letter of recommendation.

CHAPTER 10

The Three Most Important Words: Use, Location, and Approval

The goals of this chapter are:

To Remove the Misconception about "Location, Location, Location"

To Open Your Eyes to the Bigger Picture

For aeons the misdirected cliché about real estate has been that the three most important words are "location, location, location." This misconception about real estate is the root of most investors' problems. But once you grasp the truth of the matter, you will see why some people fail to achieve their desired goals in real estate investing, while others excel at it.

Let's look at this from a fresh point of view. There is no doubt that being in the right place at the right time plays an important role in any kind of investing. The first prospectors to reach the Yukon found and staked out the best locations for their gold mining claims, and those who showed up a year later were lucky to survive the first winter. Still, many millions of dollars were made later, not by prospectors but by people who made big profits serving the needs of those who came to find their fortunes. Still the right place, but a different time.

Those soon-to-become millionaires benefited from the fast pace of events that were taking place. These events caused new laws to be put into effect that imposed controls where none had existed before. For example, the Canadian government established strict criteria for any new prospector seeking permission to enter the Yukon area from the Alaskan ports of Sitka and Ketchikan, which were the major jumping-off points for the influx of prospectors. Those restrictions required each prospector to have a tremendous stockpile of food and other supplies—enough, in fact, to last a full year. This meant a heavy outlay of cash prior to leaving the port for British Columbia, where the gold fields were located. Why did the Canadian government impose these restrictions? Because it became evident after the first six months of the gold find that most of the new prospectors would not be successful, and it was not uncommon for those who ran out of supplies to steal and murder to get more.

These new restrictions brought about great opportunities for a new, nonprospecting breed of enterprising men and women. These were the shop keepers, mule team drivers, bartenders, and other tradespeople who kept things working. The flow of prospectors entering the area became their source of gold. Again it was the right place and, for the new ventures, also the right time, but with a twist thrown in, as they had to learn to adapt to the new rules that were evolving.

Most communities in the United States began to evolve their development rules and regulations, which are a mix of zoning ordinances and building codes, as the need arose. The concept of zoning, which would ultimately segment a community into zones where only certain types of development could take place, grew slowly in some areas of the country and faster in others. The concept is sound: Protect the community from certain types of development being next to each other. Clearly, no one wants to build an expensive single family home and have a junkyard go up next door.

As these early mining communities grew, those who arrived early began to adopt new, more restrictive rules. These rules would impose greater costs for development on those who would come later, but they also placed restrictions on land that had already been purchased. Owners who became complacent about these new rules and regulations and failed to comply with the new order of things lost the rights they had to their property.

Opening your eyes to the bigger picture is critical in commercial real estate investing. Your real estate investment will always be tied to its location—there is no doubt about that. Its value will always be affected by this location as well. However, there are other, perhaps more important elements to consider. The trio of *location*, *use*, and *approval* are the three most important words in real estate. Lock these concepts into your mind so that you learn how to use the rules and restrictions to your best advantage.

Remember, however, nothing about real estate terminology is ever etched into stone. What is a restriction today may be history tomorrow, replaced by a new rule or ordinance. In general, the trend is for more restrictive rules and regulations. Because everything from building to setback distances can become more restrictive, it is critical for all property owners to pay attention to what is happening in their city. As with most governmental changes, there is ample advance warning of a pending change, but only if you are observant and watch for those warnings. They occur in newspaper announcements, often in the legal section of the paper. Unfortunately, they are usually impossible to understand. They generally have a heading that will alert you to the area of town, or even which town it is, that a pending change is to be discussed or voted on. Beyond that, the jargon used in the announcement may not be very clear, in which case you should call the city clerk or other person that might be listed in the announcement and ask for a full explanation of the impending change. The process of change continues.

Virtually every community in the United States is undergoing evolution in its use of rules and regulations, and the process by which this use is policed. Very lax zoning and use regulations still exist in some areas of the country. When you find such an area, do not assume you have found a utopia for real estate investors. Shoddy zoning laws, poor building codes, and a lax policy toward them, can create communities where businesses are on top of single family residential areas, and poor construction tends to make for quickly deteriorating neighborhoods.

Key Words and Concepts to Build Your Insider Knowledge

Access
Demographics
Traffic Count
Traffic Flow
School Districts
Plats

Each of these elements has an effect on the location of any property. They are discussed here as to their impact on specific properties where the zoning has already been determined to be adequate for the intended project or for the investor's needs.

Access

Access to any property can be the most critical aspect to maximizing its use. Too often access is taken for granted, when in reality it is not uncommon for two properties across from each other at an intersection to have quite different degrees of accessibility, by both pedestrian and vehicular traffic. Clearly, with all other elements equal, the property with greater ease of access will have a higher value than one with more limited access. Difficult access can render a property valueless to a user dependent on good access for clientele and employees.

Properties that front on more than one roadway do not automatically have the right to access all those roads. This is a critical mistake many investors make when purchasing vacant tracts of land that have considerable frontage on more than one roadway. The authority that governs this access will generally be the city or county department of transportation (DOT). If the road is a state highway or tollway, the local county DOT can direct you to the proper person to deal with. The questions to start with are, "Can I obtain a permit to install a curb cut and drive lane to access the roadway? If so, can I obtain more than one, and where can I install them?

The answers to those questions will give you a good start toward solving the access problem. Keep in mind that a site located at the corner of an intersection may have limitations to where the entrance and exit to and from the roadways can be, and which direction the traffic must turn when exiting back to the roadway. If a deceleration lane and storage lane are needed to stack traffic that would turn off the roadway onto the property, then there must be sufficient space to accomplish this task, and generally the cost of constructing this turn lane would be an added expense to the investor. If there was not sufficient space to accomplish this, then access might be limited to a side road, which may not be satisfactory for the intended project.

There are other limiting factors that can come into play when dealing with vehicular access. High-traffic intersections may have turning restrictions that limit access for traffic traveling in one direction only. For example, a site located at the northeast corner of two main roads might be accessible only by traffic flowing north on one road and traffic flowing west on the cross street. In addition, many cities have alternating one-way streets, which could create a situation where southbound traffic would have to go several blocks out of the way to get in position to approach the site in a northbound or westbound direction.

If the site has existing access, it must be verified as a legal entrance and exit for the future use of the property. It is not uncommon for an existing business to have been established at a time when codes or DOT regulations allowed curb cuts, turn lanes, and entrance and exit driveways that are no longer allowed. The existing ones may be ruled a nonconforming use and allowed because they were at one time legal. However, if that use is discontinued, or the buildings are removed, the authorities may take the position that the new rules and regulations must now be applied to any such entrances and exits. The new rules may prohibit the entrances and exits as they now exist, and construction of new ones may not be feasible for the intended use.

Demographics

Demographic data will tell you the economic and physical makeup of a community: the number of families, a breakdown of earning power and age, areas of concentration, growth trends, and so on. Such information can be important in ascertaining whether a prospective tenant will be successful in a built-to-suit situation where you are the builder or owner of the resulting building. There are companies that provide demographic reports at a modest cost. A report of the basic information for a 10 mile radius should not run more than $250, and if you shop around you may find if for under $175. These reports can be obtained on a fast turnaround, and the companies that provide them update their data frequently.

Demographics play an important role in establishing the value of a location for any specific use. A full-service high-priced restaurant operator may find every factor of a site to be ideal for the intended use, except that the demographics indicate there are very few people in the market area who could afford to eat at such an establishment.

Traffic Count

Traffic counts are made by the local authority that deals with the roads that provide access to any property. These counts are available to the public, often at no charge or at a nominal charge if the report is extensive. To find out where to get these reports for the city or street in question, start with the city or county department of transportation and ask them where you can obtain a recent traffic count. It is a good idea to ask for and then compare older reports for the same area to see the trend. A drop in traffic on a road from one year to the present year may not indicate a decline in population or traffic to the general area, as there may be one or more new roadways now serving the area. However, a decline in traffic with no new roads in the immediate area may indicate that a new, limited-access road is picking up traffic that was previously passing through your area, and is now routed around to form a better flow of traffic from one distant area to another. Many cities situated along future routes for interstate or tollways have encountered this situation. This can cause a decline in the number of clientele using local motels, gas stations, and other services that are located at or near interstate access points. While this is usually a detriment to those kinds of businesses that are bypassed by the traffic they counted on in the past, these situations can create a boon to more local types of business as the traffic within these cities, blessed by the reduction of nonlocal traffic, makes these former businesses ideal candidates for economic conversion to other uses.

Because roadways of any kind have long planning stages, the savvy investor pays close attention to what is in the long-term plans for all the departments of transportation that control the flow of traffic in the area, or in nearby areas that may benefit from a new type of traffic due to new or expanded roadways.

Traffic Flow

Which way and at what times of day the traffic flows the most, or the least, constitutes traffic flow analysis. Any intersection will have a difference in traffic flow counts depending on how the traffic moves. The morning drive to work will establish a pattern that should be counterbalanced by the afternoon and early evening drive from work. A quick study of the roadways that serve an area should give you a good idea of how much of that morning and afternoon flow is local residents. If there are better routes for more distant residents to take to and from work, they may not be a part of the flow in the area you need to study. A strong local traffic flow will suggest that tenants patronized by people close to the business will have more clientele than a business that needs a wider circle of traffic to draw from. Again, if you ascertain that the main road you are checking is scheduled to be expanded to double or triple the traffic load in the next year or two, you need to consider whether that expanded traffic will aid or hinder a project you are planning for the site.

Remember that any change in infrastructure of a community will open opportunities, but may also temporarily reduce the value of the property. Heavy road construction may shut down local traffic to the existing businesses; tenants may move, and owners of vacant centers may not be able to hold out until the new road is open. Banks foreclose—and then resell to you or me, because we were sitting by, waiting for this to happen.

Traffic flow is important to both physical access to a site as well as the visual access of that same location. The combination of ease of access from a road to a site, traffic flow, traffic counts, and demographics help an investor pick between competing sites to ascertain which will best serve that investor's needs. Naturally the overall price will be a determining factor as well. But a lower price will not cause an investor to chose a site that does not have decent access, or one that has a poor demographic clientele base.

School Districts

It is a good idea to get to know the head of the local school board. This is usually a county level position. If your real estate interests are near a county line, it is a good idea to get to know the adjoining school board as well as the one in which your real estate is located. Like roadways, new schools generally take a long time to plan, build, and open. The school boards, however, are very good at obtaining statistics to support the need for new schools or expansion of older ones. All this information will help you ascertain whether there is going to be an influx of school-age children in a community that was previously a retirement area. Information such as this can indicate that economic conversion may be an ideal development plan to take advantage of the multitude of businesses that cater to children, moms, and young working families that may have a greater disposable income than a retired couple. Rental apartments that cater to families may suddenly be the hot item in such an area, as would fast-food restaurants, day care centers, and so on.

Plats

A plat is a document that contains a recorded and approved drawing of a tract of land. It may be an entire subdivision, or a single parcel of land that was broken off from a former subdivision or from a vacant tract that was itself unplatted. The document will contain varying amounts of information, depending on the rules and regulations of the city, county, or state in which the land is located. Almost always the plat will include the following basic information:

- Legal description. This description may be as simple as "the Cummings Plat number 10," or it could be "a re-plat of Coral Ridge Isles Section B." Whatever the legal description, from the point of time that the plat is approved by the local governing body (the county commission and city council, generally), the property will no longer be known by its former legal description. The tax assessor will pick up the new legal description, and any future sale will be made by reference to that new description.

- Property dimensions. In essence each property within the plat will have all its dimensions shown.

- Plat items. This will include roadways, easements for roads and utilities, and other elements that are contained within the plat, such as a pond, canal, and so on.

- Plat notes. These are notations that the approving bodies have added to the plat, and they are one of the most important things to pay attention to. They are generally restrictions that were worked out between the platting authorities and the property owner at the time of submission for approval, and they supersede any normal restrictions that might be imposed by the application of a zoning or building code. These restrictions may establish the maximum square footage of buildings that can be developed, what their precise use would be, and other limitations that could be disastrous to you as a buyer of this property when you have relied solely on the zoning ordinance.

- Date of the plat. This may sound like oversimplification, but the date of the plat is also a critical item. A seller may show you a plat that describes the vacant tract where you would like to build an industrial park. The plat shows no problems for that intended use, and the zoning that the county has approved for the property also supports that kind of development. But wait a moment here. Last year the owner replatted the property to accommodate a tenant who wanted that owner to build an office building for them. The notes on the replat state that the new use is to be office use—which required a variance of use which was granted—and that the site, as now platted, cannot be used for what you would like to build. "But the old plat said . . ." Old plats are like last month's racing results. You can't make today's bets based on them.

It is a good idea to double-check the plat and survey you have been provided by the seller to make sure it is the latest version of such a document. Double-check the plat notes, and confirm that they match the zoning and your desired use. Cover yourself with a provision within your purchase agreement that the review of these documents is part of your due diligence period, and that the seller is to cooperate fully in delivering these documents to you and/or your inspection team. Be sure your lawyer is a member of that team.

Why Zoning Ordinances Are the Key that Opens the Door to Use

There are four factors that need to be considered when it comes to any rule, regulation, or ordinance, or any trend of interpretation of those rules, regulations, or ordinances, that can in any way affect your use of a specific property. These four factors are as follows:

1. Use is a controlled element.
2. Use governs value.
3. Use and real estate laws that govern use can change.
4. Real estate laws are not homogeneous from city to city.

All four of these factors must be reviewed at the start of any real estate investment. If, for example, you are about to purchase a shopping center with the idea of changing its image by adding a food court to bring more clientele, then you must be sure that every possible ordinance, rule, and regulation, and the interpretation thereof, does not stand in your way. Let's look at each of these factors in detail.

Use Is a Controlled Element

From the commercial point of view, if you expect to generate revenue from your ownership of the property, you will want to examine carefully what factors control your use. A specific zoning may be very clear in listing what you can and cannot build or operate at any given location. However, zoning alone is not the deciding factor. Your ability to use the property in a specific way may still be ruled out if such use would violate other rules or regulations. The zoning may allow the use, but these other, sometimes hidden regulations prohibit it.

A simple example of this would be the parking code. You may want to add a restaurant to a shopping center you own, which is located on a property with zoning for that use. However, as the existing tenants' parking needs have already nearly peaked out your parking capacity, the inability to add sufficient parking to meet the code for the restaurant may eliminate that use. Certain cities will have their own peculiar building codes that create such roadblocks, and you need to make sure you get the final okay from all the possible building departments prior to going ahead with the project.

The development review committee (DRC) is often the first step in getting tentative approval for a project. This is the place where the investor or developer presents to the city the idea, together with the full documentation that the city requires for a formal presentation. Each city may vary in the complexity of plans and proposals a developer needs to present, but there is generally a printed checklist you can follow for all such submissions.

Notice I said *tentative* approval. In many cases a DRC approval is like gold in the bank. But if the project must also have a site plan approval, or if a special variance is required prior to a DRC submission, there is always the chance of getting turned down even before you get to first base.

Site plan approval often creates a new set of difficulties. When the city allows a project to go through the site plan process, this is generally accomplished before a planning and zoning board. Their approval by a majority vote is generally a final approval. However, the city commission (or county commission, if in an unincorporated area of the county) may have the right to call up the project for final approval, no matter what the planning and zoning board voted. To make this even more complex, if the planning and zoning board does not approve the project, the applicant may still have the right to present the project to the commission, in the hope that the commission will overrule the planning and zoning board. This process is often very expensive and time consuming.

So even when the zoning code seems to indicate that the project should be allowed, and that there should not be any roadblocks to stand in its way, often some seem to appear. The professional investor knows that nothing is approved until the last possible "no" vote has been overcome and the time for an appeal has passed. Yet even then, something like a countywide building moratorium (halt of all new projects) can and sometimes does occur.

When the approval has been granted, it is up to the investor to act on that approval, to obtain the building permit (if one is needed), and to start and finish the construction in a timely manner. A delay at this stage can still cause a halt to the project. Various elements can create hindrances to the extent that, while they may not stop the use from occurring, they create such additional cost that the project is no longer feasible. A community or building impact fee imposed by the city or county can force the developer to make improvements to traffic ways or drainage, or to make contributions to the parks fund, or some other demand that is routinely imposed on developers in the area. I have seen developers walk away from projects when faced with such impact costs that the project was no longer financially viable.

What all this demonstrates is that you must protect yourself by doing as much due diligence as possible prior to the contract stage. If you feel relatively comfortable that your intended use is allowed by the zoning and would be approved by the authorities, then move forward with the development of a legally binding purchase agreement or construction contract. Be sure that this agreement spells out exactly what your intent is, and states that you will purchase the property only after you have obtained all the approvals you feel you need.

In development of any kind, most investors will want the approval process to extend all the way to the issuance of a building permit. Usually investors can be satisfied that a site plan approval is sufficient, but this is a situation-by-situation determination. To go all the way to a building permit application stage and then get caught in a building moratorium can cost hundreds of thousands of dollars. Time is money, and there is a point where hands are thrown up in the air and developers just give up.

Once you understand this process, it is easy to see that the approved project, the development that is ready to go, is far more valuable than the plot of land with a "For Sale" sign on it that says "Zoned for a shopping center."

Use Governs Value

A use that has been approved can suddenly make a plot of land truly valuable. Fortunes have been made by people who learn this approval process and option vacant land, spend the time and effort and money to get the property approved, and then sell the project to developers who are ready to go and need ready-to-go projects. Often the process to obtain these approvals appears far more complex than it actually is. If the investor/developer has done his or her homework on what the authorities are likely to approve, and works toward that end, then the entire process can be relatively smooth sailing. It is still time consuming, but the gold ring at the end of the ride is visible all the way.

This process is what makes the Donald Trumps of this world rich. It is a goal that is attainable by nearly anyone. All it takes is to learn the ropes of this game, find out what the authorities want, match that want with a void (a lack of affordable housing, or a need for full-service restaurants, hotels, or other community services for example), find a property that is zoned for that use or can be rezoned for it, and tie it up. If your purchase agreement gives you enough time to get the approvals, and the development will project to be financially profitable, then you will be able to sell your approved project or move forward to complete the project yourself.

Use and Real Estate Laws that Govern Use Can Change

I introduced a new concept in the previous section. If the current zoning does not allow what you want, or even what the city officials want, you can initiate a process to rezone the site to a code that allows a greater use than the current zoning. If, for example, your shopping center has a limited commercial zoning, and you want to add a hotel to the site, you may be successful by obtaining a new zoning for the part of the property where the hotel would be constructed.

I have been successful in acquiring vacant land by option or a purchase agreement conditioned on my obtaining rezoning or other such approvals so that the use of the property can be enhanced. I have had values jump from $10,000 per acre, in 30- to 60-acre tracts, to over $50,000 per acre as a result of such efforts that took less than a year to accomplish. I have brokered transactions for clients who have acquired 10-acre sites for high-rise apartment development, who have walked projects through the city and made millions on an instant flip of their purchase contract of the site to another developer, who in turn would make even more millions after completion of the project.

The key is to start with what the zoning allows. If that is not sufficient for your needs, see what new zoning you might be able to get. If the cards start to fall in your favor, then tie up the land and go for it.

Real Estate Laws Are Not Homogeneous from City to City

Many commercial investors have gotten burned by making the assumption that a real estate ordinance in one city means the same as the same real estate ordinance in another. I have brought this up earlier, yet it is so easy to make that mistake, more details about this subject are worthwhile.

I live in Fort Lauderdale, Florida, which is one of the cities that constitute Broward County. Neighboring counties include Dade to the south, of which Miami is the principal city; Palm Beach to the north, of which West Palm Beach is the principal city; and Collier County to the west, of which Naples is the principal city. These three counties are each made up of many cities, some as small as a few hundred residents, others in the hundreds of thousands of residents. One thing they all share is that many of their city codes, ordinances, and building rules and regulations sound like they are the same, but they are not.

Many of these cities are still attempting to better define their existing real estate laws which frequently causes internal conflicts with the different departments and boards that must make decisions based on these different rules. The attempt to have all the necessary decision makers be acting on the exact same code with the same interpretation can become a muddled mess. Some new regulations may be adopted that are vague and leave loopholes in the code as to exactly how the regulation is to be applied. Situations like this occur all the time but are often ignored by the officials because of their lack of clarity. This causes decisions to be made that are inconsistent and may lead to litigation.

When you are faced with a vague ordinance or any city code, it is important to get a ruling from the head of the appropriate department as to how that law is applied and specifically how will it affect your situation. Get this ruling in writing, and if you think it is still vague, then get the city attorney to give you a legal opinion as to the exact meaning of that law.

The Power of Absolute Approval

Without the final and absolute approval to proceed with the allowed use, the real estate investor is the bridegroom without a bride. The process of obtaining approvals can become very political in nature, and most communities fall into one of three categories:

1. The politics is prodevelopment.
2. The politics is antidevelopment.
3. Prodevelopment and antidevelopment advocates are locked in battle.

The reality of responsible community administration is that development should be viewed as an important process of renewal. Building codes and city ordinances should be written in such a way as to encourage upgrading of older parts of the community, while at the same time maintaining the rights of the property owners to utilize their properties as the zoning allows, without undue bureaucratic hassle. Too often building departments and the other authorities that make decisions as to what gets approved and what is denied are allowed to be lenient and to bend the rules from time to time. This practice occurs in most communities and makes it very difficult to establish a standard by which all projects should be measured.

Because this may well be the situation in your community, it is important to learn how the important decision makers are apt to vote when it comes to these rule-bending situations. This is especially important if your project might need to have a rule bent to get approved.

It is far better to go with the flow than to fight a battle with City Hall. Just remember that the final approval can be money in the bank.

CHAPTER 11

Future Vision

The goals for this chapter are:

To Demonstrate the Benefits of Changing the Use of a Property

To Give You Insight on How to Accomplish This Goal

To Provide Examples to Help You See What Is Not Already There

A visionary is a person who is able to see beyond the present situation and imagine what could be in its place. The ability to envision a new shopping center where there is only a pasture at present, or new affordable homes in place of existing warehouses, is invaluable in the commercial real estate field. This ability is something that you can develop and fine-tune—you do not have to be born with it.

You can learn how to do this by first understanding the benefits to you, and to the neighborhood, of being a part of such future changes. The next step will be for you to discover what is possible, which of those possibilities would fill a need for the neighborhood, and which of those would be financially viable.

This chapter is designed to lead you down that path to accomplish the three goals stated above.

Key Words and Concepts to Build Your Insider Knowledge

Land Use Master Plan
Current Uses Allowed
Already Approved Infrastructure Changes
Rezoning Possibilities
Project Economics
Economic Conversion

Land Use Master Plan

Most states have mandated that each county should have an overall master plan to enable better-planned growth and uses of land and to allow for a longer-range development outlook than previously possible. The cities within each county are then given a timetable to bring their own development plan into sync with the overall county plan. A major part of the countywide plan would be the placement of employment areas; population controls by means of density caps within zones established by the county; and other elements that may include schools, parks, traffic ways, and the like.

As with anything devised by man, no such plan is ever perfect, so there is an administrative procedure to effect changes in these plans. Cities have some leeway to make adjustments when development does not flow the way the plan had dictated, or when the city or county itself needs change.

The overall county plans are generally designed to show what the different areas of the county should ultimately be used for, and it is then up to the cities to zone those areas according to the master plan. This procedure also has some flexibility. If the master plan shows that the northeast section of a city is to be used for commercial development, the city may have the leeway to choose what kind of commercial development it would like for that area. Accordingly, the city would assign appropriate business and commercial zoning for that area, provided those zoning uses did not violate the intent of the master plan.

If you are fortunate enough to be in a county that is in the process of adjusting or readjusting its development plan to match the county master plan, you will have the opportunity to participate in this process. Most such new plans give developers a chance to see how the development politics are shaping up for the area, and the very long-range outlook these plans present.

If your community development plans have been in place for a long time, this does not mean the whole world knows about those plans. The majority of people who live in a community don't know the names of the people who live three doors down from them, let alone pay attention to such mundane things as the master plan for their city. Do, however, learn everything you can about the master plan for the county and how the different cities have developed their plans to coordinate the overall development. You will find opportunities abound.

Current Uses Allowed

The very first question you should ask of the zoning department of the community where the property you want is located is this: Is the existing use allowed under the current zoning? Sometimes the answer is no. This might mean the zoning code has changed and the existing building or use is no longer permitted but is allowed to remain as a nonconforming use. When this occurs, some communities will not allow that use to be transferred to another owner, while others are more flexible in that respect. Clearly, if you were buying a building because it was a pawn shop, and the zoning department tells you that you will not be able to get a certificate of occupancy with that use because of the change of ownership, then that is likely to make you reconsider the purchase of that property.

Most zoning codes include a specific list of businesses and uses that are permitted in that zoning. Some of these uses, however, may require separate approval as a prerequisite to being able to apply that use to that zoning. This prerequisite approval is called a *special exception*. The special exception is generally obtained through the city commission or other such authority, and will be valid for that specific use, such as a gas station, a day care center, or other specific use that is shown in the zoning book for that zoning code. The approval of a special exception will expire if not acted on or extended.

Other uses which are also shown as permitted may require something additional, like a minimum size for the site, or some other criteria that may not be available in all areas where that zoning code is present.

The example of the City of Tamarac, Florida, zoning ordinance for B-1 and B-2 business zoning will give you a good idea of what is included in zoning code books.

DIVISION 14. B-1 NEIGHBORHOOD BUSINESS DISTRICT*

Sec. 24-326. Purpose.

The B-1 neighborhood business center district is intended primarily to meet the neighborhood-shopping and service needs of surrounding residential areas.
(Code 1975. § 28-137)

Sec. 24-327. Permitted uses.

In a B-1 district, no building, structure or land and water use shall be permitted except for one (1) or more of the uses permitted by the master list of business uses as set forth in division 19 of this article.
(Code 1975. § 28-138)

Sec. 24-328. Property development regulations.

(a) Minimum lot area and dimensions in a B-1 district shall be as follows:

Area	1/2 acre
Width	100 feet
Depth	200 feet
Frontage	100 feet

(b) Minimum yard setback requirements shall be as follows:

Street	50 feet
Side (interior)	25 feet
Rear	25 feet

---

*Cross reference—Minimum landscape requirements in certain districts. § 11-8.

(c) Maximum building height and total floor area shall be as follows:

Maximum building height	35 feet
Maximum gross floor area of building	35% of the total lot area

Exceptions:

(1) The maximum building height may be increased by ten (10) feet to accommodate elevator towers, mechanical equipment and screening, including parapet walls, clock towers or other ornamental devices: provided, however, that the top horizontal area of all height encroachments shall not exceed more than fifteen (15) percent of the area of the roof.

(2) The minimum interior side or rear setback shall be fifty (50) feet when abutting a residentially zoned district or an S-1 zoned district, excluding golf courses, with a landscaped buffer as provided in section 24-329(5).

(3) For properties less than one (1) acre, the minimum interior side setback may be reduced to zero feet on one (1) side provided that one (1) of the following conditions exists:

a. No building or structure exists on the property adjacent to the proposed zero-foot setback.

b. The existing adjacent development would abut the proposed zero-foot setback.

(4) Wherever two (2) commercial buildings are proposed to abut each other, the side access to the rear of the buildings shall be unobstructed for a

(Continued)

minimum of thirty-five (35) feet. The access shall be designated and posted as "fire access lane" and comply with section 28-16 of the American Insurance Association Fire Code. In addition, roof overhangs shall not extend beyond the property line.
(Code 1975. § 28-139)

Sec. 24-329. Special regulations.

The following are special regulations for B-1 districts:

(1) *Enclosed uses.* All uses shall be operated entirely within enclosed buildings, except where permitted in division 19 of this article, for a limited period of time, upon application to and approval of the city manager or during specified holidays for the sale of seasonal potted plants.

(2) *Lighting.* In order to minimize offensiveness to persons on neighboring property and to eliminate distractions to and temporary blinding of drivers of vehicles passing illuminated property, all artificial parking lot lighting shall either be shaded or screened in a manner that will limit spillover of lighting onto adjacent property and rights-of-way. Spillover shall not exceed three (3) footcandles vertical and shall not exceed one (1) footcandle horizontal illumination on adjacent properties or structures measured at grade. An outdoor lighting installation shall not be placed in permanent use until a letter of compliance signed and sealed by a registered engineer or architect is provided to the city stating that the lights

have been field tested and meet the standards set forth above.

(3) *Outdoor storage.* Outdoor storage of merchandise is prohibited except where permitted in division 19 of this article, for a limited period of time, upon application to and approval of the city manager or during specified holidays for the sale of seasonal potted plants.

(4) *Off-street parking, loading and trash containers.* No off-street parking, loading or outdoor storage area or vehicular drive shall be located within ten (10) feet of any abutting residentially zoned or S-1 zoned district. No trash receptacle, fixed or mobile, shall be located in a required street setback area or within fifty (50) feet of any abutting residentially zoned district property. Loading zones shall be permitted only in the side or rear yard setback.

(5) *Fences, walls and landscaped buffers.* A six-foot-high, solid masonry wall, stuccoed and painted, shall be required along any line abutting a residentially zoned or an S-1 zoned district excluding golf courses. A ten-foot landscaped buffer strip on the interior side of such wall shall be planted with shade trees, eight (8) feet to ten (10) feet high at the time of planting, spaced no farther than twenty-five (25) feet apart, center to center. An optional design of such a wall may be approved by the city council.
(Code 1975. § 28-140)

Cross reference—Minimum landscape requirements in certain districts. § 11-8.

Secs. 24-330—24-345. Reserved.

DIVISION 15. B-2 PLANNED COMMUNITY BUSINESS DISTRICT*

Sec. 24-346. Purpose.

The purpose of the B-2 district is to encourage the development of an intensive commercial facility, providing a wide range of goods and services, located adjoining at least one (1) major arterial roadway and servicing a consumer market of a substantial territory. (Code 1975. § 28-146)

Sec. 24-347. Permitted uses.

In a B-2, no building, structure or land and water use shall be permitted except for one (1) or more of the uses permitted by the master list of business uses as set forth in division 19 of this article. (Code 1975. § 28-147)

Sec. 24-348. Property development regulations.

(a) Minimum lot area and dimensions in B-2 districts shall be as follows:

Area	1 acre
Width	200 feet
Depth	200 feet
Frontage	100 feet

(b) Minimum yard setback requirements shall be as follows:

Street	50 feet
Side (interior)	25 feet
Side (corner)	35 feet
Rear	50 feet

*Cross reference—Minimum landscape requirements in certain districts. § 11-8.

(c) Maximum building and total floor area shall be as follows:

Maximum building height	40 feet
Maximum total floor area (not including exterior mall space)	30% of the total lot area

Exceptions:

(1) The minimum interior side or rear yard setback shall be fifty (50) feet when abutting property is either a residential or an S-1 zoned district with a landscaped buffer as provided in section 24-349(5).

(2) The maximum building height may be increased by ten (10) feet to accommodate elevator towers, mechanical equipment and screening, including parapet walls, clock towers or other ornamental devices: provided, however, that the top horizontal area of all height encroachments shall not exceed more than fifteen (15) percent of the area of the roof.

(3) For existing properties less than one (1) acre, the minimum interior side setback may be reduced to zero feet on one (1) side provided that one (1) of the following conditions exists:

a. No building or structure exists on the property adjacent to the proposed zero-foot setback.

b. The existing adjacent development would abut the proposed zero-foot setback.

(4) Wherever two (2) commercial buildings are proposed to abut each other, the side access to the rear of the

(Continued)

buildings shall be unobstructed for a minimum of thirty-five (35) feet. The access shall be designated and posted as "fire access lane" and comply with section 28-16 of the American Insurance Association Fire Code. In addition, roof overhangs shall not extend beyond the property line.
(Code 1975. § 28-148)

Sec. 24-349. Special regulations.

The following are special regulations for B-2 districts:

(1) *Enclosed uses.* All uses shall be operated entirely within enclosed buildings unless otherwise approved on a site development plan. Any exposed activities such as garden supplies or automotive installations shall be fully screened from horizontal view from any point off the site.

(2) *Lighting.* In order to minimize offensiveness to persons on neighboring property and to eliminate distractions to and temporary blinding of drivers of vehicles passing illuminated property, all artificial parking lot lighting shall either be shaded or screened in a manner that will limit spillover of lighting onto adjacent property and rights-of-way. Spillover shall not exceed three (3) footcandles vertical and shall not exceed one (1) footcandle horizontal illumination on adjacent properties or structures measured at grade. An outdoor lighting installation shall not be placed in permanent use until a letter of compliance signed and sealed by a registered engineer or architect is provided to the city stating that the lights

have been field tested and meet the standards set forth above.

(3) *Outdoor storage.* Outdoor storage of merchandise shall be permitted only when incidental to the commercial use located on the same premises: provided that:

a. The storage area shall not be located in any of the required setbacks.

b. The stored merchandise shall not protrude above the height of the enclosing walls or buildings.

(4) *Off-street parking and loading.* No off-street parking shall be located within ten (10) feet of any abutting residential or S-1 zoned district property. No loading shall be located within thirty (30) feet of any abutting residentially zoned district property. No trash receptacle, fixed or mobile, shall be located in a required street setback area or within fifty (50) feet of any abutting residentially zoned district property.

(5) *Fences, walls and landscaped buffers.* A six-foot-high solid masonry wall, stuccoed and painted, shall be required along any line abutting a residentially zoned or an S-1 zoned district, excluding golf courses. A ten-foot landscaped buffer strip on the interior side of such wall shall be planted with shade trees, eight (8) feet to ten (10) feet high at the time of planting, spaced no farther than twenty-five (25) feet apart, center to center. An optional design of such a wall may be approved by city council.
(Code 1975. § 28-149)
Secs. 24-350—24-385.   Reserved.

City of Tamarac, Florida
A community located west of Fort Lauderdale

A partial list of uses for B-1 and B-2 Zoning Categories

Note: Items shown as x* require a special exception approval from the City Commission

BUSINESS USE	B-1 Neighborhood Center	B-2 Community
Abstract company	x	x
Accounting office	x	x
Advertising company	x	x
Air-conditioning equipment, retail only	x	
Air-conditioning equipment, retail repairs		x
Air-conditioning equipment, wholesale		
Alcoholic beverages (accessory use), special exception*	x*	x*
Ambulance service, special exception*	x*	x*
Amusement centers, indoors, special exception*	x*	x*
Amusement center, exterior, special exception*		x*
Animal clinics (no boarding kennels for animals and no exterior runs or pens)		x*
Animal clinics, pet hospitals		
Antique shops	x	x
Archery range, indoors, special exception*		
Armored car service offices		x
Art galleries	x	x
Art schools, special exception*	x*	x
Art supplies	x	x
Artists' studio	x	x
Associations (civic, etc.)	x	x
Athletic clubs, indoors, special exception*	x*	x*
Auctioneers, enclosed, special exception*		x*
Auditorium		x
Auto parts, equipment—Accessories, new, retail—Also new, wholesale*	x	x

Auto repair:

    (1) All major repair shall be done within an enclosed building.

    (2) Outside storage or display of parts is prohibited. Outside merchandise display

(Continued)

BUSINESS USE	B-1 Neighborhood Center	B-2 Community
is limited to petroleum products and tires only, and these products shall not be displayed beyond the pump island areas.		
(3) Outside storage of vehicles shall be restricted to vehicles with valid license plates and valid inspection stickers. All vehicles stored outside after business hours shall be parked in an orderly manner and only in approved parking spaces and shall not be visibly dismantled and shall not appear to be junked or abandoned.		
(4) Paint and body shops and paint and body work are prohibited. Special exception.*		x*
Auto tag agency and license bureau	x	x
Auto tires, new retail and installation		x
Auto tires, wholesale		
Auto wash racks, as accessory use*		x*
Awning stores, sales only*	x*	x*
Bait fish (other than artificial)		
Bakeshops, retail, limited preparation	x*	x*
Banks, commercial:		
If any bank, whether freestanding or not, is to have drive-in facilities, this use is allowed only if a traffic circulation plan is submitted which will be sufficient to satisfy the maximum projected usage of the drive-in facility on the site with no disruption of traffic off the premises or disruption of customers seeking to park their vehicles and to physically enter the bank. Each drive-up lane must have stacking capability of one hundred (100) feet minimum.	x	x
Banks, commercial, not in freestanding buildings, with no drive-in facilities	x	x
Barbershops	x	x
Bars, not in restaurants, special exception*		x*

BUSINESS USE	B-1 Neighborhood Center	B-2 Community
Bath and closet shops	x	x
Beauty parlors	x	x
Bicycle stores and repair shops	x	x
Billiard rooms, poolrooms		x
Bird stores, retail only	x	x
Blacksmith shops		
Blood bank		x
Boat rentals		x
Boat sales, showroom enclosed, accessories, special exception*		
Bondsmen	x	x
Bookstore, by special exception*	x*	x*
Bottled gas, outside storage only, special exception* (all outside storage to be in location approved by the City Commission)		
Bowling alleys, special exception*		x*
Broadcasting studios, no towers	x	x
Building supplies, retail from buildings only; no open-air sales or storage facilities		x
Burglar alarm company	x	x
Bus terminals, special exception*		
Camera shops	x	x
Candy stores, retail	x	x
Car rental agency, special exception*		
Carpet and rug sales, cleaning on premises, special exception*		
Carpets, rugs, floor covering, retail, special exception*		
Carpets, rugs, floor covering, wholesale, special exception*		
Carryout foods, no kitchen preparation	x	x
Caterers		x
Ceramic, retail, limited preparation	x	x
China, crockery, glassware, earthenware, retail	x	x
Chiropractic clinic	x	x
Churches, places of worship, Sunday schools, convents, parish houses	x	x
Clothing stores, except secondhand	x	x

(Continued)

BUSINESS USE	B-1 Neighborhood Center	B-2 Community
Clubs, lodges, civic, noncommercial	x	x
Cocktail lounges, special exception*		x*
Community garage		
Concrete products, retail		x
Confectionery and ice cream stores	x	x
Conservatories (arts and music), special exception*	x*	x
Corsetieres (sales and fittings only)	x	x
Modiste, wearing apparel, furrier, retail	x	x
Motels		x
Motorcycle sales and service, special exception* (no exterior display, all repairs to be performed in fully enclosed areas)		
Municipal buildings, parks, playgrounds, reservations, parking	x	x
Museum		x
Music and radio stores, retail	x	x
Music instruction	x	x
Newspaper bureau	x	x
Newsstand	x	x
Notions, variety stores	x	x
Novelties (handbags and handicraft), retail	x	x
Novelties (handbags and handicraft), wholesale or retail and wholesale		
Nursery sales (see 24-349(1))		x
Nurseries (horticulture)		
Office building, general	x	x
Office furniture, business machines	x	x
Office stationery and supplies	x	x
Offices for doctors, dentists, pediatrics, architects, realtors and related professions	x	x
Optical stores	x	x
Optometrist	x	x
Outdoor (sidewalk) sales:	x	x

(1) For a limited, temporary period of time not to exceed 4 days.

(2) In conjunction with an authorized, licensed business use, verified by the supervisor of occupational licenses.

BUSINESS USE	B-1 Neighborhood Center	B-2 Community
(3) Outdoor storage and display of merchandise during business hours only from 10:00 a.m. to 3:00 p.m.		
(4) Requires that an application be submitted to the supervisor of occupational licenses. The city manager, fire chief, chief of police and supervisor of occupational licenses shall ensure that the application for outdoor (sidewalk) sales meets the technical requirements of this Code.		
(5) The application must be submitted 10 working days prior to sidewalk sale, in writing, to the supervisor of occupational licenses, with a permit fee of $5.00.		
(6) Outdoor storage/display of merchandise shall not impede normal pedestrial movement via the sidewalk or interfere with the entrance-exit of the subject premises or that of adjacent businesses.		
Package and liquor stores	x	x
Paint stores, wall covering, retail only	x	x
Parcel delivery service		x
Parking, commercial, special exception*		x*
Parking garage, commercial		
Pawnshops		x
Pet shops		x
Pharmacy (prescriptions, drugs, prosthesis only)	x	x
Photograph, developing and printing for others, retail, pickup and delivery only*	x*	x*
Soft drink stands		x
Souvenir stores		x
Sporting goods store		x
Sprinkler system; shop, storage and service		
Stationery stores		x
Stock exchange and brokerage office	x	x
Sundry stores	x	x
Supermarkets		x

(Continued)

BUSINESS USE	B-1 Neighborhood Center	B-2 Community
Surgical and orthopedic appliances, sales and accessories		x
Swimming pools, supplies and accessories		x
Tailor shop	x	x
Taxi service establishment		x
Taxidermist		
Telephone exchange building*	x	x
Television sales and repairs	x	x
Theaters, special exception*		x*
Tire, battery and accessories, automotive; retail and installation, as enclosed accessory use only*		x*
Towel and uniform supply		
Travel bureau	x	x
Tropical fish shop, retail	x	x
Upholstery shop:		
Those locations in B-1 zone may not exceed 5,000 square feet in area and may not engage in manufacturing on the premises.	x	x
Utilities, public offices	x	x
Vehicular and boat maintenance, special exception* (all repairs to be performed in fully enclosed areas)		
Vehicular and boat maintenance, as accessory use*		x*
Video, sales and exchange clubs	x	x
Waiting rooms and ticket offices for transportation system	x	x
Water conditioning sales, residential and commercial		x
Water treatment, pool equipment and chemicals (no manufacturing)		x
Wearing apparel stores	x	x
Wearing apparel, wholesale		
Wholesale merchandiser, retail trade		
Window blinds, draperies and curtains, retail	x	x
Woodworking machinery, sales		
Wig shop	x	x

(Code 1975, § 28-171; Ord. No. 88-5, § 1, 1-27-88; Ord. No. 89-32, §§ 1, 2, 10-10-89; 5-22-96)

Already Approved Infrastructure Changes

When there is a master plan in place, long-range infrastructure changes and development are easier to plan for and to finance. The kinds of infrastructure changes most important to a commercial real estate investor will be anything that will have a long-range benefit to a neighborhood, to the businesses of that neighborhood, and to the values of the real estate in the affected neighborhood. There are several interesting and not so apparent factors that occur when future plans are approved for changes in present infrastructure. Let's look at a proposed new entrance/exit from a turnpike that passes through a county.

The process generally would have included many meetings that the public could have attended, if the public had seen the notices in the local newspaper and had understood the significance of those meetings. The first tier of meetings would have dealt with the reason for the new entrance/exit, then the location. This lets cities in the area of the proposed entrance/exit make proposals as to why it should serve their area, or why it should not be anywhere near their area. There would be a point of view for both sides of those proposals, as any change in infrastructure can have both a positive and a negative effect on the immediate area where the changes are made.

One thing is sure, whatever the public learns from these early meetings is often quickly forgotten after the decisions have been made. Why? Because any change in infrastructure goes through the hurry-up-now-wait progression of events. The wait part of the plan might be several years or longer. Real estate investors who understand this process can take advantage of this situation by keeping in touch with what is happening. If an opportunity arises to buy land or buildings in the area that will receive benefits from the future change, then look into that potential. Only remember this: Some infrastructure changes cause an immediate rise in value the day the newspaper announces that the work is going to start next month. Then, when the work starts, and traffic flow in the affected area becomes a quagmire of dirt, dust, and delays, businesses in the area watch their customers leave, perhaps never to return. If the infrastructure changes will produce that kind of immediate effect, then be careful. The best buy might be a few months into the work, when owners become desperate and prices drop dramatically.

Rezoning Possibilities

Most communities have some flexibility within similar zoning codes. Business zoning, for example, many allow multifamily use as well as mixed use of residential and business. As business zoning uses approach a more industrial category, the list of possible uses starts to thin out. Sometimes the community is receptive to rezoning a tract of land from one category to another. This can go either up or down the scale of use, depending on the site, what is around it, and the direction of development the community would now like to see occur in that area. For example, 40 years ago the land in question may have been zoned for heavy industrial use that might have allowed metalworking, smelting and foundry operations, junkyards, and so on. Over the years those businesses have disappeared from the scene, and now the city would like to see affordable housing replace the abandoned warehouse structures. If this fills a void and the land can be purchased at a reasonable price, and there are no insurmountable environmental problems to overcome, going with the flow is the smart thing to do.

From another perspective, a 50-acre tract of land zoned for single family homes at one to the acre, which was once part of a much larger tract of land, has been cut off by the right-of-way of a new turnpike. This highway has 18-foot-high solid concrete sound battens on both sides of the roadway, so the 50 acres is now like an orphan. Development adjoining the 50 acres is mostly multifamily residential zoning that will allow medium- to high-density condominiums and upscale rental apartments. It would be reasonable to assume that the community would entertain a rezoning of the single family 50 acres to allow a greater residential use.

Keep in mind that when adding density to an area, there may be population caps that have to be considered. For many communities this is a relatively recent addition to the zoning and planning concept. Counties are often divided into zones that are given population maximums that will be allowed in the future. The maximum zones tend to be the ones that are already in place, so areas of new development generally have a lower overall density per acre than more urban locations. When the maximum population assigned to that zone when the master plan was last reviewed and approved has been reached, it may still be possible to obtain more units from underdeveloped adjoining zones, or by an amendment to the masterplan, approved by the state legislature.

The concept of population caps and how to deal with them is not uniform across the United States, and it may not even be an issue in some states or counties. But when you are confronted with this problem, be sure to seek good legal advice before attempting to rezone to a higher-density residential use.

Project Economics

The economics of any investment will vary according to the market conditions of your specific area of the country. There are six main elements that are the essence of each income producing investment:

1. **Total possible gross income**. Considering the local situation, you will want to know the maximum income this property or investment will produce, and what will it cost, in time and money, to reach that point. If you determine that the property is at or nearly at the maximum revenue production without extraordinarily large capital investment, then your hope of adding value to the property may not be a realistic goal. Remember, however, that it is the bottom line that is the important issue, so stopping your analysis at this point might shortchange the issue. It may be possible to increase the yield of any property by better management, reduction of expenses, and more attractive financing.

2. **Minimum operating expense**. The least possible expenditure that will allow you to keep the property in operation is the minimum operating expense. This is the

no-frills operation that meets the needs of the property and would include all debt service, real estate taxes, insurance, utilities, a reserve for repairs and replacements, and management cost. It should allow for maintenance of the status quo, but would not allow for continual upgrades of the property. Once you think you have gotten down to a threadbare operational budget, take another look to see what could be cut. Is your debt service as low as it can be? Consider refinancing if a new mortgage would create lower monthly payments or generate some needed capital without adding to the monthly mortgage payment.

3. **Break-even occupancy.** This is the minimum level of rented space that will produce sufficient income to pay the operating cost and debt service of the property. If the property is a single tenant use, then the loss of that tenant means the property is 100 percent vacant until another tenant can be found. This is one of the hazards of having a single-use tenant. Properties that have multiple tenants spread the risk of high vacancies over a broader income base. However, most triple-net leases are to single use tenants. Fast-food and other restaurant chains, furniture stores, and big-box retail enterprises are good examples of this kind of tenant. The creditworthiness of a single-use tenant is the most critical factor in investing in this kind of property.

4. **Tenant versus customer demographics**. This is the matchup of the person or entity that rents the space and the customer or client that the lessee must have to sustain their business and make a profit. If either you or the tenant has made a mistake in selecting a good location, a great tenant won't last long if the demographics of the client or patron base are all wrong. Naturally there are other factors that can affect the tenant's ability to make a profit and remain a good, rent-paying participant in your income-producing properties. Poor business skills, supply problems, or a change in trends or competition can make that tenant no longer successful in the market area.

However, area demographics are easy and quick to obtain. A few minutes of surfing the Web will give you a choice of companies that can supply good demographic information to help you effectively match tenants to the needs of the neighborhood where the property is located. When purchasing an existing property that is already fully rented, it is a good idea to make sure that the demographics support the likelihood of all the tenants continuing to be successful at that location. A quick check of the rent collection log would give you a clue to how things are going for each tenant. A tenant who is consistently late in making rent payments may already be having problems meeting other obligations as well. Find out as best you can what is causing this problem. It could be something other than the client base. Nonetheless, demographics are a tool that all real estate investors can and should learn to use. The companies that compile the data can help you learn how to use that information. Ask for explanations to the terms they use and what the data indicates.

5. **Level of Maintenance**. The prior maintenance of existing properties you acquire should be carefully reviewed. Last-minute cosmetics that a seller slaps onto a building might look good today, but a month after you close, the paint starts to peel, the roof begins to leak (again), and problems that were hidden begin to manifest. The key to purchasing a property that has experienced poor past maintenance is to find out the actual condition of the property prior to buying it. Poor maintenance might simply mean that the current owner cannot properly manage his investment, which in turn is a highly motivating factor to sell.

   As a buyer of such a property, you make a detailed inspection of every possible aspect of the property, especially the newly painted areas. If you have the time to obtain estimates of the real cost in time and money to bring the property into great shape, then you can use the findings as leverage to renegotiate the deal. Note the words "have time to obtain estimates." Far too many buyers cut short the amount of time they allow for their inspection and due diligence review of the property. Effective due diligence not only allows for the inspections, but will give a contractor or repair person time to come up with realistic and accurate costs to correct the problems found.

   Those costs, by the way, should be in two levels. The first is what will it cost to fix everything that can be fixed and replace what cannot be fixed. The next level is to go beyond fix and replace to include making improvements. Once workmen are at a job site, it doesn't cost all that much more to carry the repair process to an improvement level.

6. **Investment goals**. How you purchase, finance, and maintain a property should be tied closely to your investment goals. It has been my sad experience to see properties

slip into decay because there was no long-term thought about what that investment could do for its owner. A well-thought-out plan would use techniques that would maximize the buyer's assets at the time of purchase. This might mean that a tax-free exchange, also called a 1031 exchange, can be used to dispose of an existing property while at the same time using that equity as part or all of the purchase price of the new property. Financing should be used to give the total overall benefit of cash flow, equity buildup, or some of both.

The maintenance and management posture of any income-producing property should also be designed to get the most out of the real estate. This would suggest that the expected life of the buildings should not be prolonged past an economic effectiveness. When the value of the underlying land can support a greater use of the property, then buildings go and a new project replaces them.

Every real estate project and income-producing investment has a point where the projected cost exceed the acceptable return that can be obtained. Before discussing this situation, it will be helpful to dissect that first sentence of this paragraph. The easiest way to do this is to ask the following questions:

- When does the project become too costly?
- What is an acceptable return?
- Is there something other than reoccurring income that sparks the investment?

You will see that although the original sentence is absolutely correct, the timing to the situation is as important as the return expected and the nature of that return. Let's look at each of these questions in some detail.

When Does the Project Become Too Costly? If you review the current income of a hotel, as an example, and discover that its revenue over the past three years does not come close to supporting the value asked by its owner, would you say the property has reached the point where cost exceeds an acceptable return? The answer will depend on several factors. If the highest and best use of the site is that hotel, and there is nothing that can be done that will improve the return, then the property is overpriced and the income versus cost is out of balance, with income at the bottom and cost skyhigh. However, if you wanted to buy the property because you had another use for the site that would turn your investment into a gold mine, then the potential income versus the cost has shifted into your favor. Naturally, when new development is to be a part of the equation, all that additional cost must be included in your overall investment.

Many developments function on a future projection of revenue. Imagine that you saw a great spot for a new Holiday Inn. If the cost of the land, the cost of the development, and the time it would take from day one to having a stabilized revenue from the hotel was all calculated, and even conservative projections offered you great returns, then in the long run who cares what the existing business (if any exists) is doing?

What Is an Acceptable Return? An acceptable return may vary from project to project and according to the investor's goals. The potential positive leverage that is possible from financing may make a marginal net operating income an excellent cash flow. For example, if a shopping center had a net operating income of $200,000 and your total price to acquire the property was $2,200,000 and you had no debt on the property, your return is approximately 9.9 percent of your invested capital.

Price	$2,200,000
Cash Flow	200,000
Return	9.9 percent

However, borrow 80 percent of the purchase price ($1,760,000) with a debt service of $149,600 per year (8.5 percent constant, including principal and interest), your cash flow is $50,400. Based on a cash investment of $440,000 your cash flow return is 11 percent.

Price	$2,200,000
Less debt	−1,760,000

Cash invested	$440,000
Cash flow	$ 50,400
Return	11 percent

Added to the fact that you are double-dipping on OPM, and your tenants eventually pay off your mortgage—even if you have no increase in NOI—your return will then be a cash flow of $200,000 per year with your same original investment of $440,000. Your return in this very conservative approach has skyrocketed to 45 percent.

Cash flow after mortgage is paid off (by your tenants)	$200,000
Your original investment	$440,000
Return	45 percent

The point here is that your acceptable return will depend on how you view return. If your goal is to establish an estate that will give you absolute financial independence in 12 years, then you might want to maximize your equity buildup and continual improvement of the center, so that within 12 years the revenue would have paid off the debt and allowed reinvestment to improve the center and its income. If you made the assumption that your NOI would increase by only 3 percent per year at simple interest (not compounded), in 12 years your NOI would grow from $200,000 to $272,000. Your original investment remains at $440,000 investment, so now, with zero debt service to pay, your cash flow is $272,000 and your return is 62 percent of your initial (and only) cash-out-of-pocket investment.

Is There Something Other Than Reoccurring Income That Sparks the Investment? Assume for a moment that you have been following an announcement made two years prior that a new federal office building was going to be built where, at the time of the announcement, there was nothing but run-down homes and businesses. Two years have now passed, and the old houses and businesses are still there. Why? Because it takes time to go through condemnation proceedings and to acquire the needed land. But all that is about to change because the last holdout tract has been acquired.

The announcement of construction is still several months away, but it is time for you to act. You end up buying a building that is half vacant, but so what—you have made a steal of a deal and can afford to wait out the next 18 months if you need that long. You have just entered the wonderful world of seeing the future, and taking advantage of economic conversion.

Economic Conversion

The balance of this chapter is devoted to the method of implementing economic conversion. This concept has been mentioned in earlier chapters, and by now you should have a good idea of how it works and what you have to do to make it work for you. This chapter, however, is designed to tie all the loose ends of economic conversion together so that you can see how to best make it work for you. The forward vision of seeing what actual use a site will allow is just the beginning. Economic conversion is taking that vision to its final stage.

Discover the Magic of Economic Conversion

There are five elements to economic conversion that you must understand to grasp the extent to which you can benefit from it. This concept is not new, and the methods you will use to turn this into your own private gold mine will require considerable effort on your part. However, the majority of that effort will go into learning everything you can about your own neighborhood and the local real estate laws, building codes, and the like, that will, in the end, be your guide to wealth. The following are the elements to be aware of:

1. Most owners lack vision.
2. Most brokers follow owner's vision.
3. How to develop a vision of the future.

4. Small steps yield big results.

5. Pitfalls to watch out for in economic conversions.

Most Owners Lack Vision

There are many different kinds of commercial investors. Most buy commercial real estate because there are usually multiple tenants involved, and that spreads the risk of high vacancy over a wider base than when dealing with single family rentals. There are investors who buy run-down property with the idea of fixing it up to improve the facility and increase rents, but they do not change the fundamental use of the property so they do not benefit from any economic conversion. Then there are investors who buy property based on present revenue. These investors generally look at the numbers and pay the highest prices because they want quality and are willing to pay for it. Those investors may make some improvements over the long haul, but often they are satisfied with the returns as they are. They like triple-net long-term leases where creditworthy tenants send them monthly checks and that's that.

The kind of investors who can make the quickest and greatest profit from their efforts are those who look for properties with improvements that are structurally sound but the existing use has become economically obsolescent. That is to say, the property no longer produces the amount of revenue that another use of those same improvements would produce.

The key is to learn how to take an underproducing property and turn it into a winner. Most properties you will see will be underproducing. This occurs most often because most property owners have no future vision. The sad fact is they cannot see that no matter what they did to the existing use, the property was going to be a losing situation. So, instead of throwing good money down the drain, they let the property continue to decline until it is no longer worth keeping the doors open. Even worse, some property owners feed the property to keep the doors open in some blind hope that things will turn around all by themselves.

The beauty of this situation, from the investor's point of view, is that these property owners are ripe sellers. They may already be up to their eyeballs in debt and are likely sick and tired of trying to deal with the situation as it presently exists. By the time owners reach this point, even if they suddenly had a revelation as to what they should do to make the property a winner, they are usually in an economic hole that is too deep to climb out of.

Most Brokers Follow the Owner's Vision

I have been an active realtor for over 35 years, and take my word, most real estate salespeople and brokers are not visionaries. First of all, the majority of them are residential salespeople, and they tend to follow the owner's vision. When a seller is motivated to sell, the salesperson who can help that seller attain that goal can be a very good person to know to help achieve that goal.

Commercial brokers and salespeople tend to be more in tune with the trends of the marketplace, but many of them are simply upgraded residential brokers who work the market. They become the "hotel specialist" or the "warehouse king," and so on. If more salespeople and their brokers were really at the top of their game, they would know what is going on in the community and what other uses the property could best be converted to. Nonetheless, from your perspective, the fact that only a few professional real estate salespeople and their brokers deal with commercial real estate anyway, and that only a few of those professionals are development oriented, means the field is wide open to you, should you take the time to learn the simple steps to mastering economic conversion.

How to Develop a Vision of the Future

It should be obvious that if you drive around your town and see only what uses are currently in existence, then you are missing the boat. I have already given you the keys to mastering the technique of becoming knowledgeable of the zoning and building codes. You've learned that as you develop the habit of inspecting more and more real estate, there will be a day when you realize that the run-down duplex you have driven by for the past six years is sitting on a parcel of land that will allow 25 apartment units to be built, or the 50-year-old frame house on a corner lot is actually zoned to allow a 50,000-square-foot office building to be built.

This kind of local knowledge is learned by osmosis. It just suddenly occurs to you how stupid you have been not to realize what's there. But if you think that is stupid, what about the owner or the real estate firm that has the "For Sale" sign in the yard and never thought to present the building to apartment developers in the community?

In general, economic conversion means taking the existing property and converting it into another use, one that will give you a greater return than is possible from the current use.

But the zoning issue is not the whole story here. It is important to know the pulse of the marketplace to the extent that you can ascertain what void will exist when your conversion has been completed. It is not enough to know if there is a need for more office space right now, for example. The key is, will there still be a need a year from now? A quick check of all the building departments in the communities within your market range for the type of use you have in mind will give you a good idea of what new projects are in the pipeline. You may discover that once all the new office buildings currently in planning stages get built, there is likely to be a glut of office space in your area. On the other hand, you might find that while there are many investors planning office buildings, no one has made any application for industrial centers, and that there is a crying need for upscale industrial-style distribution parks.

You will need to know what the lenders like, as well. It is one thing to find a void and another to rush out to fill it. If the local lenders shy away from that type of investment, and you are planning on getting your hands on other people's money to finance your project, then you will have to step back and rethink those plans. It might be possible to find funds from sources away from the local market. Or you might have to change your plans to a project more favorable in the lender's eyes.

Small Steps Yield Big Results

The Rule of Small works wonders in real estate. Often an economic conversion is a modest change in the nature of a property. A 100-unit motel is converted into 50 suites, which now attract a different category of clientele. Lower operational expenses and more cash flow might result from this kind of a conversion. Or a 400-unit hotel gets converted into a 150-apartment complex that is an assisted living facility; or a vacant, freestanding former supermarket is converted into an indoor amusement facility for children, or a bowling alley, or a self-storage facility.

Pitfalls to Watch Out for in Economic Conversions

There are five major pitfalls in economic conversions that you should be especially careful of:

1. Losing control of the project
2. Time
3. Hidden faults
4. Construction overruns
5. Environmental problems

Let's review each of these in detail.

Losing Control of the Project: Once you see a property that looks like it might be a good candidate for an economic conversion, you should take steps to tie it up. If you do not, it is possible that the word will get out that someone is going around the city building departments and is asking a lot of questions about a possible new use for that site. You might find that your preliminary efforts are picked up by another investor willing to act to tie up your dream property.

It is critical that you tie up a property early in this process. There are many reasons for this besides someone else stepping in front of you in the deal. One of the most obvious is that you do not want to commit a lot of your own money to do the necessary investigations and studies to make sure that the conversion is feasible unless you control the property.

Start with a simple letter of intent, if you like. This is a technique that is used for real estate transactions of any size, and often some of the biggest deals begin this way. A letter of intent focuses on the business issues of the transaction: price, terms, and the buyer's requirements and criteria needed to close the deal. The legal matters are generally left for the formal contract that will follow. Sellers can respond to a simple letter of intent without running up expenses with their own lawyers, as approval of a letter of intent does not bind either party to the deal. It is common, however, that the letter of intent contain a provision that spells out that although the terms and conditions of the letter of intent do not bind either party, both buyer and seller are acting in good faith and that the seller will not negotiate with any other potential buyer during a period of time (say 30 days) following acceptance of the letter of intent, while the formal agreement is drafted and reviewed by both parties.

Once the letter of intent is fine-tuned to the point that both buyer and seller accept those business issues, the key is to move quickly into a formal agreement. This agreement should be presented by the buyer to the seller within a few days of approval of the letter of intent. There are likely several legal issues that will need to be negotiated, but once the price and payment terms are set, there remains only one critical element to be established: the due diligence time.

Time: Time is an all-important factor in real estate and is most critical when it comes to an economic conversion of a property. It is one thing to buy a strip store with the plan to keep it in its present use and condition, and completely another when changes of use and structure are anticipated. During the letter of intent stage, you may not know the amount of time you will need to complete your due diligence studies. If this is the situation, you will want to avoid setting a period of time you might need to accomplish your studies in the letter of intent. Reference can be made to a "reasonable due diligence time to be contained in the formal agreement." An astute seller will push to keep the time short, and may insist on some definitive period prior to accepting the business issues in the letter of intent. If you are forced to state a specific time in the letter of intent, then try to get as much time as possible. Numbers of days should be spelled out as "business days" and not calendar days, and special attention should be given to holiday seasons when city business all but shuts down.

As I have mentioned before, the time period for due diligence should not allow for the inspections, but it should include unforseen delays, additional inspections, or more advanced environmental inspections in the event that hazardous elements or chemicals are discovered. If rezoning or other special factors must be dealt with within governmental departments, you need to find out how much time those can be expected to take, and then double that time.

Time is an issue that may be very costly in any real estate acquisition. Many investors deal with this issue by their willingness to pay for the added time they need, either by direct payments to the seller to extend the closing on a month-by-month basis, or by building in increases in the closing price as delays are encountered.

The important issue for you as a buyer of such properties is to know the maximum you can afford to pay for the property, and to build a worst-case scenario into your due diligence timetable. You do not want to run into a situation where the four months you allotted drags into a year and four months, and you are forced to either step up to the plate with more cash to the seller, or to walk away from the project because you still need more time to get city approvals.

Hidden Faults: When your construction workers begin to make the necessary changes to effect the economic conversion, it is not uncommon to find problems that can be costly to correct. Some of these problems I discuss in the last item in this section, "Environmental Problems," but others can exist as well. One of the worst construction problems is when the building is not constructed according to the original plans. This happens quite often when there have been one or more remodeling stages in the building's life. Some of this work may have been done without permit and may not meet code. Other code issues can include changes in the code that would have allowed the existing building to continue in its nonconforming-use status, but now, because of substantial remodeling, the city and, most often, the fire department may require expensive upgrades or changes to the property. The amount of remodeling that may trigger this will vary among city codes, so be sure to check out the appropriate building codes in the city where the property is located.

Construction Overruns: I have never seen a remodeling or economic conversion that did not cost more than the original estimate. This happens not so much because of the problems that are encountered, but because additional changes are often made while the remodeling is in progress. One of the best ways to limit this is to pay more attention to the existing plans. If you are lucky enough to be dealing with the original owner of the property, have them warrant that the building is built according to the plans filed with the city, and that no "unpermitted" construction has ever occurred. This gives you a potential claim against the seller if your construction team finds this not to be true.

With accurate existing plans, the remodeling can be made with a minimum of changes and without the need to make unnecessary additions in the process. Holding the contractor to the construction bid estimate will be your best way to keep the costs within your original budget and estimate.

Environmental Problems: All due diligence should allow sufficient time to do all the environmental inspections that will possibly be needed. The initial phase one inspection is when the properly licensed inspection team checks out the property for any obvious problems. They look at the plans, make special note of the year the property was built, look at the past use of the vacant land prior to buildings being erected, and ascertain if there is any reason to anticipate possible contamination of the subsoil or the presence of hazardous materials. This additional inspection would be the phase two environmental inspection, which may in turn trigger other, more time-consuming inspections, such as a well to monitor levels of hazardous gases seeping from the ground, as well as potential asbestos testing for areas that may be removed during construction or remodeling of the building. A formal contract should allow for additional due diligence time being added to the time contained in the contract when these additional inspections are required.

Buyers should attempt to have the seller warrant that there are no such problems, and that if any are found, the price will be adjusted according to the cost to correct the problems. Sellers, and their lawyers, will generally always balk at this by saying that all they can claim is that "to the best of their knowledge" no such problems exist. A modification of this all-or-nothing attempt would be to have the seller warrant that no such problems were created during the ownership period when the current owner had the property.

CHAPTER 12

The Six Most Powerful Negotiating Tactics

The goal of this chapter is:

How To Maximize Your Present and Future Benefits Through Effective Contract Negotiations

Buying and selling real estate is not a simple, take-it-or-leave-it situation. The methods you use to buy or sell property are a combination of many different investment tools at your disposal. The idea is to be able to negotiate a deal that takes you closer to your desired goals, while at the same time giving the other party the potential of a win-win situation.

There is an old saying in this business: "I can pay your price, if you accept my terms." This is nearly always true, because the terms of a deal can easily modify and reduce the overall cost to reach that price. For example, assume a seller of a property I truly want to buy is asking $100,000 for a lot I would like to build an office building on, but the price is at least $20,000 more than I feel the lot is worth. I also know that it will take me at least two years from the day I have the lot under contract to get the plans approved by the city, get construction bids, obtain financing, and construct the office building. This time is something I can use in the negotiations. So I offer the seller $10,000 for a 12-month option with the right to extend for another 12 months for a second $10,000, with a final $80,000 at the end of the second year—which totals $100,000. This is just one way to pay the price on my terms.

Key Words and Concepts to Build Your Insider Knowledge

Rent Adjustments
Contract Negotiations
Soft Letter of Intent

Rent Adjustments

There are several important adjustments that are generally a part of every commercial lease. They are real estate tax adjustments, cost of living adjustments, common area maintenance, and percent of gross sales adjustments. In general these charges can be negotiated separately by the tenants.

Real Estate Tax Adjustments

Some leases may allow the lessor to collect increases in the real estate tax over the amount assessed the year the lease was written. This can occur when the lessor has already taken into account the existing tax structure as a part of the base rent. In other leases, commonly found in larger properties such as shopping centers or office buildings, the tax is a separate item that is charged to the lessee in accordance with the percent of the property occupied. The lessee would be charged a corresponding percentage of the total tax assessed for any given year. For example, if there were 25 tenants in a shopping center and the center consisted of 200,000 square feet of rental area, and the annual real estate tax for any given year was $100,000, then that would amount to 50 cents for each square foot any specific tenant occupied. This adjustment is generally a part of the general common area maintenance (CAM), which is discussed in this section, but it can be found separate from that adjustment and is, in that case, an additional adjustment to those items contained in the CAM.

Cost of Living Adjustments

A cost of living adjustment is a provision that is often in a separate paragraph of the lease, but it may also be incorporated in a section entitled something like "Lease Adjustments." However, it may also be incorporated into the CAM adjustment.

The actual adjustment is usually a formula that allows the lessor of the property to increase the rent during the term of the lease, often on an annual basis, but any division of time can be used, such as quarterly, semiannually, or even monthly.

A benchmark date is given against which the lease is adjusted. This is often the "all items" index as published by the United States Department of Labor. This index (or a commonly accepted replacement of that index, should the government stop calculating that specific index), should be identified with the base year which is to be used as the benchmark. If the lease was originally established in July 2005, then the benchmark could be stated as follows: "This lease is subject to semiannual adjustments in the base rent based on any increases in the U.S. Department of Labor All Items Index from the benchmark date of May 2005. The first increase shall occur on [a date would be inserted] and then every 6 or 12 months following that date." Note that I used May 2005 as the benchmark date for adjustments. This is to allow the adjustment to be calculated a month prior to the actual implementation of the increase.

As with all terms and conditions of a lease, the form of base rent adjustments is open for negotiation. Often there is a cap on the amount of an increase that can be applied, such as "not to exceed 5 percent increase during any adjustment period."

Common Area Maintenance Adjustments

CAM is a catchall adjustment package that is charged to tenants of commercial rental properties. It can be very inclusive, so much so, in fact, that it will cover every possible outside cost to manage and maintain the property during the tenant's lease. These charges can include items such as a reserve for replacement of major mechanical items, such as air conditioning and heating equipment, outside lighting, and other such equipment; a management fee, usually based on a percentage (say 5 to 10 percent) of the gross rent of the property; cleaning services; security services; utilities; sales tax (where applicable); parking lot maintenance; building and roof maintenance; a budget for center advertising and promotion; and so on. These charges may be divided equally among all tenants, or certain tenants, such as the anchors of the center, may receive a break on some of the charges.

Percent of Gross Sales Adjustments

This is a shopping center type of adjustment and is often negotiated separately with each tenant. It is often a percent of the revenue earned by the store or shop, over and above a base that is negotiated in the original lease—say, 3 percent of gross sales each quarter, when they exceed $5,000,000 in gross sales. All numbers and percentages are subject to negotiation.

Contract Negotiations

No matter how standard any contract appears (a lease, a purchase agreement, or an option agreement, for example), much of the contract is subject to negotiation. It is rare for any agreement between two or more parties to be accepted as presented. When the agreement is very comprehensive, as many commercial leases tend to be, it is necessary to pay close attention to every item contained in the document.

It has been my experience that contracts drawn by overly conservative lawyers can often be hard to understand. Some lawyers attempt to make every statement so perfectly clear and cover every potential problem or circumstance, and use court style language to protect their clients.

Other contracts might be rather loose and not cover every item very well. These agreements work well until there is a problem created by one or other of the parties.

The point here is that the time to negotiate a contract is in the beginning, and not when you are headed into a legal battle. Spend time with a good real estate lawyer and make sure any agreement you are to sign and commit to has been fully read and understood, and that your potential difficulties are understood. Before you sign the contract, renegotiate to remove any potential difficulties.

However, when you are purchasing an existing income property with one or more tenants in place, you will have to accept that property with its existing leases. In larger properties where there are dozens of leases, it is not uncommon to find that few of these leases are identical. Different lawyers, different owners over the years, and sloppy management companies may all account for what is a nightmare of lease documentation.

Other contracts that you inherit when you buy an existing property can also be employment contracts, equipment leases, and service contracts. This documentation is also likely to be a mixed bag, where each item is unique. Future problems can occur when these documents are not carefully reviewed.

A major part of your due diligence in purchasing such properties is the review and detailing of these different documents. I have found some hidden time bombs when doing such reviews, as well as some hidden gold mines. When a lease has periodic adjustments built in, and management has not applied the formulas correctly, an understatement might be a windfall for the new owner. Sloppy management may not even be aware that some leases have expired, or that the percentage of gross income is due for a big jump the month after you take over the property.

Because these reviews are very time consuming, this is one of the first due diligence items to get into. When problems are discovered that affect the income negatively, start your renegotiations on the purchase agreement right away.

The Six Powerful Negotiating Tactics

1. Soft letter of intent

2. Option contracts

3. Split funding

4. Floating seller-held mortgages

5. Partial releases

6. Real estate exchanges

These six negotiating tactics are just part of your negotiating tools. They are powerful enough, however, to warrant a special place in this book. Learn to use them well and you will be building your future with every contract you execute.

Soft Letter of Intent

I have discussed the use of letters of intent in earlier chapters. This section will deal with what I call the "soft" letter of intent. First of all, letters of intent are widely used in all forms of real estate, with the exception of single family residential properties, which tend to go directly to contract to purchase. Even so, there is no reason that you can not use a letter of intent for that type of property as well. Secondly, the advantage of any letter of intent is that it enables you to negotiate the business part of the deal early in the contact stage. By keeping the letter as a nonlegal-looking document, it is often easier to cut to the chase, to move through the important number items (dollar amounts, number of days or months to close, etc.) and hammer out the basics of a deal prior to getting the lawyers overtly involved to the extent that your lawyer is dealing with their lawyer, rather than buyer to seller.

A soft letter of intent is a person-to-person approach. It requires some advance due diligence to discover something about the seller and a good understanding of the property in question. Read the sample which is shown on page 248.

A letter like this one does not look like the usual letter of intent—in fact, nowhere is that term used. It is a direct and complimentary letter to the owner of a property you want to own. As an investor for over 40 years, I have discovered that it is relatively easy to find out something about the owner of a property, and even easier to find out a lot about the real estate in question. One thing will lead to another, and before you know it you find a point of common interest. If it is not Toastmasters International, it might be the Fort Lauderdale Bill Fishing Association, or another sport you share, or a university you or a relative attended.

Develop the use of this soft letter of intent" and it will open many doors to opportunities.

Option Contracts

The option contract uses time as your tool. It is highly effective in allowing you to tie up a property for little money, and it gives you the added advantage of softening the overall purchase price. You will use an option best when you already know that you want to buy the property and *will close on it if the seller gives you the time you ask for*.

Dear Mr. Alan,

I have heard many nice things about you from a former member of the Toastmasters International Club of which you served as president a few years ago. I, too, am a former member of that club and commend you for your devotion to its good cause.

It was especially interesting then when I discovered that you are the owner of a 25-unit apartment complex that I have admired for some time now. This is a property I would love to own, as I already own and manage several other apartment buildings in the same area of town.

As an owner of such properties in the same area, I appreciate the time and effort that go into the upkeep and management of such a property. Equally, I believe I am a good judge of a fine investment like that one, and I am willing to pay you a very fair price for the property.

Recent sales of smaller but similar properties have closed at the $62,500 to $65,800 per unit range. Without knowing the details of your existing leases, I would say that would be a fair range for your property.

I am actively looking to fulfill my needs to find a replacement property for a 1031 exchange, and I have only 40 days to identify such a property. I do not need to close on the property for several months but can close immediately if that would be of benefit to you.

I would like to meet with you as soon as you like to discuss the purchase of your property. Would you be available for lunch on Wednesday at 1:00? If so, we could meet at Alexander's. Please give me a call to confirm or reschedule our meeting.

Sincerely yours,

Jack Cummings

At the beginning of this chapter I showed you an example of an option. Here is another example:

I wanted to tie up a tract of oceanfront land in the area south of Vero Beach, Florida. After several months of looking at different tracts in a 10-mile stretch of beachfront, I found a potential site. It consisted of 103 acres that had approximately 1000 feet of beachfront and ran across the main beach road, called A-1-A, to the wide Indian River that is part of the intracoastal waterway in that area. Much of the riverfront land was contained in an old, mosquito-control area, and I knew there was the potential that the 60-plus acres in that control area may never be buildable. But the real value was the beachfront and the 30-plus acres across the beach highway that was high and dry.

My intent was to put together a small group of investors and to syndicate the property. I believed if I could first get the business terms down pat, and then tie up the real estate for a period of time, I could form the syndication and see some advance appreciation prior to having to close on the property.

I used a soft letter of intent directly to the owner (through a real estate broker that was the listing agent on the land) and described my interest in acquiring the tract. I spelled out what I needed to accomplish to do that (form the syndication), and I was so confident that I was willing to pay him $10,000 as early as next week if he would agree to sell me the property within six months if I was successful in putting the deal together. If I could not accomplish it within that period of time, he could keep the $10,000.

In that initial contact I did not discuss the price or terms of the deal. What I wanted to stress was that $10,000 would go directly into his pocket next week, if he could act that quickly.

He and I maintained a dialogue for several weeks, slowly working out the details. In the end I handed him a $10,000 check, which his broker would hold in escrow for 15 business days while I checked out his title and the details of the mosquito control district's legal position on the 60-plus acres within their district. The deal was that unless I found something I did not like within that first 15 days (for any reason), he could keep the $10,000.

Then I had a period of six months to put my syndication together. I would then close on the land, giving him an installment sale, which would benefit him at that time for tax reasons. (An installment sale is when the seller takes back a mortgage and you pay him over a period of more than one year. Capital gains tax is not due on the sales price at closing this way, but is paid over the period of years the payments are received).

By the time I handed over the check, I was already well into putting the syndication together. Within the first 5 days I was satisfied with the title and other details of the property. By the end of the 15 days (three weeks, counting only business days), the investors were on board. There was no need to rush to close, as we had six months to go.

A word of caution: options are not so good if you have to pay a lot of money to tie up the property with no assurances that you can use the property as you intend to.

Split Funding

Split funding is a halfway measure to fill a full cup. By this I mean that the buyer will meet the demands of the seller, but not all at once. This is an effective way for the buyer to show the seller that he or she is trying to be accommodating to meet the seller's terms. In a way, it is like the manager of the complaint department. The key is simply to listen to the complaint, to nod that you agree and understand the problem, and then to offer some form of consolation to make closure to the complaint.

Here is an example of split funding. Jake is a buyer who really wants to purchase the 50-room motel that Alan would like to sell. Alan is a very motivated seller and has another use for the capital he has tied up in the motel, which was a business that he discovered he was not cut out to deal with.

The price of the motel was $2,500,000—a bit on the high side. There was a first mortgage of $1,750,000 that could be assumed by a qualified buyer, and Alan wanted to cash out his equity of $750,000. Jake knew the business and believed he could turn the property into a real boutique establishment and end up with a winner, but he would have to make an immediate investment of $250,000 into the property to update some of its systems and to give it a new look. The problem for Jake was that Alan wanted all cash to the mortgage at closing. The most that Jake could come up with was $700,000, and that was after putting a first mortgage on his home and cashing out most of his stock portfolio. Of that amount, he would need to hold back $250,000 for the improvements.

But Jake really had confidence in this investment. He knew that in one year, or 18 months maximum, he would have made a major improvement in the business operation and would be able to support a new value close to $3,500,000. With that kind of new value, he would be able to refinance the motel and obtain a 70 percent new first mortgage. That would bring in a total of $2,450,000—almost the total original purchase price.

Jake made his offer. He would assume the existing first mortgage and pay the balance of $750,000. However, the cash part of the deal would come in two installments, $400,000 at closing and another $400,000 18 months later. The additional $50,000 would be treated as interest on the delayed payment.

Alan's need and motivation helped this deal come together. Jake more than met the obligation to pay the $750,000, only he did so in two payments 18 months apart. To sweeten the deal, Jake agreed to escrow the $250,000 he was going to spend on improvements, to show Alan that he was sincere about the property and that the $250,000 would improve the real estate, which would go back to Alan if Jake failed to make the second part of the split fund.

Split funding can be used in many different ways. The first payment could have been an option payment, with the actual closing coming later on. It could have been a lease payment on a lease with option to buy. The key is that it can and does work.

Floating Seller-Held Mortgages

This is a technique most real estate investors have never heard of, but if you include a few simple words in your purchase contracts, it can generate profits when you never thought they were going to materialize.

Let me set the stage first. Often you are able to obtain some or all seller financing when you are purchasing your real estate. As I have mentioned earlier, the motivated seller is a primary lender in many transactions. When this is apparent in your negotiation stage, it would be to your benefit if the seller-held mortgages were drafted so that you could sell the property without having to either pay off the mortgage, or let a buyer assume it. The following is an example of such a situation.

Fran negotiated to purchase a 20-unit apartment building owned by Julie. Julie was, as it turned out, a highly motivated seller, as she had been transferred to a distant city and could no longer look after the property. Besides that, she needed to get some of her equity out of the property to give her cash to purchase a residence where she was moving. Her price was eventually negotiated down by Fran to $800,000. There was an existing first mortgage, which could be assumed in the amount of $500,000. Fran was able to come up with $150,000 in cash, which left $150,000 still unaccounted for. To close the deal, Julie agreed to accept a second mortgage from Fran in that amount, payable at interest only for eight years at 7 percent interest, with a 10-year amortization at the same rate after that. Fran had attended one of my lectures, so she had inserted the following clause in the offer:

"At any time during this second mortgage, the guarantor of the mortgage may elect to substitute the security of the mortgage for another property, provided that the substitute property was not encumbered by a first mortgage greater than 50 percent of its assessed value, and that the combination of the existing debt plus the outstanding balance of this second mortgage would not exceed 70 percent of the assessed value of the substitute property."

What this simple paragraph did was allow Fran to float (often called *slide*) that second mortgage to another property. Notice that I said "another property," as it would not matter who owned that substitute property, as long as they agreed to accept that added obligation.

In the event of this small $150,000 mortgage, it may not have meant much to Julie, as she was happy holding the mortgage in the first place. So as long as it was secured, she agreed.

But what this did was allow Fran to sell the property later for $900,000 cash, pay off the existing first mortgage of $500,000 (less whatever principal had been amortized by that time), and pocket the balance of $400,000. But what about the balance of $150,000 due Julie? As long as Fran had another property, or a friend who had another property, that mortgage would simply slide off the 20-unit apartments and over to the substitute real estate.

What kind of friend would it take to allow this to happen? How about you, if you were Fran's friend and you had a property you were trying to sell. If your equity would meet the test, you might make a deal with Fran to let her slide that $150,000 debt to your property in exchange for, we'll say, a $175,000 investment in another property Fran owns. Now your equity is reduced and you have picked up $175,000 of equity in her other deal. Your reduced equity in your property also makes your property more attractive to a buyer who has a little cash (which you can now accept).

Or Fran, without such a friend, will slide the mortgage over to one of her other properties and take the full $400,000 cash out of the deal to invest in another property.

Okay, lets go big-time. If the deal was a $20 million hotel package, and the seller was willing to hold a soft purchase money second mortgage (*soft* means below market rate interest and on payback terms) in the amount of $5,000,000 at interest only for 10 years with a balloon, you would be highly motivated to hold on to that debt as long as you could. It is like cash in the bank.

So five years from now a buyer offers you $25 million for the hotel package, cash to the existing debt. But you can slide $5 million of that to another property. You would do it in a heartbeat.

Welcome to the big time.

Partial Releases

Partial release is a technique used by land and multifamily housing developers to allow the development and sale of their product prior to paying the full price of the land. First let's look at several examples of how this technique is used.

Jim is a single family home developer and wants to buy a 100-acre tract of land on which he will build 200 homes. He estimates that it will take him five years to complete the project, so he wants to enter into a purchase agreement with the seller and pay for the land over that period of time. The seller is willing to hold a mortgage on the entire tract. Jim agrees to the basic terms of the deal, which is 10 percent down, with five annual payments of the balance plus interest. This is okay so far, but as the seller is to hold a first mortgage on the land during these five years, they have to find a realistic way to allow Jim to build and sell the homes in the meantime.

A provision for partial releases is inserted into the purchase agreement. This will allow Jim to get releases of the lots on which he will be building homes as the project progresses. The per lot price Jim has to pay to release the lot from the security of the mortgage is at a small premium of the overall balance owed, so that as Jim pays for the lots, he is prepaying the mortgage at a faster rate than the five-year terms. This insures the seller that his security is actually increasing as the payments occur.

Assume the land was sold for $4,000,000. Ten percent down leaves the balance owed at $3,600,000. This works out to $18,000 per home lot ($360,000 ÷ 200 = $18,000). The release price is set at $25,000 per lot, with a minimum of 36 lots to be released at the end of each year. The $25,000 will apply against the principal outstanding on the loan ($3,600,000) and interest will be extra.

With this partial release schedule, by the time Jim has released 144 lots, he will have retired the full amount of the mortgage ($25,000 × 144 = $3,600,000). Keep in mind that in addition to the land price, Jim will be making improvements to the area with streets, utilities, and so on. This also raises the value of the property and enhances the security of the balance owed to the seller.

Any formula of a partial release that is mutually agreeable between the parties will work. The releases could have been at par, which would have been $18,000 per lot, plus outstanding interest, or even a staggered price, say $30,000 for the first few lots, then a gradual reduction to below $15,000 per lot as the project winds down, or a flip-flop of that situation.

Some land developers bring in an equity partner to bank the land while the development is under way. In that situation the lender, perhaps a Wall Street brokerage office or a major insurance company, takes title to the land and advances the cash needed to complete the development of the lots, then releases them from their security package.

Richard is a high-rise condo developer. He puts his whole product in one building, then sells the apartments. He must obtain a similar provision to allow whoever is holding the development loan to release those units so that they can be delivered to the buyers. Most lenders require a certain percentage of sales to occur prior to the start of the building. In this situation, the lender can see that the projections Richard had made are correct, and by the time the building is substantially completed and a certificate of occupancy of the units is made, there should be sufficient income from the closings of those sold apartments to pay down the loan to a point where the lender's security is increasing at each closing. The developer's profit can be weighted to the last sale as additional incentive for the project to be completed on target.

Ned purchases a 20-unit apartment building with the idea of converting it into condo apartments. The seller is asking $1,000,000 for the building and is willing to hold a purchase money first mortgage in the amount of $600,000 following a down payment of $400,000, but she is reluctant to give any releases. Ned suggests that the seller agree to four bulk releases of five units each. None of the apartments will be released until Ned has completed the remodeling of the units, and together with his original down payment to the seller, Ned guarantees that he will verify an investment in the remodeling of $300,000. Each of the bulk releases will be at a different price. The first five will be at $20,000 per apartment, or a total of $100,000. This reduces the amount still owed from $600,000 down to $500,000. The second five will be released at $30,000 per apartment, so the balance owed is now reduced to $350,000. The next five will be released at $40,000 per unit, so only $150,000 is remaining. This sum is paid off when Ned has sufficient sales or has already made enough profit to take the seller out of the picture.

Aaron has been accumulating single family homes for nearly 10 years. He took 30 of them and financed them with a blanket mortgage. This was one single mortgage that was secured by the package of the 30 homes. This was done for several reasons. It created one mortgage in the amount of $4,500,000 that was at a better rate than 30 much smaller mortgages. Aaron had one lender and one payment a month.

However, Aaron made sure that if he ever wanted to, or if a new owner of the package ever wanted to, they could have the homes released out from the blanket mortgage, one at a time. This would save Aaron, or a new owner, from having to pay off the entire $4,500,000 owed just to sell one or two homes, and would allow the protection to sell them all, one at a time.

Now that you see how this works, let's look at some pitfalls in partial releases from the seller's point of view, and how to overcome the problem.

The major pitfalls come from too cheap a release, and releases that take the cream of the security and actually reduce the value of the security to the seller. For the most part, this is a difficulty that can occur with vacant land, say the housing project we looked at as the first example. If the developer is able to release in a random fashion, the best lots might be the first to go. This can leave the cheaper lots left over or, worse, hidden in the back of the project. If this is a possibility, as would be ascertained by review of the project, then the releases can be set to follow a pattern within the overall tract. Release patterns I have used in large acreage tracts I have purchased generally followed a formula that allowed for releases of so many acres at a time, say five acres at a shot, starting at the back (or the presumed lowest-value area) and working toward the road or higher-value areas. All releases following the first would have to be adjacent to the previous until the highest-value release was made. Several passes of such releases might be needed to continually start again at the back and work toward the front, but no tract could be left unreleased that would be separated from other unreleased tracts. In using this formula, I was always able to show the seller that a release at par was more than fair, as the seller always had the highest-valued land left until last.

Real Estate Exchanges

The Internal Revenue Service has a tax section called Section 1031. This is a part of the code which offers real estate investors (and other types of investors as well) the opportunity to roll over their investments without ever having to pay the capital gains tax on those properties.

The essence of this section of the tax code as it relates to real estate is that a property owner who holds the real estate as an investment (not your home, but an office building, or land bought for speculation, or any real estate that you can show is currently owned for income or appreciation, for example) can use the equity in that property to acquire another "like kind" of property and not pay the tax.

There has been a lot of confusion about the term *like kind*, and it has been shown by thousands of examples permitted by the tax courts that *like kind* simply means that the replacement property must also be for investment purposes.

Like kind does not mean that if you own an office building, you can only exchange it for another office building. You can exchange your equity for any other investment real estate, provided the transaction is at arms length (no special deals with the kids or your girlfriend), and that the property is not in a foreign country.

Okay, so how does this affect a real estate transaction?

Say that 15 years ago you purchased a vacant lot for $20,000 down, and over a period of 15 years made mortgage payments on a $180,000 mortgage. Let's not consider the interest or taxes that you paid during this time, as you would have taken them as business or investment expenses and gotten appropriate tax shelter from those payments.

Fifteen years have gone by, and your tax basis in the property (this is like the book value of the asset) is $200,000. Profit of a sale is established as what you get that exceeds your tax basis. Sell for $500,000 and your profit would be $500,000 less $200,000 or a total of $300,000. If you had to pay the tax on this in the year of the sale (keeping in mind that all your other income will be taken into consideration to find your tax rate), you could end up paying $60,000 or more to Uncle Sam.

In the early days, in order to use the IRC (Internal Revenue Code) Section 1031, you had to actually make a direct or multileg (three or four party or more exchange) exchange where you got something and one or more people were involved in the exchange process.

However, along came a guy named Starker, who came up with a process that eventually was accepted by the Internal Revenue Service and is now called a Starker Exchange. This process, which is really the way to go in most tax situations, allows the owner of a property that has a potential tax at the time of a sale not to have to pay. In this event, and assuming that the seller will agree to reinvest the equity from the sale into another investment property, the property can be sold for cash. The cash is turned over to a person or company that acts as a facilitator to the exchange. The cash is basically used to go out into the market and purchase exactly what the seller really would like to own. Gone is the idea that "you take mine, and I'll take yours," and exchanges have become big business.

Now, there are some rules that have to be taken seriously, or several years down the road, when you get audited for something else, the IRS auditor finds that what you thought was a valid 1031 tax-free exchange, is really something more like a "lots of tax to pay" exchange.

I've listed the basics of the 1031 exchange, some of which I have already touched on.

As with any tax code, the IRC 1031 needs to be continually reviewed. A new tax court case could open up new opportunities, just as did the Starker case. Or it could tighten up some of the benefits that are now available to investors.

I am presently in the process of writing a new book to replace one which I wrote several years ago, also for John Wiley & Sons, Inc. Because of the constant flux of the IRS, the old book is out of date and the new one not ready for the market yet. Don't wait for my new book to do a real estate exchange. Follow the tips listed here and you should be okay.

Basic Rules of 1031 Exchanges

- Neither the sold nor the replacement properties can be located in a foreign country.

- Neither the sold nor the replacement properties can be for personal use or considered as a noninvestment category.

- Direct person-to-person exchanges are still allowed.

- Multileg exchanges are also allowed. This is the kind of exchange where Jim gets Bill's property, Bill gets Jack's property, and Jack gets Jim's property.

- A partial exchange is allowed, where not all the equity is able to be put into other "like kind" real estate. The part of the value that is outside the replacement real estate is taxed.

- Mortgages on property can throw a monkey wrench in the deal, but it is still a workable exchange. For example, you want to exchange your $500,000 present-value lot that you only paid $50,000 for 10 years ago. However, recently you borrowed $350,000 against the lot to purchase something else (it doesn't matter what). When you borrowed the $350,000 the IRS did not tax you on that money. Now the lot is still worth $500,000 but your equity is only $150,000 because of the existing mortgage that the lot secures. So you give me the lot for my office, which I value at $150,000, and I take the lot and the obligation to pay off the $350,000 sometime in the future.

  This is okay, but the IRS will now consider that you have gotten *boot* (a term to cover cash or anything else you get or are relieved of that is not a qualified replacement property). In essence, you get taxed on that $350,000 the year of the sale, just as if you had gotten cash.

- Depreciation has a somewhat similar effect as the mortgage situation, but with a different slant. I have owned an apartment building for over 40 years. I built it on a lot for which I paid $5,000, and I have fully depreciated the building, which cost me around $60,000 to build. Its present value is $375,000 or more. My tax basis is not $65,000, but a simple $5,000. The land was the only item that I could not depreciate. To sell the property I would be faced with a taxable gain of $370,000 or more.

- When you enter into a Starker Exchange and sell your property in a normal buy/sell agreement, you can allow the funds to be processed according to the rules of the Starker. This means that the funds are banked by the facilitator, and that the facilitator is not related to you in any way (not even a business relation). You have no control over the funds other than to direct how they are used to purchase a replacement property.

- In the Starker example there are two important time periods you must adhere to. Both these periods begin the day you pass title on the property you sold. Many people are confused about this and think the time periods start when you sign a contract to sell. Not so. The first period is 45 calender days and is the time that you have to identify your replacement property. By the end of that 45 days, you should have chosen a limited numer of replacement properties. You do not have to acquire all, but you can if that is what it takes to use up the proceeds of the exchange.

- The second period for a qualified Starker is that you have a total of 180 days, from the date you passed title to the property you sold, to close on the replacement properties. This is often where the problems begin to mount. It is very easy to get to the 180th day and not to have been able to close on the replacement property because of a problem with the new property, the title of the property, or the fact that the owner has died or disappeared, or a multitude of other difficulties that blow real estate transactions apart.

Tips on Making Real Estate Exchanges

- Remember that you do not have to do a real estate exchange solely for tax purposes. Many times you can throw something you don't want to keep into the pot of an outright purchase. I have purchased property using, as either all or part of my equity or down payment, gem stones, time-share weeks, the use of a time-share week, consulting time, vacant lots, and other properties. Most of those deals had nothing to do with trying to save on capital gains tax, only that I would use the odd item as a bonus to the seller, or an opportunity for me to clean that asset out of my inventory.

- Find one or more local realtors who are up on real estate exchanges. There are clubs of such real estate people who specialize in exchanges and usually open their meetings to investors as well. To find one, you should check with the nearest board of realtors in your area (check several neighboring cities as well).

- Surf the Web. Put in as your search criteria, "real estate exchanges in [your city]," and see what results that produces. You may have to play with this search a bit, and when you get some names do not assume they are experts. But they are a personal source you can approach to expand your sphere of reference.

- Get to know a lawyer who knows about real estate exchanges. Generally the best such person will be a CPA who is also a lawyer. Check with both CPA and law firms and you will find several good ones.

- Find a local real estate exchange facilitator. These are the people who devote their business to keeping you from having your tax-free exchange fall apart during an IRS audit.

- Do independent evaluation of the property you are going to get as all or part of an exchange.

- Remember, any exchange that moves you closer to your goals can be a good exchange.

Graduation Time

Okay, unless you have jumped to this page after reading the title, I will presume that by now you have successfully read this book. This means that you are properly armed to tackle commercial real estate. Income realty investments are out there waiting for you to come along. But do not think that this is going to be as easy as falling off a log. You will have to put in time and make the contacts that will ultimately be your source of knowledge that will lead you to profits. Continue to expand that knowledge at every opportunity. Never think your learning is finished. Your brain is far from empty, but there is lots of room to go.

Good luck.

Index

Index

Index